THE UNIVERSITY OF KANSAS PUBLICATIONS
SOCIAL SCIENCE STUDIES
1962

The West Indies Population Problem

Dimensions for Action

THE UNIVERSITY OF KANSAS

COMMITTEE ON SOCIAL SCIENCE STUDIES

JOHN G. GRUMM
JAY JACKSON
CHARLES E. STALEY
CHARLES K. WARRINER
DONALD R. McCOY, *Chairman*

The University of Kansas Social Science Studies are offered in exchange for similar publications by learned societies, universities and other academic institutions. All orders and all matter sent in exchange should be addressed to The Library, The University of Kansas, Lawrence, Kansas.

SOCIAL SCIENCE STUDIES

THE KANSAS INDUSTRIAL COURT: AN EXPERIMENT IN COMPULSORY ARBITRATION, by Domenico Gagliardo, 1941 (paper cover, $2.00).

TERRITORIAL KANSAS: STUDIES COMMEMORATING THE CENTENNIAL, 1954 (paper cover, $2.75).

PERSONALITY IN A COMMUNAL SOCIETY: AN ANALYSIS OF THE MENTAL HEALTH OF THE HUTTERITES, by Bert Kaplan and Thomas F. A. Plaut, 1956 (cloth, $3.25).

THE MAKING OF THE MEIJI CONSTITUTION: THE OLIGARCHS AND THE CONSTITUTIONAL DEVELOPMENT OF JAPAN, 1868-1891, by George M. Beckmann, 1957 (paper, $2.50; clothbound edition, published by the University of Kansas Press, $3.00).

COLLECTIVE FARMING IN RUSSIA: A POLITICAL STUDY OF THE SOVIET KOLKHOZY, by Roy D. Laird, 1958 (paper, $2.50; cloth, $3.25).

MASKS AND MEN IN A MELANESIAN SOCIETY: THE VALUKU OR TUBUAN OF THE LAKALAI OF NEW BRITAIN, by C. A. Valentine, 1961, illus., 17 photos., 3 color plates (paper, $2.75; cloth, $3.50).

SPECIMEN RECORDS OF AMERICAN AND ENGLISH CHILDREN: PRIMARY RECORDS IN PSYCHOLOGY, by Roger Barker, Herbert Wright, Louise Barker, and Maxine Schoggen, 1961 ($4.00).

The
West Indies Population Problem

Dimensions for Action

By

E. GORDON ERICKSEN

The University of Kansas

THE UNIVERSITY OF KANSAS PUBLICATIONS

SOCIAL SCIENCE STUDIES, 1962

LAWRENCE, KANSAS

© 1962

COMMITTEE ON SOCIAL SCIENCE STUDIES

UNIVERSITY OF KANSAS PUBLICATIONS

Library of Congress Catalog Card No. 62-63207

PRINTED IN THE U.S.A.

TO

DANA

Acknowledgement

Work on this book began in 1956, after my return from the Lesser Antilles where I served for two years as consultant in housing and town planning for the International Cooperation Administration. It was during this assignment that I became acquainted with Sir Stephen Luke, Controller of Development and Welfare in the British West Indies and Crown Representative for the federation of the Islands. He suggested that I prepare this book, feeling that my unique experience of working on most of the islands and among all social strata, especially suited me for a project of this kind. I am grateful to him for the original idea.

However, without the generous financial support of the University of Kansas, and its Endowment Association, this project would never have reached fruition. Beginning with a modest but adequate grant from the University's Graduate Fund, I was able to work up a sizable bibliography (a portion of which is published here), most of the best material being scattered in diverse books, journals, pamphlets, and government reports inaccessible to the casual student of population. During the ensuing three years, with two generous awards from the General Research Committee, plus a travel grant from the Endowment Association I was able to return to the Islands in the summer of 1959 and move the project to completion.

I make grateful acknowledgment of the invaluable assistance received from my colleagues in the Sociology and Anthropology Department of the University of Kansas in the form of informal discussion of the manuscript. The statistical skills generously offered by my close colleague, Dr. Ray P. Cuzzort were especially helpful. My gratitude is extended to Dr. George F. Jenks, Department of Geography, who gave generously of his time as cartographic consultant. To research assistants Sushil Bhatia and Jeffrey Hadden I am exceedingly indebted for their untiring library research and cartographic assists. To Marilyn Holmberg and Joy Hadden who endured the tediousness of typing and re-typing tables and manuscript, I am equally indebted. Of course, to my many friends and informants in the West Indies, I send my thanks for their sincere efforts to portray for me the life and problems of the inhabitants. I are particularly indebted to Dennis Malen-Smith and Norris J. James of Grenada and Leo St. Helen of St. Lucia for their efficient field work.

I am also indebted to all the publishers, editors, and authors who gave permission to reprint both copyrighted and uncopyrighted materials. Many of them went beyond the bounds of formal assent; they gave warm support and substantial help.

However, my greatest obligation is to the many students in my courses during the last five years upon whom I have, so to speak, "tried out" the ideas set forth in this book. While they are too numerous to mention by name I hope they will accept this simple statement of my gratitude and affection, for their constructive criticism and for their patience and forbearance.

My wife has helped enormously through years of encouragement and loyal support during which time the chapters were conceived and written. I cannot find words to express the full sense of my obligation to her.

E. GORDON ERICKSEN

Contents

Tables

Figures

Preface

About ninety million people were added to the world's numbers during 1957 and 1958. That increment is comparable to the population of Japan, and twice that of France. Such growth is unprecedented in human history.

One demographic trouble spot is the new West Indies Federation, a cluster of ten British islands struggling haltingly toward political autonomy under the sympathetic, guiding hand of Whitehall. At current growth rates, these Caribbean peoples, mainly Negroid, will double their numbers within a generation, from three to six millions. Like the world itself, they are caught in a demographic dilemma; modern low death rates have made their traditionally high birth rates anachronistic. No one, however, would suggest a return to the death rates of only a few years ago. But the hope of these island peoples for joining together in the solving of their economic and population problems is clouded. At this writing, the Federation is being dissolved through inter-island disagreements concerning the principle of free movement of people and goods, the right of the federal government to tax incomes and profits, and the full operation of a customs union. Jamaica and Trinidad have proclaimed their autonomy. However, the premier of Barbados and the chief ministers of the Leeward and Windward Islands are advocating a second start. The need of Barbados' bursting population to find living space stands at the core of the dissension, with more prosperous Trinidad and Jamaica standing firm against any mass invasion from their neighbor.

The world's masses, of which the West Indies is but a tiny proportion, have yet to come to grips with the task of bringing births and deaths into some kind of balance. In fact, the technical aid programs of the United States, Britain, and the United Nations, are abetting a world revolution in death control as they carry modern medicines, wonder drugs, miracle-working insecticides, and the best of public health methods to the most remote communities of the globe. While laboring to reduce the death rate of the world's less fortunate people, they seldom pause to consider the ultimate consequences. Yet, while it took 200,000 years for the world's human population to reach 2,500 million, it will now take a mere thirty years to add another 2,000 million. If nothing happens to prevent it, in 600 years the number of human beings on earth could be such that there will be only one square meter for each to live on. Just how a reduction in births is to be achieved in our less advantaged nations, is open to wide differences of opinion. But that some simple, inexpensive and generally accepted way must be found is

1

beyond question. This complex problem as it concerns the West Indies,[1] prompted this book.

Until very recently, population growth rates were most rapid in countries more advanced techno-economically, with highest levels of literacy, and an abundance of food and natural resources. Now the greatest growth is taking place in the more agriculturally-based regions, where more than half the world's population lives in comparative poverty. In these territories, death rates are falling spectacularly while birth rates remain high. In the Federation, with its agricultural base, the birth rate has, since 1935, held steady at about 32 per 1000 population while the death rate has declined from 23 (1932) to 11 per 1000 (1952). With no place to expand, her rate of increase in the last ten years has exceeded two per cent (for the United States the figure stands at 1.8). The demographic pattern is roughly parallel to that found in China and Egypt.[2]

With staggering prospects for continued world population growth, future trends of human living standards must depend largely on the effects of social ingenuity upon fertility. Untried experiments in fertility control may be expected to soon take their places beside long-term economic, geographic and technological programs. Indeed, the world social-economic picture has improved somewhat in vital sectors in the last two decades. There have been substantial improvements in health, food consumption, education, and gross national income. But this optimism is dampened when we recognize that in the presence of vast poverty and need in the world today, this improvement is but a fraction of the potential for improved standards of living. The increases in national income in such poor countries as the West Indies, have often been accompanied by a growing unevenness in the distribution of this income within the population, and by a growing dissatisfaction on the part of groups that have not benefited as much by the rising incomes as they have suffered from the rising prices. Improvements in standards of living are unevenly distributed by area and status. Furthermore, urbanization has been proceeding more rapidly than industrialization; cities are growing at the expense of smaller towns. Since the agrarian economy is unable to meet the increased food requirements it is necessary to import high cost food from abroad, generally from highly industrialized countries. The result has been

---

[1] The terms West Indies Federation, the Islands, West Indies, and Federation will be used equivalently.

[2] Each month, mainland China grows by more than a million individuals. The birth rate is estimated to be between 37 and 42 or even higher, while the death rate, estimated at 16 to 21, is believed to be falling rapidly. In the seven years immediately after World War II the death rate in Egypt dropped over forty per cent. In those seven years her population increased from 18.5 to 21.5 million. Her present rate of natural growth is approaching three per cent.

one of transferring poverty and underemployment from the country to the city and of the city inheriting the overflow of rural distress. With their low income potentials the cities are unable to supply the necessary services for comfortable living.

The faster the population grows in the Federation, the larger the share of each year's income that must be invested in increasing the stock of productive equipment merely to maintain the existing level of equipment per worker. Yet most workers have difficulty saving and investing out of their meager incomes sufficient to permit economic development to keep pace with rapid population growth. Furthermore, many would neither save nor invest if their incomes were ample. And with their high birth rates, but low death rates, they create a heavy load of dependent children for the working population generally.

If a disorganized society may be identified by the loss of common orientation and objectives between individuals and groups of individuals, and by a situation where aimlessness, inter-personal exploitation, economic defeatism or apathy appear as more effective forces in the game-of-life than positive logical thinking, then the Negroid peoples of the West Indies are disorganized. As a consequence of their low level of morale, I would call them brothers in abandonment. The old plantation slavery structure of relationships in which definitions, expectations and symbols were ordered within class and caste-like divisions is breaking down as valuations and thoughtways find their locus in permissive local communities. Here the definitions of objects may be tenuous or quite firmly rooted in past preconceptions. The demographer must take into account this transition in human assessment—it may not be viewed as external to his task. He cannot merely assume a structure but must emphasize action and definitions of objects and conduct *in-the-making* within and between communities. Now as the economic and power structure, carved out of the colonial past, is upset the English whites are withdrawing in order to escape the problems which attend an over-populated, economically broken possession.[3] The new burden of self-determination comes somewhat as a shock to these folk who now inherit the land, lacking as they are in a self-imagery adequate for tomorrow and its questions: For whom will a new Federation speak? Whose ideologies are to be served?

This population is confronted with a dual world of meanings, definitions, and objects: those in the present world of reality and those of the not-too-

---

[3] See Philip D. Curtin, *Two Jamaicas—The Role of Ideas in a Tropical Colony, 1830-1865* (Cambridge: Harvard University Press, 1955).

distant past. Current events, centering on the cities, are upsetting the old system in which a person of European stock and light skin was considered higher in the social scale than any other. The rise of the mixed bloods, persons with Negroid features but with some education and property, into vacated positions of power suggests new definitions of "ambition" and "success" in the making. New elites are emerging as resident whites slip downward—people who but for their color might be at the bottom of the heap. "Misplaced" persons are the harbingers of the break-down of the old system leaving the observing Negro peasantry in an ambivalent state of jubilation and anxiety.

In this island society, the demographer soon discovers that he is in the presence of not a single "population problem" but many population problems, each having dimensions (both physical and social) within islands and between islands. He cannot with confidence engage in "averaging averages" for truth does not rest here. Each island has a history of acquiring its own rather peculiar combination of racial stocks, religions, incentives, and cultural strains through isolation and through importation of labor from various parts of the world. Despite some common elements of cultural heritage and a "consciousness of kind" there are great contrasts—in physical environment, historical pursuits, customs, and institutions. And now, with the waning dominance of the extra-territorial English and without an endogenous social continuity, the Negroid people are both compassless and rudderless. Their gains and their dilemmas are created by themselves. While biological and geographic forces are always significant in achieving what the classical demographer calls "elemental balance," nevertheless man is seldom completely at the mercy of these factors for he is capable of side-stepping or controlling them in various ways. The population problem is significantly bound up with technological, economic, psychological, and most certainly, ideological factors.[4]

There are a number of points of interest to be viewed in this context. One is the problem of an island society built upon a single institution, namely the slave plantation. With its disappearance, the economic base has not only undergone a modification but the inner assessments of persons have likewise changed. Under the slave system the Negroes became a combination of a forced lower laboring class and a charter member minority of people living under allegedly "foreign" masters in their "own land." Now as free people they face not only the problem of the man-land ratio but must

---

[4] After J. O. Hertzler, *The Crisis in World Population* (Lincoln: University of Nebraska Press, 1956), p. 44.

tussle with the problem of keeping or changing the proportionate number of the various racial groups appropriate to the socio-economic system they want for the future. After all, West Indian society was built on the assumption that all whites have property, a business, or an independent income from outside, and that Negroes should pursue only the lowest type of work at a modest wage. Now there are "too many Negroes." The cost of schooling them, policing them, sponsoring them occupationally, is quite upsetting when viewed in the matrix of the pre-established system. In contrast with Spanish and French conquerors and exploiters who solved the problem of the mixed-bloods by permitting the status-line to be flexible so far as race was concerned, the English generally insisted on strictly keeping the line. Thus race contact in the West Indies has always been a class contact, with caste tendencies—or at least with very limited opportunity for rising from the bottom class to the managerial class. Thus with the breakdown of the old system the task of sponsoring the "right" people into the "right" status categories is poorly charted, there being but one guidepost: "This is now the black man's country."

The reproductive practices of these culturally disinherited people have always fit the expectations of the time. But all this is now in flux; many communities are reproducing their numbers in terms of the satisfactions attending a plantation slave economy but suffering from the anxiety which goes with freedom to move and improve one's lot. And no less anxious are the experts. The classical demographers are no exception. Convinced that human incentives and expectations have no place in applied demography, they confine their advice to the biological and material spheres of their discipline and hope for the best.

Thus some of my colleagues will recoil from the perspective which spawned this book: Students of population, in full recognition of the interlocking character of material and non-material forces in human events, are obliged to join the subjects of their investigation, mutually identifying ends as well as means in the pursuit of "progress."

Social scientists' knowledge about social change makes this suggested role obligatory, though certainly difficult. In deeply rooted cultures it is admittedly difficult to propose successful techniques for modification of human incentives. However, in the Federation, the inhabitants are not so set in their ways. Hardly more than one hundred years removed from slavery and indentured servitude, almost everyone is a part-time social innovator, borrowing from other cultures and reinterpreting everything to suit his personal tastes, twists and biases. I contend that in this setting "outsiders" can sympathetically and cooperatively intervene in the interpreting process. The

5

present trend of human events suggests an approaching socio-economic crisis requiring emergency planning. The long-term approach will be of little value. Students of overpopulated areas must not abdicate their responsibility to help these people spell out their goals and chart the possible routes of action. Scientific *laissez-faire* should be left in the ivory-tower.

WHAT THE BOOK IS NOT ABOUT

This book is not intended as a compendium of the latest census facts on the population of the Islands. To the contrary, it is a book of scientific and social facts about a redundant population. It is a book about a problem. With figures from the latest available censuses, together with the annual enumerations published since 1946 (all of which are deficient insofar as accuracy is concerned), I have assembled the data sufficient to permit an excursion into a theory of social action. This requires the introduction of such non-demographic concepts as norms, social control, and human expectations. The concept of countervailance stands at the core of my theorizing.

Chapter I

The Dimensions of Population Theory

To accomplish anything worthwhile in science (and in nearly everything else, for that matter), a man has first to persuade himself that things may be different from what they seem. This is a most difficult step to take for it involves "taking on all comers." When someone asked Einstein how he came to discover relativity, he replied: "By challenging an axiom."

I have long been dissatisfied with orthodoxy in population theory and would join those who are challenging its axioms, particularly the theory of *stable equilibrium*. Those of us who come from the behavioral sciences into the field of population are struck by the ethnocentrism in both content and method and especially with the absence of research that has anything to do with conduct. The time is appropriate for the introduction of hypotheses and tools of analysis showing the linkage of population phenomena to motivations and meanings. Now, vital statisticians and economic "theologians," having generally pre-empted the theory and method of demography, accept the roaming in this vineyard by anthropologists, sociologists, philosophers and even physicists so long as their basic orthodoxy is neither disturbed nor desecrated. The result, in my opinion, is that many elements or "variables" vital to the field (for example, infanticide), are ignored because established investigators consider them "empirically deficient." With a tight neo-positivistic approach to their data, they discover that non-material forces in the demographic scene do not yield readily to quantification. They are all too inclined to maximize description, and minimize synthesis on the ground that the closer they stick to their figures the less opportunity there is for generalization but the greater is the validity.[1]

But conventional demographic "facts" do not always fit reality. The parsimony of demography, predicated upon the notion that changes in human numbers are rooted to forces conceived as external, is proving unfruitful and unrealistic. Permeating the literature is the thesis that ideas are a mere reflection of the material foundations of society, implying that human beings are mere passive responding agents. However, the material conditions of existence, are never external causes carrying their own meanings. People telescope their definitions, evaluations and expectations into those objects that they would take into account. Demographic "variables" never "speak for themselves." They must be selected by the participants, mar-

---

[1] After Rupert B. Vance, "Is Theory for Demographers?", *Social Forces*, October, 1952, p. 11.

7

shalled, linked together, and given a voice. To the Negro West Indian, for example, life is first for leisure, interrupted occasionally with work so that leisure itself be possible. The separate individual has a genius for whole-hearted friendship but on the level of mundane existence he is prone to be a sensualist. He needs material things for life, to be sure, but he is not squeam-ish how they are to be acquired. Since leisure and ecstasy mean so much to him, he is (at least by middle class American Protestant-ethic standards) coldly indifferent to how the material needs of life are to be achieved. If it requires the exploitation of his neighbor he does so without much feeling of guilt. How can the impact of such a mentality upon survival, reproduction and migration be ignored by students of population?

The dynamics of human numbers needs to be integrated with some basic theory of social change. The whole problem of causal interrelation which demography faces is proving most complex. Simpson and Yinger write:

.... The word "cause" ... is a slippery concept. Many scientists and philosophers have stopped using it entirely because of the misunderstandings that result from its naive application. Only the use of the concept of many "levels of causation" can prevent the attempt to explain a phenomenon by one surface relationship. Behind each cause is another cause and behind that another, and the third may, in turn, affect the first. Science is not interested in finding the "ultimate" cause but in describing the total group of interacting forces which occur in connection with the phenomenon being studied. Some forces, to be sure, may be more im-portant than others. This is determined by a simple criterion: How consistently does the force occur in connection with the phenomenon which other forces are controlled? How well can one predict the occurrence of the phenomenon by analysis of the "cause"?[2]

By assuming that changes in human life are either due to heredity or to physical environment we are not only failing to simplify the problems of explanation but are actually complicating and obscuring them. To de-mographers the "environment" is usually defined as an external and sur-rounding condition, distinguished from an organism which is a living thing. This dichotomy marks an attempt to draw clear distinctions between "in-dependent" and "dependent" variables and ignores their interdependence. Robert Bierstedt describes the problem this way:

.... The historical courses of different societies follow no single track; by different routes they arrive at different destinations. The tempo of change itself is different in different periods and in different societies and even in different parts of the

---

[2] George Simpson and J. Milton Yinger, *Racial and Cultural Minorities* (New York: Harper & Brothers, 1953), p. 170. By permission.

same society. The metronome of history beats now faster now slower in separate ages and epochs. Where can we begin amid this welter of difference, to discover the principles that guide and inform the processes of social change?[3]

There have been any number of approaches to the West Indian population problem: economic, geographical, technological and biological, to name a few. They are single variable analyses in the main. Most of the chapters in this book show how the single explanation, taken alone, is superficial and that a multiple-causation approach is equally sterile when each component of population is viewed singularly, one after the other. Simple and multiple approaches come to grips with those kinds of human events encountered least often. A cause produces an effect, but likewise the effect may react upon the cause. Increase in activity complexity engenders an increase in the complexity of interaction; the reverse is also true. We are in the presence of mutual interdependence.[4] The total configuration of mutual dependence carries the seeds of emergent change and control.

THE BIAS OF CLASSICAL EQUILIBRIUM THEORY

The science of economics with its concern with land, labor and capital has been the usual source of theoretical excursions into population problems. The preoccupation with these three elements has seemed to be less interpreting of reality than building a model economic society—thus demographers become evaluators although they would hesitate to acknowledge it. A definition of economic competition is made to fit the requirements of an ideal state and is tied to the notion of equilibrium of numbers to resources. Newcomers in demography must contend with this rigidity in point of view in dealing with their data.

The equilibrium or equivalence theory of "optimum numbers" is a frequent battleground of demographic theorists. The equilibrium concept synthesizes a body of doctrine whose essential ingredients have been the products of a long succession of famous theorists including Adam Smith, John Stuart Mill, Karl Marx, Ricardo, Cannan, on up to Carr-Saunders, Wolfe and Thompson. Wolfe meant by optimum population the size which furnishes the labor supply which, when fully utilized, is necessary to operate the total resources of land, materials and instrumental capital at the point of least labor cost per unit of product or income. And Warren Thompson reacted by saying that such an economic optimum is the chief enemy of a spiritual or

---

[3] Robert Bierstedt, *The Social Order* (New York: McGraw-Hill Book Company, Inc., 1957), p. 497. Used by permission.

[4] See George C. Homans, *The Human Group* (New York: Harcourt, Brace and Company, 1950), p. 98.

personal optimum. The notion that the economic optimum *is* the welfare optimum is hard for sociologically grounded demographers to digest because it fails to appreciate the complexity of human personality and culture. However, economist Manuel Gottlieb accepts this limitation as being a mere complication:

Optimum theory searches for a maximum output by (hypothetically) varying population size. It must be admitted that this procedure invests the theory with a certain bias which must be corrected. In actual fact, population policy will endeavor to impress its aims on a population which is already in a process of movement and which may only gradually over the course of a period of time be affected by a given policy. During this prolonged transition, changes in the arts and resources may supervene and easily make it desirable to aim not at a fixed size but at a desirable trend of change, or, to use the phrase of Cannan, a "right movement." The argument of Gunnar Myrdal that "the amount of applicable technical knowledge is changing and increasing all the time" may thus constitute not an insuperable objection for the optimum concept but merely a complication for the practical task of its ascertainment. The problem of an optimum population is, consequently, "not so much that of adjusting a variable population to a given quantity of land and given stage of the arts but that of harmonizing its changes with the changes that take place in respect of the latter also." To this extent the theory is, if one chooses, "dynamic rather than static."[5]

If, as Professor Gottlieb points out, the optimum is a continuous unfolding operation, I can take no serious issue other than saying that technical knowledge is seldom a "mere" complication. With this in mind, the West Indian optimum number was defined long ago as the product of a succession of generations husbanding, re-arranging and consuming a limited and partially exhaustible resource supply, the resulting diminishing returns bringing on inflated costs, and contributing to a mental state of collective hopelessness. The niggardliness of nature long ago lent in some measure to the ordering of life in terms of the glories of the personality, suitably conditioned, however, by fluid small community moralities.

My point is this: there is no assignable limit on island growth rates. Each community, living close to the margin of subsistence, has built a partial culture, predicated upon socio-economic pessimism—a mind-set which serves as a buttress to the shocks of periodic economic dislocations. Such shocks do not carry an ominous threat of catastrophe to the populace. Hence the word "shock" itself becomes inappropriate.

---

[5] Manuel Gottlieb, "The Theory of Optimum Population for a Closed Economy", *The Journal of Political Economy,* Univ. of Chicago Press, (December, 1945), as quoted in Joseph J. Spengler and Otis D. Duncan, *Population Theory and Policy* (Glencoe: Free Press, 1956), pp. 164-165. Used by permission of the University of Chicago Press.

Many population theorists would not only reject the thought of a dynamic interpretation of optimum members, they would reject my insistence that the West Indies has no optimum number whatsoever. Vigorously defending their theoretical status-quo, they offer two mutually reinforcing assumptions for the support of equilibrium doctrine. One of these is the notion of the inevitability of things—the idea of the influence of an "unseen hand." The other is the tendency to study demographic phenomena in a prism beginning all dissertations with the statement: "All other things being equal. . . ."

Assumption 1: "The Unseen Hand"

One of my teachers at the University of Chicago, demographer-technologist William F. Ogburn, once remarked that students of population can be divided into two camps: the "do-nothingers" (defending the *laissez-faire* bias) and the "for-Godsakers" (the reformers). He preferred the former. This dichotomy, while perhaps extreme, points up the theoretical predicament in the field. The "do-nothingers" fall back on a kind of static fatalism suggesting that the "invisible hand" will inevitably control population. They employ those familiar concepts "balance," "equilibrium," "maladjustment," "function," "evolution," and "culture lag," in describing empirically observable situations, thus giving a *laissez-faire* valuation to population phenomena. But when they speak of the various elements of human life moving toward balance there is the almost inevitable implication that an ideal of some sort has to be attained—an ideal in terms of a given "common welfare." Thus unwittingly they become evaluators. They formulate their problems in nineteenth century Spencerianism, proclaiming that man must never interfere with the obvious trends of things. An obvious contradiction in this perspective is that these same people would try to interfere with those of us who would change things. If they are convinced that things will change anyway, then why try to change the changers? If they believe in *laissez-faire* they would leave the changers alone too. With some controlling hand dictating a balance between resources and numbers of people, they are caught up in a particularistic fallacy, attributing population change to a single cause or a package of "external" causes, forgetting that human beings are themselves dynamic participants within the causal order. The external force is thought to call the tune and the human organism to play it. But man is not a mere agent responding to the stimuli of geography, economics, diet, or machines. These "determinants" become significant only when embraced by the initiative of the conscious agent.

11

The *laissez-faire* point of view has predominated as a demographic guide in the study of overpopulated and depressed countries. The danger in this doctrine is that valuations are hidden behind preconceptions that are not discussed or even known to the investigators. The theory is arbitrary because it is not founded upon a definition of relevant interests. "Poverty" and "misery" are relative conditions of existence placed in this Malthusian-like doctrine as impersonally as income or wages. In a world of variation, change, and human capriciousness, there can be no such thing as an ideal index or ratio. For, in the final analysis, the weights have always to be *chosen* on the basis of one's interest in the study.

I recognize that this observation sounds trite to any scientist who is at all aware of his methodology. Unfortunately, too many demographers fail to recognize that all choices are valuational. They cannot circumvent valuations by restricting their research to the discovery of "facts." And the very attempt to avoid evaluations in this way involves in itself a valuation. While I recognize that data-finding is indispensable for the solution of problems, my complaint is that too much data-seeking goes on without a problem. Louis Wirth once remarked:

. . . . The full statement of a problem, including the decision of scope, direction, hypothesis, classification, principles, and a definition of all terms used, render explicit evaluations necessary in fact-finding research. The author can, of course, explicitly disavow any practical interest and declare that he personally finds that the topic and the hypothesis appeal to him aesthetically — or that he has made all his choices at random. If, however, practical usefulness is an aim in science, even the direction of research becomes dependent upon much wider valuations concerning society.[6]

Assumption 2: "All other things being equal. . . ."

As for the second equilibrium supporting assumption, demographers will often proceed in their studies on the presupposition that all other things can be held constant (and thus ignored) either in the procedure of analysis or in any recommendation for action. They refuse to recognize that all other things are rarely, if ever, equal in the human realm or that we can only point to the "more or less" heavy impress of one or the other positive factors upon human conduct and community building. While man's control over his external surroundings is limited it is increasingly effective. His actions do change his physical environment. Modern man interferes with the total

---

[6] Gunnar Myrdal, *An American Dilemma* (New York: Harper and Brothers Publishers, 1944), p. 1058.

physical situation. He plays back on his physical world through his interests and attitudes.

The theories of the "classical school" of economics were concerned with the causes and consequences of population changes in the effort to discover the "laws" governing the levels and trends of production, wages, interest, rents, and profits. From these theories flowed arguments, far more sophisticated than Malthus' ratios, to support the thesis that population growth tends to depress wages and create poverty.

Early nineteenth century writers had commonly believed that manufacturers were subject to constant or increasing returns and that the augmentation of production in the extractive industries involved increasing difficulties in rising costs in spite of technical progress. But before the close of the century the idea was accepted that, *other things being equal,* average output per worker would fall in non-extractive as well as in extractive industries after the ratio of workers to the resources with which they work passed a certain point. It was soon discovered, however, that other things were not equal, and that the effects of population growth upon wages and *per capita* income depended upon accompanying changes in social organization, technological skills and productive wealth. The latter factors might change from independent causes in such a way as to feed back upon the tendency toward diminishing returns.

Ultimately there emerged, then, the notion of a dynamic and variable optimum population advanced by Cannan and other writers. Cannan defined optimum as a population that was moving in the right direction with respect to the increase of output *per capita.* "The right movement is that which will give the largest returns to industry in the long run, the interests of the people of all the generations being taken into account." Cannan envisioned a "point of maximum return to all industries taken together," that is, a population in which the productivity of labor would be at the maximum. He indicated that the optimum magnitude changed as circumstances changed, usually faster than the actual population.[7]

In general the majority of writers toward the end of the nineteenth century and early in the twentieth were more optimistic than the earlier nineteenth century writers in their estimate of man's ability to control his numbers. Their optimism, still framed in laws as much social as physical, had its origin in the spread of contraceptive practices and the decline of birth rates

---

[7] *The Determinants and Consequences of Population Trends* (New York: United Nations, 1953), Chapter III.

in economically advanced countries, and was reinforced by the thesis that the birth rate tends to decline with the "advance" of civilization.

Many writers now hold that the decline of the birth rate in Western civilization is to be associated with industrialization, urbanization and accompanying changes in modes of living. However, they still *look upon man as a passive respondent to forces which are considered generic.*

Attempts to formulate mathematical "laws" of population growth are still with us. The increasing availability of statistics relating to population trends has encouraged this tendency. Quetelet in 1835 had initiated such an effort. He asserted that "the resistance or the sum of the obstacles opposed to the unlimited growth of population, increases in proportion to the square of the velocity with which the population tends to increase." *All other things being equal,* (i.e., in the absence of a change in "social state") a population tends to grow more and more slowly. At Quetelet's request, Verhulst submitted this principle to examination. In 1838 he suggested that a symmetrical theoretical curve which he named the "logistic" was suitable to describe the course of population growth. A few years later he made use of it to estimate the population of Belgium. Initially he supposed that the obstacles increase "exactly in the same proportion as the super abundant population," but he soon replaced this supposition with the hypothesis that obstacles "increase in proportion to the ratio of the super abundant population to the total population."

For a long time the logistic curve was little used, in part because census data were lacking. As a result the work was generally forgotten until after 1920, when the logistic curve was rediscovered by Pearl and Reed. Pearl's law of growth was based on biological and geographical assumptions. Any population, he believed, began its cycle by a slow increase, the rate of increase rising steadily until the midpoint of the cycle was reached. Density, he said, was the key to the decline in reproduction. Environmental and cultural conditions *must be held stable* for the normal development of a logistic population curve. New economic systems (such as the shift from agriculture to industry) can start new cycles and interrupt an old one before it is complete.[8]

Others such as R. Wilcox, H. P. Fairchild and H. F. Dorn added their limitations to the mathematical logistic curve to those noted by Pearl and Reed, with the following conclusions: first, the logistic was not always the type of curve that best described the past population growth of a given

---

[8] See Raymond S. Pearl, *The Biology of Population Growth* (New York: Alfred A. Knopf, 1925).

country or region; second, even where a logistic described the past growth more precisely than other curves it may not continue to do so in the future; third, it had not been established that a population must pursue the path of a logistic even when there were strong grounds for supposing that an S-shaped curve would be traced; finally, and most important, it was asserted that the logistic law did not effectively take account of the changes in culture which permitted a population to exploit its resources more effectively and to alter its relations with other populations, nor did it anticipate changes in aspiration, in tastes, and hence in reproductive behavior. Critics of the logistic "law" were not content to look on it primarily as an empirical formula which sometimes described the past course of population growth and might well represent the future tendency under certain conditions.

Today, despite the recognized limitations, numerous ideal-type S-curves have been hypothesized in the literature. Four of these simple theoretical patterns are: first, a cycle marked by an initial rising birth rate terminated by a subsequent rise in the death rate; second, a pattern showing a stationary birth rate, then a falling death rate which rises again to terminate the cycle; third, a cycle initiated by a rising birth rate brought to an end by a drop of the birth rate, while the death rate remains stable; finally, the most used theoretical pattern characterized by both falling birth rates and falling death rates, but in the first stages the death rate dropping more rapidly than the birth rate only to be overtaken by a more rapidly falling birth rate in the later stages of the cycle.

From Figure 1 below it will be seen that the logistic pattern does not seem to fit the facts of West Indian experience for the period 1922-1948. Of course, one never knows the time span required for a logistic curve to reveal its dimensions. Thus the predictive value of such a theory is weak. One might argue that "through time" (an inference that time carries its own causal determinants—an absurd assumption) the cycle will eventually be reached, or that under the impact of a culture a logistic curve might evolve. Donald Cowgill says: "It is common knowledge today that population tends to increase with the influences of industrialization, the widening of commercial trade areas, the development of mechanized agriculture, improved medical science, and mass education. Pearl's logistic curve does approximate the growth cycle of most areas subjected to these influences."[9]

Unfortunately for these claimants (like the psychologists who insisted on the reality of a closed number of instincts, like the sociologists who searched

---

[9] Donald O. Cowgill, "The Theory of Population Growth Cycles", *The American Journal of Sociology*, (September, 1949), pp. 167-168. Copyright by the Univ. of Chicago.

FITTING AN S-CURVE TO WEST INDIAN GROWTH PATTERN

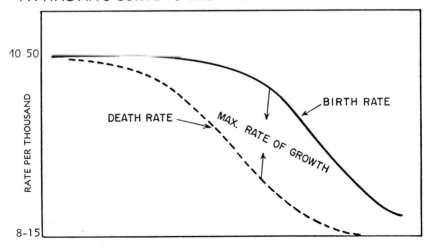

RATE PER THOUSAND

10 50

8-15

DEATH RATE

MAX. RATE OF GROWTH

BIRTH RATE

MODEL OF WORLD DEMOGRAPHIC REVOLUTION

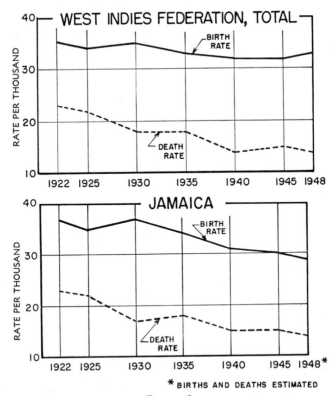

WEST INDIES FEDERATION, TOTAL

RATE PER THOUSAND

40

30

20

10

BIRTH RATE

DEATH RATE

1922 1925   1930   1935   1940   1945 1948

JAMAICA

RATE PER THOUSAND

40

30

20

10

BIRTH RATE

DEATH RATE

1922 1925   1930   1935   1940   1945 1948*

*BIRTHS AND DEATHS ESTIMATED

Figure 1

16

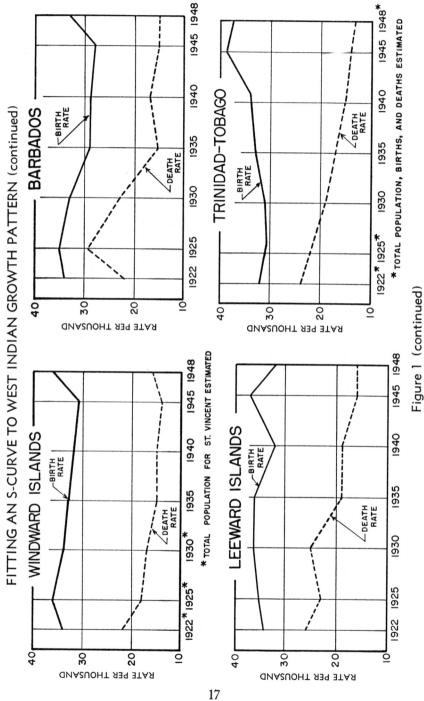

FITTING AN S-CURVE TO WEST INDIAN GROWTH PATTERN (continued)

BARBADOS

TRINIDAD-TOBAGO

*TOTAL POPULATION, BIRTHS, AND DEATHS ESTIMATED

WINDWARD ISLANDS

*TOTAL POPULATION FOR ST. VINCENT ESTIMATED

LEEWARD ISLANDS

Figure 1 (continued)

17

in vain for the closed number of wishes that motivate men), they have now hypothesized so many S-curved possibilities that together they explain nothing.

THE PRINCIPLE OF COUNTERVAILING POWER

In the West Indies, the course of demographic events points to an un-crystalized and changing socio-physical base. Population change is both the product and cause of continuous inter-force pressures, even though the degree of these pressures varies in time and place. The unstructured pressures affect human numbers. The result is that the interaction of forces are either moving, or, if not moving, they are in tenuous accommodation poised to move. When one force, e.g., economics, moves in one direction it tends to encroach on the course of some other force, e.g., religious sentiment. Thus movement is in the nature of pressure and as such encounters resistance, may conduce acceleration or acquiescence, i.e., countervailance. Whenever such contacts are initiated, the entire mode of relations changes. Furthermore, whatever structure is involved in demographic phenomena it is vitally influenced by human assessments. That is, so-called external forces become forces only insofar as they are made socially significant. This bare statement merely sketches the fundamental fact that *demographic phenomena in the Islands are intrinsically unstable and inherently disposed toward rearrangement.*

In this multi-island region, with its broad range of quasi-cultures, combinations of forces replace each other, like instruments in an orchestra, so that there is a larger polyphonic configuration for the society as a whole. Indeed, one can argue that a population curve will show some tendency toward symmetry because it is a composite of curves for several activities. This is an axiom in the teleology of most classical demographers. However, there is enough variability in the population pattern to make it uncertain, to these theorists, whether growth is typically expressed by a logistic curve or by a first-phase symmetrical normal curve. Furthermore, the duration of growth can range from as little as two or three decades to as much as five hundred or a thousand years. The population growth patterns for the Islands (Figure 2) indicate this problem. Because of the reciprocal influencing of such forces as technology, ideology, geography, and economics, each with varying power in different periods, even in a homogeneous society the duration and direction of growth cannot easily be predicted.

To attempt to pull various attributes or variables out of the culture content and examine the effect of each separate from its interlocking variables

18

POPULATION GROWTH, 1871-1961

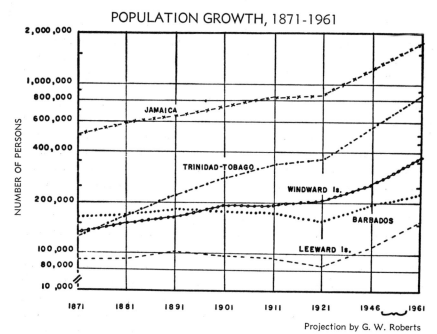

Projection by G. W. Roberts

This Graph covers a 90-Year Period. The Slope of the Graph Shows the Rate of Growth or Decline in Population, Plotted on Semi-logarithmic Scale. (1901 not available for Barbados and Jamaica.)

Figure 2

is to engage in spurious analysis. With culture content inclined to grow cumulatively, each element must be studied in its matrix. The development of natural resources, for example, cannot be studied in isolation from the technology, diets and norms of a culture. The economic base as a factor in population may not be studied meaningfully if it is removed from valuations.

The principle of countervailance is based upon the proposition that the components of society (the domain of sociology) and the components of aggregation (the domain of demography) are not mutually exclusive as the theoretical literature has trapped us into believing, but two complementing aspects of every form of group life, emphasizing that every social group exists in a territorial, physical and substantive as well as social-psychological bond, respectively. Countervailance is a theory of causal dynamics, stating that any force will start a chain of action moving in one direction or the other, as the case may be, with a speed depending first, upon the complex of the initial push and second, upon the interceding causal interrelations within

19

the matrix. Thus the entire change-configuration may either turn back on itself or enter an uncharted course. For example, starting with poverty as the impeller, infanticide may or may not ensue depending upon the collision or permissiveness of the system of female life styles, the values attached to marriage, to infants, to masculinity, and to sexual license within the community. If the colliding force of any of the above mentioned conditions is heavy, its volatility can bend the flow of energy coursing along the main stream toward the act (infanticide). Should this colliding force be an expression in the defense of the sanctity of life, it will blunt the established momentum, i.e., the impetus of poverty will be lessened by this intervening counter-force. It is in this sense that the impersonal "struggle for existence" and human values mutually interact, fuse, even cause each other.

The principle is built upon the work of others. Economist John Galbraith may possibly have been the first to use the term in his book *American Capitalism: The Concept of Countervailing Power*. He used it as a tool to show how those in our economy who have controlled the means of production are now subjected to the counter dictates of giant consumers (entrepreneurs) in the determination of prices, volume and quality of goods to be produced. In this treatise on the transfer of economic initiative, Galbraith pays sole attention to two forces, saying nothing, unfortunately, about the place of home, local governmental units, and other value clusters in their countervailing relations to the entrepreneur. Then, Gunnar Myrdal's "theory of the vicious circle" plays upon the notion of cumulative circularity.[10] Robert M. MacIver, with his "principle of circularity" explains how, in the flow of events, effects can be spread differently along the time axis. Frederick J. Teggart, in his *Theory and Processes of History*, argues that the process of change is actually a set of discontinuous changes. He takes to task the tendency of science in assuming that there is such regularity in the operations of nature that these may be described in stated terms, that events will follow from one another in fixed chronological order. To the contrary, continuous modification is present through the operation of processes that collide with the process under observation. What we find throughout the course of history is the unmistakable result of constant processes manifested in fixity or persistence, tempered by other processes which gradually effect a modification of this rigidity.

Theories of change are all too inclined to ignore the volitions of men as intercedents in the causal process. On the matter of population change, human aggregates and their spatial arrangements are everlastingly bound up

---

[10] See Gunnar Myrdal, *An American Dilemma* (New York: Harper and Brothers, 1944), pp. 207-209.

20

with sociological phenomena. In his scientific mission, the demographer is cautioned to remind himself and his colleagues that human groups are real and that group life is a vast interpretative process in which people singly and collectively guide themselves by defining the objects, events and situations which they encounter.[11] The definition of infants, families property, mother versus father rights, may not be ignored as "imponderables." The definitions must not be viewed as external or incidental to the population research problem. The investigator cannot assume a social structure, but must be aware of action, objects and conduct in-the-making.

People live overwhelmingly in a habitat which they have made by themselves and which is constantly changing. Indeed, men, as animals, are in a position to dig for roots just like the lower forms (and they do), but the more explanatory roots are those of tradition, sentiment, values, skills, and prejudices. The concept of countervailance embraces the forces which conduce population change, and is offered here as a counterpart to nineteenth century concepts of fixed change. My effort is to reconstitute the demographic perspective along fresh lines, looking first and foremost to the person to find out how he affects other persons (autodemography) and indirectly to his interaction with the physical environment (syndemography) in order to live.

---

[11] See Herbert Blumer, "Sociological Analysis and the 'Variable' ", *American Sociological Review*, (December, 1956), p. 686.

Chapter II

"Always Begin With the Land":
The Geographic Dimension

The noted West Indian economist, Arthur Lewis, avows that "the problem of the land is usually the crux of the matter." To start with the land is a first principle. West Indian observers usually respond to such advice, pointing not only to the competition for space but also to the lack of irrigation and water, soil erosion, lack of seeds and fertilizers, poor transport, and uneconomic farm units.

Innumerable writers since antiquity have recognized the influence of the geographical environment on population. Some have used the "geographic environment" to include all the conditions and phenomena which exist independent of man's existence and activity, specifically topography, climate, natural resources, and location. Others have used it to explain almost every conceivable aspect of man's life and history: his physical and mental traits, racial differences, the density and distribution of population, the social organization, including the progress and decay of cultures.

Few readers will question the fact that geographic conditions vitally influence the size, composition and distribution of population. After all, the very existence of man and society is dependent upon the natural environment. The problem, however, is to determine the nature of this influence, and the extent and degree to which it accelerates or retards demographic change. In dealing with the West Indian physical environment each element may vary independently of the others, for example, two islands may have a similar climate but differ widely in topography. Moreover, each component will be expected to have its separate influence on segments of an island population by reason of the definitions or assessments given to these components as they are made to fit into the mosaics of the social and personal life organizations. The separate influences of geographic elements may all be positive, i.e., favoring the "development" of society, or one may be positive and the others negative. Their influences thus may countervail each other. Again, one factor may tend to influence human numbers in one direction of development and the others in another direction. The difficulty in measuring these influences is in holding all other forces for change constant. In any case, the geographic environment must be considered a complex of various forces, affecting the make-up and re-composition of societies not only in their totality but also individually.

As physically constituted, can the West Indies become an efficient and powerful nation? Kingsley Davis would say no, finding the following conditions necessary for greatness· (1) a rich and extensive territory, (2) an industrial economy, (3) a high proportion of people in non-agricultural pursuits, (4) a high degree of urbanization, (5) a great amount of public education, (6) a low agricultural density, (7) a balance of low fertility and low mortality.[1] Few nations in the world have all of these attributes and certainly the West Indies are not included among them. Unqualified on all counts, the Islands' chances of acquiring these qualities in the foreseeable future are small. Assuming for the moment the reliability of Davis' conclusions, I envisage a predicament in which improvement of any one component to the neglect of others can invite more chaos than order. The noted geographer, Otis P. Starkey writes:

Increased prosperity in the islands will not result from increased production of the present import industries alone: the resource base is too limited and increased exports might not find a market. Increased efficiency by further mechanization will result in further unemployment. However, most of the islands would benefit substantially from improved internal transportation, and better inter-island connections. An increase and improvement in fishing, animal husbandry, and the growing of local food crops to help reduce the high level of food imports would help if it does not reduce present exports.

Further economic opportunities must be sought in manufacturing and tourism although unfortunately both of these require heavy capital investment. . . .[2]

This is not a "rich and extensive territory."[3] And even if it were, such would likely encourage rather than discourage population growth by reason of the inertia of historically-rooted demographic practices.

At the outset, I recognize the general influence of the physical environment not only upon certain forms of culture but also upon people and customs. But the physical environment furnishes the materials, not the plan, out of which man develops his culture. Geographic factors exert a limiting rather than a determining effect. Not only will the same environment be met by different reactions from peoples in different periods of development

---

[1] Kingsley Davis, "The Demographic Foundations of National Power," in *Freedom and Control in Modern Society,* ed. by Morroe Berger, Theodore Abel and Charles Page (New York: D. Van Nostrand Company, 1954), pp. 206-242.

[2] Otis P. Starkey, *Commercial Geography of the Eastern British Caribbean* (Bloomington, Indiana, University of Indiana, June, 1961), Technical Report No. 1.

[3] The term "underdeveloped country" has often been applied to the West Indies. Unfortunately, the term has been carelessly used and ill-defined, usually referring to a low level of economic development, quite apart from the potentialities of an area. The West Indies is "developed" in the sense that its natural resources have been tapped, "underdeveloped" in the sense that its *human* resources are still untapped.

but similar environments reveal dissimilar cultures.[4] Furthermore, the cultural factors may be quite as effective, or even more effective, than geographic factors; and psychic inertia as the underlying cause of persistant cultural traits must always be taken into account.

Man and culture are the dynamic factors in demographic development; the physical environment is mainly static. While the cultures of great historical areas have undergone tremendous changes, the physical surroundings within the same areas have changed but little.

We are not dealing with an equation in which the geographic components are the independent variables, or the causes, and the number of people are the *dependent variable*, or effect. If there is such a thing as a geographic optimum for the West Indies, it will not be attained by a formula that takes population as a dependent variable but rather would consider the number of people (with their expectations) to be the moving force. In analyzing the populace we must start and end with human wishes—what human beings would make of themselves.

However, to ignore completely the role of geographic factors is to commit a serious demographic error. My intent is simply to caution the reader in assigning more significance to the conditioning factors than is warranted.

The geographer's terms "site" and "situation" will be used here to organize my data and observations on the geographic factors in population dynamics. By the term "site" is meant the characteristics of the local environment, i.e., the immediate area on which a community is built. Probably the greatest importance of site lies in its influence on the configuration of settlement. While site embraces the influence of the local environment, "situation" refers to the position of the territorial community on the earth's surface and becomes important in determining the relation of a site to the resources and human development of the world. To study the situation necessitates an appraisal of the population composition and the accessibility of diverse population groups to one another. Thus while "site" is a geographical fact determined by function in time, "situation" refers to the site in relation to the larger total conditions or circumstances.

The function of island societies, like cities, frequently changes in the course of time in response to changing demands made by the surrounding territory for which they serve as centers. Islands, cities, and social institutions tend through time to exist for reasons other than those which brought them into existence. An island site may be selected in the interest of protection from invaders, for military strategy, and only incidentally for com-

---

[4] A. A. Goldenweiser, "Culture and Environment", *American Journal of Sociology*, (March, 1916), pp. 628, 633.

mercial purposes. For the West Indies, situation or position is becoming more important than site in determining the growth potential. Because of poor situations many islands are being ignored. Excellent sites with poor situations often remain unutilized, but poor or mediocre sites are frequently developed because of excellent situations. Observe how the military and foreign aid programs of the United States have demanded a revised definition of the importance of the West Indies in so far as American self-interest is concerned.

SITE COMPONENTS

The only common physical characteristic in the Islands is the surrounding water. This makes insular temperatures milder than those of the large land masses in the same latitude and makes the Islands on their windward shores subject to the influences of the unbroken sweep of the wind of the sea. Water is so much a part of the island dweller's environment that he has turned to the sea for a portion of his subsistence and for transportation. The fullest use of the sea for livelihood does not necessarily follow, however, since other occupations are more profitable. An island such as Barbados, with fair soil, is the home of farmers who consider the surrounding sea a barrier to marketing their products, and who turn to fishing only to add variety to their diet. Barren or mountainous islands such as St. Lucia push their people toward the seas as an easier avenue to livelihood.

The infinite variety in the economies of the Islands, due in large part to variations in their local environments, make them fascinating studies in geography. Of course, the size of an island and the number of people it will support are of great importance in determining the influence of its insularity. As noted in Figure 3 below, there is considerable range of density from island to island. Barbados is the most heavily populated. Its density is unique, not only in the Caribbean, but anywhere in the world. In 1946, Barbados had a population of 192,800, crowded into her 166 square miles. There are few areas in the world which can compare with this density of 1159 per square mile. Malta, which has a population one-third bigger than that of Barbados, on only two-thirds of the area, is the only island in the world which has a greater density. Java, with 964 persons per square mile in 1941, is the only other area in the world which approaches Barbados.

The area in square miles of the many islands of the Federation ranges from Montserrat with 32 to Jamaica with 4,207 (Table 1). Please observe that most of the islands are much smaller than Jamaica. Trinidad, which is slightly less than half the size of Jamaica, has 1,863 square miles. The next

TABLE 1

Areas and Chief Towns, West Indies Federation

Island	Area in Sq. Miles	Chief Town
Jamaica with its dependencies	4,207	Kingston
(a) Turks and Caicos Islands	224	Grand Turk
(b) The Cayman Islands	90	Georgetown
The Leeward Islands, including:		
(a) Antigua & Barbuda	170	St. John's
(b) St. Kitts	68	Basseterre
(c) Nevis	50	Charlestown
(d) Anguilla	35	The Road
(3) Montserrat	32	Plymouth
(f) Dominica	305	Roseau
The Windward Islands, including:		
(a) Grenada	133	St. George's
(b) St. Lucia	233	Castries
(c) St. Vincent	150	Kingston
Barbados	166	Bridgetown
Trinidad-Tobago	1,979	Port-of-Spain

largest island, Dominica, with 305 square miles is only about one-sixth the size of Trinidad. The rest of the islands are less than 250 square miles. Thus we gain the picture of two large islands (Jamaica and Trinidad) and a dozen much smaller ones. Mountainous terrain leads to a concentration of the population on ocean fronts and results in a low overall density when compared with such other small countries as Java and Madura, England and Wales, Holland, and Puerto Rico.

The climate of the Lesser Antilles is characterized by a prevailing high temperature, yet there is relative comfort in the shade when the northeast tradewind is blowing. These islands lie far down on the track of the Atlantic tropical hurricanes of late summer or early fall, and these scourges rival volcanic outbursts in their destructive effects. However, as land obstructions, these islands provoke rain from the tradewinds. The lower islands not infrequently suffer from drought while the loftier ones have a plentiful rainfall, e.g., Dominica and St. Lucia.

Unfortunately, it is precisely in the lower islands, where agriculture is most extensively developed, that the rainfall is most deficient. Yet when rain does fall there it may be heavy, because condensation begins at a high temperature, where a moderate measure of cooling precipitates a large volume of water. Erosion has taken perhaps one-quarter of all the top soil from the mountain areas. Rain, falling with tropical fury, will sometimes remove

27

DENSITY PER SQUARE MILE, 1911, 1946

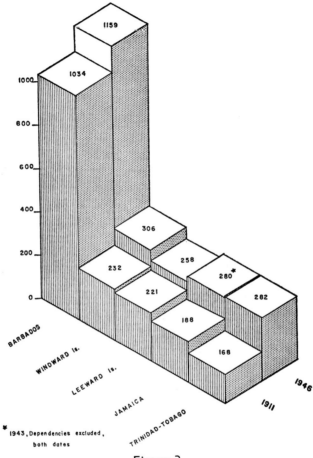

Figure 3

several inches of soil during one storm. Rainfall in all the islands varies from a low of 25 inches per year to a high of 200.

A first obstacle then is the nation's physiography: 8,095.6 square miles of land most of which is hilly to mountainous. With a population estimated at 2,933,000 in 1955, this means a density of 362 persons per square mile. Not all the islands are arable. Only a little less than one-fourth is well suited to farming.

The large percentage of arable land in Barbados, 57.5, can be accounted for in two ways. First, Barbados has less mountainous area than any of the other islands. Secondly, the tremendous population density which existed for over two hundred years has caused its inhabitants to work and re-work every possible acre of land in order to maintain subsistence. There is an average of 1,391 persons per square mile of farmland or approximately 2.2 persons per acre: a little less than a half acre for each inhabitant.

It is generally estimated that there are approximately four billion arable acres of land on the earth. Estimating the world population at 2.5 billion, this means that there are approximately 1.6 acres of crop land per person on earth. The less than one-half acre per person in Barbados becomes even smaller when compared with the United States which has almost four acres of arable land per inhabitant. (And the United States depends primarily on an industrial rather than an agricultural economy at that.) Christensen[5] has estimated that one man needs 2 to 2.5 acres of arable land for subsistence, a figure four to five times greater than the actual amount of land available in Barbados. With an annual population increase of approximately two per cent, the intensity of the problem is certain to increase in the next generation.

These conditions might not be so serious were the island economy not so dependent upon agriculture. Employment and net income both show the extent of this dependency. Almost 73.3 per cent of the total labor force is engaged in agriculture. The income of Barbados in 1942 is reported at 5,585 thousand pounds sterling and total income from agriculture was 2,580 thousands for that year, which is 46.2 per cent of the total island income. Similarly in Jamaica, the net income for 1942 was pounds sterling 33,300 thousands and income from agriculture was 14,636 thousand, which is 33.9 per cent of the total island income compared to 39.8 per cent in 1938.

Agriculture and the Labor Force

Man has swarmed over the arable flatland of the Federation in such large numbers that housing, and commercial and agricultural land uses are locked in a struggle for dominance. Acre by acre, plantations are yielding to non-agricultural uses, terrain permitting. But in the case of Jamaica, although 86 per cent of the surface is less than 2000 feet altitude, the limestone plateau is by no means flat. Only 10 per cent of the land is under cultivation by reason of its irregular terrain. Of Jamaica's 4,450 square miles, only 600 square miles or 14 per cent are classified as flat and much of this is unsuited for cultivation. Many of the streams have carved deep valleys back from the coast,

---

[5] Christensen, J. J., "Technologies of Increasing Food Production," in *World Population and Future Resources,* ed. Paul K. Hatt (New York: American Book Company, 1952), Chapter 8.

and the limestone is, in many places, honey-combed with caverns, leaving many square miles unfit for agriculture.

The Blue Mountains occupy the eastern third of the island. It is a mass of complex folds reduced to a stage of maturity, and rising to an elevation of over 7,000 feet above sea level. Surrounding and projecting westward over the greater part of the island is a highly dissected limestone plateau, marked with deep valleys and broad basins. Here are found fertile limestone soils, which support some of the best agricultural communities in the island. Bordering the island is a discontinuous coastal plain that varies in width from practically nothing to more than five miles.

The distribution of population on certain islands presents several points of interest. Geographer William M. Davis[6] points out that it is only on the relatively low limestone islands like Antigua and Barbados that the whole surface is well enough occupied for the partition of estates and the location of villages to be developed. On the mountainous islands such as Dominica, St. Lucia, St. Vincent, and Grenada, villages are almost wholly limited to the shore and plantations to the shore-facing valleys. The high interior of these mountainous islands remains a forested wilderness, only here and there cultivated in small patches. On St. Lucia, St. Vincent and Grenada, which have more indented shore lines than Dominica, shore settlements are almost wholly determined by the bays in front of them. The larger towns on all the islands are on the leeward or western coast, where navigation was safer for small sailing vessels on which the islands long depended for overseas transportation; consequently holiday cruising steamers touch only at the chief ports, seldom seeing the windward, or eastern, side of the islands.

The arrangement of highways is in accord with the distribution of population. The low islands are crossed by a network of roads, many of which are of excellent surface; the high islands are served chiefly by coastwise roads, along or near the shore, with valley roads leading inland and occasionally crossing over the axial mountain range. On several of the more embayed high islands, however, the coastwise roads are by no means level, for they lie a moderate distance inland so as to pass behind the bay heads and therefore have to make many ascents and descents over the enter-bay spurs. On Dominica and St. Lucia the coastwise roads fail to make the entire circuit of the island by reason of the boldness of parts of the coast.

The Case of Barbados. No part of the Barbados landscape has escaped alteration by man. During the first century of settlement the indigenous

---

[6] William Morris Davis, *The Lesser Antilles* (New York: American Geographical Society of New York, 1926), pp. 1-11.

flora and fauna were almost completely destroyed and were replaced by exotic forms. The soil was greatly altered except where it was too thin for cultivation. Pests and diseases from other areas were accidentally added to the Barbadian environment by man. It is also possible that the clearing of the forests decreased both the rainfall and the sensible temperatures. Whereas most of the Lesser Antilles have a good position for trade, Barbados has the additional advantage of being eastward and windward from the main chain. Thus it was the logical stopping place for sailing vessels from Europe wishing to transship cargo for the other Lesser Antilles and proceed to Trinidad or Jamaica without encountering adverse winds or currents.

The lack of extreme temperatures in Barbados is due to the moderating influence of the surrounding ocean. No part of the island is more than five miles from the sea, and the moderating influence of the water is the more penetrating because of the almost constant winds across the island. Such differences in actual and sensible temperatures as exist among the various parts of the island are largely due to differences in altitude and exposure to the wind. Even when the weather is oppressive, the unpleasant heat lasts only from noon to about four in the afternoon. Temperature conditions are also suited to most warm-temperate and tropical plants, and agriculture is not greatly restricted by the temperature factor alone. By reason of the warm weather, germs, pests and plant diseases are not destroyed during the winter, but this is partly balanced by the sterilizing power of the bright sunshine and by the ability of the winds and rains to carry away many germs and pests. The life of the people of Barbados is patterned by temperature conditions, not so much as a matter of necessity as a matter of convenience. Barbadians rise early, and slacken their pace during the middle of the day, but the stores do not close, nor does business cease. Sports and amusements are adjusted to the temperature; strenuous games are played early in the morning or late in the afternoon. However, the temperatures are not oppressive enough to have forced the abandonment of English style dress.

On the average, about sixty-two inches of rain falls annually on Barbados, but this average includes stations with twenty inches of rain and stations with over one hundred inches. Sugar production oscillates with the changes in annual rainfall.

The bulk of the unplowed land is untilled because of thin, infertile or exhausted soil. Even the cultivated areas have remarkably thin soils and would lose their fertility were it not for heavy fertilization. Improved methods of soil cultivation are responsible for a large part of the increase in Barbadian productivity. Nearly half of the acreage is occupied by cane

31

fields; and since two successive crops overlay, fields of cane are always a conspicious feature of the Barbadian landscape.

The mineral resources are limited to those commonly associated with sedimentary rocks and are of small importance to the Barbados economy. The coral limestone has provided building stone, building lime, and lime for fields. Tile bricks and crude local pottery are made from clay in the Scotland district. Oil has been known for some time to exist in this area also. Small quantities of petroleum have been obtained within the last decade and explorations are continuing.

When the slave trade was abolished in 1806 there were 60,000 Negroes in these British islands, and in 1834, 83,176 slaves were emancipated. But the Negroes had to continue working for white men or starve. There were several hundred sugar plantations in the hands of white men and this discouraged emigration by freed Negroes. Thus the racial-economic relations were not greatly changed by freedom. A plantation system is still in operation in Barbados, although some Negroes have acquired modest plantations of their own.

In passing, Barbados is the most intensively agriculturalized island of the Federation. There is a total absence of mineral resources such as coal and iron.

The Other Islands. Trinidad has the broadest economic base in the region. Although petroleum products account for about three-fourths of her exports, there is still a fairly well balanced commercial, industrial and agricultural economy. Sugar, cocoa, citrus fruits, and coffee are the main commercial crops. But balance is hardly the term to describe the economic geography of the other islands. Where the king, sugar, has been dethroned there has taken place not a diversification of crops but rather the substitution of one staple for another. Thus bananas have replaced sugar in Jamaica, as they are displacing limes in Dominica and arrowroot in St. Vincent. Since the carnage, by the 1955 hurricane, of her nutmeg trees Grenada too has gotten the "banana fever."

Because attention is concentrated on the cultivation of export crops, food (flour, fish, meat, milk, butter) must be imported along with textiles, building supplies and variable quantities of capital equipment. And nothing is more fantastic in the economy of these Islands so bountifully endowed by nature than the high percentage of food in their imports. About eighty per cent of Trinidad's food comes from outside her shores. Densely populated Barbados cannot afford the luxury of growing foodstuffs. Meal, fish, beans, and peas figure largely in Barbadian imports. The situation in Jamaica is even worse. There are insufficient cattle on the island to provide fresh milk, so tinned milk is imported. At present, well over a million dollars are spent annually on preserved fish from North America. Ironically, the island dependencies of Jamaica exist largely on the export of salt to Canada for the curing of imported fish.

The large plantations, typical of the slave system, still dominate the island chain. The difference between black and white is essentially one of the landlord and laborer. The invasion by Negroes of the white man's occupational domain centers in the cities and in entrepreneurial pursuits. The proportion of independent cultivators to plantation laborers is instructive: in Trinidad 1:4, in St. Vincent 1:24, in Barbados 1:28, in St. Kitts 1:73. Even in Jamaica more than half of the total area was comprised in 1930 of less than 1,400 properties, averaging 1,000 acres each. The alternative to the plantation system with its landless, discontented-to-apathetic proletariat, is a system of peasant-proprietorship as in Grenada.

The evolution of Negro peasantry in the face of persistent opposition from planters and governments, makes a most fascinating story. Beginning with the food crops, the peasants showed by the end of the nineteenth century that the cultivation of plantation crops was not beyond them. In Trinidad, the story surrounds the golden age of cocoa, a permanent crop which requires little cultivation after it has been planted and which is well suited to cultivation by peasants. Coffee also played its part in the development of peasantry, as did arrowroot in St. Vincent, nutmeg in Grenada and lime in Dominica. Bananas in Jamaica owe their beginning to the genius and courage, industry and capacity of the people of that colony. The little man in Jamaica is the largest producer of bananas. While the large planters no longer despise banana cultivation, the peasants have maintained their positions. Land holdings under twenty acres represent over 30 per cent of the acreage under bananas. Today 44 per cent of the cane grown in Trinidad comes from properties of less than five acres. Whatever the economic merits of large-scale cultivation, the plantation lacks the social stability which inevitably accompanies peasant-proprietorship. The memory of slavery is as indelible in the West Indies as it is in the United States, and agricultural labor for wages is to the Negro West Indian a badge of slavery. The Negro will work his own land, but is increasingly unwilling to work for field wages.

The total proportion of the working population engaged in agriculture is high when compared with the industrialized areas of the world. As observed in Figure 4, 45 per cent of the gainfully employed labor force of Jamaica was engaged directly in agriculture in 1946. Both the Leeward and Windward Islands had approximately half of their labor force engaged in

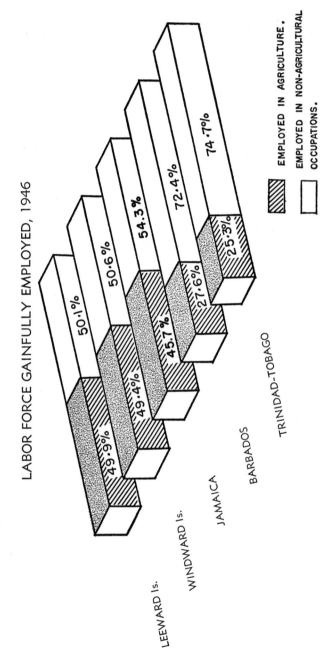

LABOR FORCE GAINFULLY EMPLOYED, 1946

49·9%
49·4%
45·7%
27·6%
25·3%

50·1%
50·6%
54·3%
72·4%
74·7%

LEEWARD Is.
WINDWARD Is.
JAMAICA
BARBADOS
TRINIDAD-TOBAGO

EMPLOYED IN AGRICULTURE.

EMPLOYED IN NON-AGRICULTURAL
OCCUPATIONS.

Figure 4

34

agriculture. It is interesting to note, however, that Barbados and Trinidad-Tobago have only about one-fourth of their total labor force occupied in agriculture, or only about half the proportion of the other islands in the Federation. This phenomenon can be accounted for on both islands by the introduction of technology. In Barbados, agricultural production, chiefly sugar, accounts for more than 95 per cent of her exports and more than 45 per cent of the gross domestic product (1951-55). But introduction of technological innovations in sugar production has caused a steady decline in the proportion of workers needed in agriculture.

In the '50s sugar planting held its position in Barbados, accounting for 90 per cent of the whole agricultural working population. It was also the largest single item in Trinidad and Tobago. In St. Lucia and Jamaica although still important, it was outnumbered by "mixed farming" and "general farming," respectively. In Grenada and St. Vincent, the 1946 census shows the proportion engaged in sugar planting small by comparison with mixed farming while in Montserrat and Dominica, sugar planting was of still less importance.

The census states that in Jamaica, "mixed farming" accounted for 70,878 persons in the 1946 census area and "general farming" for 128,703. A further 4,636 were engaged in "farming" without any further specification as to type, and no doubt many of these properly belonged to the mixed farming item. In addition to Jamaica, mixed farming predominates in Montserrat and all four Windward Islands.

Judging by the ratio of small farmers to farm laborers, the Leeward Islands and St. Vincent are most like Barbados in having few peasant cultivators (at least, few whose *principal* occupation is reported as cultivation). In Trinidad and Tobago, in Grenada, St. Lucia, and Jamaica, both peasant cultivators and wage earning laborers are numerous.[7]

The census, furthermore, reports that the ratio of unpaid helpers to wage-earning laborers is again lowest (1:33.4) in Barbados. The Leeward Islands, St. Vincent, Grenada and Trinidad-Tobago show ratios less than 1:10. Dominica shows the highest ratio of one unpaid helper to 2.6 wage earners, Jamaica 1:4.8, St. Lucia 1:6.3.

All persons other than farmers were asked by census enumerators whether they engaged in cultivation on their own behalf, subsidiary to their

---

[7] Jamaica shows a number of employing farmers, much larger, in fact, than all other colonies combined, but neither foremen or managers are high by comparison with other colonies. The fact that 4,000 of the 18,933 agricultural employers in Jamaica, or 21 per cent, were illiterate seems to indicate that their farms cannot have been very large or efficiently operated.

principal means of livelihood. A summary of those persons who gave an affirmative answer to this question is shown in Table 2.

TABLE 2

Persons Engaged in Cultivation as Principal Occupation and Those in Subsidiary Agriculture (Except Jamaica), 1946[a]

	Total Cultivators	Farmer, Farm Managers Stock Raisers	Cultivators Subsidiary
Barbados	29,611	875	28,736
Leeward Islands:			
Antigua	4,387	1,550	2,837
Montserrat	2,772	795	1,977
St. Kitts	6,995	1,013	5,982
Trinidad-Tobago	45,401	18,186	27,215
Windward Islands:			
Dominica	7,956	4,741	3,215
Grenada	9,974	3,389	6,585
St. Lucia	8,367	3,296	5,070
St. Vincent	5,463	1,789	3,674

[a] Census of Jamaica, Part A, 1946, p. 119.

SITUATION

From the standpoint of situation alone, the West Indies is certainly one of the most heterogeneous and geographically dispersed political entities in the world. Between Jamaica in the northwest, whose nearest neighbor is Cuba, and Trinidad in the southeast, lying off the coast of Venezuela, are a thousand miles of open sea.

History has shown that the sea may be either a barrier or a bridge. For Jamaica, Trinidad, and Barbados, with reasonably good harbors close to areas of dense population, the sea is a bridge. The surrounding water acts as a connecting link rather than a cause of isolation. But Grenada and Dominica are subject to the same social and economic results of isolation as found in many mountainous regions of the world. Their social environment provides the evidence, this being particularly true in the case of Dominica. Distance from markets puts a premium on a self-sufficient economy, and social and cultural conservatism characterizes these islands.

The Federation: Where Peoples Meet

Racially, the West Indies are so diverse, the forces for a national existence are countervailed by this racial pluralism. The Leewards and Windwards

36

have largely a Negro population with very few people of pure (so-called) European descent. In Jamaica about sixty per cent are predominantly of West African origin, but there are important European, Indian, Syrian, Chinese, and Jewish minorities (minorities in the numerical sense). What is commonly called the middle class is chiefly composed of colored people of mixed African and British stock with a mixture of other races, while the "working class" is principally Negro with some Indians. Small business is largely Chinese and Indian; big business is Syrian and Jewish. The nearby Cayman islanders are inbred and the descendents of English, West Country sailors and buccaneers.

On the other hand, Trinidad was once a Spanish colony and has also had a considerable French influence. A century ago, Trinidadian officials carried Spanish titles yet church services were held in French. Today, a number of place-names recall these influences and many "Creole" families bear French surnames. The two chief races today are the Negro and the Indian (the latter being so defined locally). Indians are outnumbered by Negroes and have generally expressed opposition to federation of the islands, possibly through fears of being inundated, politically, by the blacks. In addition, Trinidad has its Portuguese (businessmen), Venezuelans and Chinese.

Densely populated Barbados likes to call itself "Little England," and it reproduces with great fidelity the strict social divisions of the England of a century ago. But there is a difference: in Barbados, the divisions are on a "shade" basis—the more European the color, facial features and hair texture, the more upper class their possessor.

Mention should be made of the Maroons in Jamaica. These are descendants of slaves who fought the Spaniards and declined to be re-enslaved when the British conquered the island. They took to the hills and successfully opposed all attempts to dislodge them, so that the British government finally signed a treaty with them. Now they enjoy considerable self government in a remote and roadless cockpit country and discourage visitors. Capital offense cases are, however, sent down to Kingston for trial.

An analysis of the racial and ethnic make-up of the West Indies could fill a book. And this fascinating subject has been touched upon here only for the purpose of making the generalization: the political unity of these British possessions will always be fraught with tension and power struggles within and between islands by reason of gradations in racial composition. Each island has a population problem peculiar to itself.

To help the reader visualize in his mind the variability in racial make-up, a three-dimensional drawing (Figure 5) is included to portray these similarities and contrasts.

37

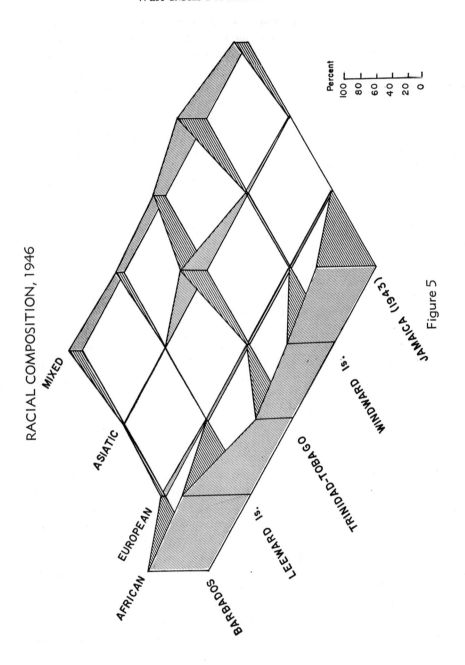

RACIAL COMPOSITION, 1946

Figure 5

Situation and Idle Hands

Since the sugar-prosperous eighteenth century, when the West Indies were Britain's prize possession, colonialism has gone out of style, and the Islands have turned into economic liabilities, many of them now on a steady dole. Unemployment is high. And idle hands make people seek more gainful settings, either on some other island or in an urban center. If the Islands are to emerge as an enduring nation, a customs union must not only be enacted[8] but the problems of urbanism and migration must be faced. Cities are becoming the abode of the rural unemployed. The hordes of jobless in Jamaica and Barbados are unable to move with ease to more prosperous Trinidad. Even island officials must put up with far more red tape than most American tourists in traveling from island to island.

Inflow-Outflow. While out-migration undoubtedly slightly improves the employment picture of the region, at the same time it depletes that part of the labor force which is valuable in the strengthening of the economic life of the Islands, particularly industrial expansion. The more highly trained personnel are those inclined to migrate to England. G. W. Roberts writes concerning Barbados:

While the present organized emigration forms a valuable limb of the population policy of Barbados, the past exodus from this island furnishes an excellent example of the limits of emigration as an agent of lasting population control. For although the outward movement sufficed to assure a 14 per cent fall in population from 1891 to 1921, its cessation in the 1920's was followed by a resurgence of growth. In fact in the thirty-four years following 1921 the increment of the population threat (72,000) placed it at a level 25 per cent above that of 1891. Half a century's continuous emigration in no way impaired the capacity of the population to reproduce itself.[9]

Only sharp and early declines in fertility can offset massive overcrowding in the Islands. So far only Barbados has publicly committed itself to a policy of fertility control.

Felt population pressure connotes dissatisfaction with the habitat and is expressed in a readiness to move. Centering on Jamaica, Barbados, Grenada, and Trinidad, this predisposition to move is reflected in statistical records.

---

[8] Tariffs are now a jumble. Antigua collects duties on goods in transshipment to St. Kitts, which in turn collects another duty upon arrival. Jamaica's industries are protectively walled off, and will presumably suffer from competition from other islands. Legislation will have to eliminate these barriers, create a common market, set common tariffs, and provide for negotiating commercial treaties with other nations.

[9] G. W. Roberts, "The Caribbean Islands", *The Annals of the American Academy of Political and Social Science*, (March, 1958), p. 135. By permission.

Felt population pressure serves to make people unadjusted to old settings, to make them psychologically ready for movement.[10]

Migration out of the Federation by the Negroid peoples, however, is not flowing so smoothly as to maintain any condition of balance between population and resources. Thus the disjunction between equilibrium theory and observed facts necessitates some subsidiary postulates: a comprehensive statement of the conditions under which migrations would or would not occur. One may never encounter a "perfect" mobility situation—where ability and readiness to move in response to an opportunity for improving one's competitive position is in operation. The conditions for mobility must always be understood in terms of the particular historical circumstances. Noneconomic forces, writes Saunders, become "frictional factors"—factors in constant operation preventing the "ideal" mobility from occurring. Economic competition, he insists, is not sufficient to account for mobility. False or misleading reports on relative opportunities result in movements into areas where the scale of living is actually lower. Many Barbadians in migrating to England have discovered this fact. Under such circumstances these migrants return if possible to Barbados or wander aimlessly and disillusioned in the mother country. "When such wasted movements become known to other potential migrants, they serve to produce inertia and impede further movement."[11]

Increased economic opportunity and the spatial reorganization of the population result in a permanent reduction of population pressure only when reproduction is so controlled as to allow for a rising scale of living rather than a mere increase in size of population. With the great disparity between the birth rate and the death rate in Jamaica and related islands, the departure of migrants from the West Indies to the United Kingdom has not had a significant effect upon population size or its redistribution.

One can anticipate political barriers being thrown up by England as the West Indies again tries political autonomy. The difficulty for West Indians is that there are essentially no places in the world where these predominantly Negroid peoples, untrained and relatively illiterate, are wanted.

Actual migration is not governed simply by high and low congestion, but is governed by economic costs, political barriers, ethnic attitudes, and limited horizons, all in countervailance. It is not safe to predict the volume of future migration on the basis of impoverished density alone.[12]

---

[10] Harold W. Saunders, "Human Migration and the Social Equilibrium," *Journal of Business,* University of Iowa, (March, 1942), p. 221.

[11] *Ibid.,* p. 225.

[12] Kingsley Davis, "Future Migration Into Latin America", *The Milbank Memorial Fund Quarterly,* (January, 1947), p. 44.

The six charts in Figure 6 (and Appendix Table 1) indicate first, the net changes in the population on the basis of a calculation of the excess of births over deaths if no migration occurred and second, a comparison of this natural increase with the inflow-outflow of the population, pointing to considerable outflow for Barbados and the Windward Islands in the 1940 decade. The indicated inflow is obtained by subtracting the excess of births from the amount of change in total population from the end of one period to the end of the next period. Increases in population by migration are indicated when the slope of the population curve is greater than that of the natural growth curve. The reader should be mindful that the six charts show only net changes, not the total amount of population turnover.

The present story is one of outflow. One will observe how the densely populated island of Barbados has experienced a net outflow since the middle '30s. This emigration is noteworthy. G. W. Roberts believes that the effects of the Barbadian outflow upon Trinidad are unmistakable. He reports that in the six decades prior to 1921 the contribution of Barbados to population growth in the other islands, in fact, was more than one-eighth of the total net emigration into the region.[13]

Lord Simon of Wythenshawe in his 1955 report entitled *Population and Resources of Barbados* observed that between 1891 and 1921 the number of emigrants was so great that in spite of a moderate excess of births over deaths, the population fell in those years from 193,000 to 157,000. Between 1921 and 1950 the net immigration amounted to about 29,000; just under an average of 1,000 each year. This, he believes, was due to the return of Bar-

TABLE 3
Population: Rate of Increase, Barbados, 1921-1953[a]

Period	Mean Population	Average Birth Rate per 1,000	Average Death Rate per 1,000	Rate of Increase %	Total Natural Increase over 5 yrs.	Increase due to Migration over 5 yrs.
1921-25	155,043	35.03	32.89	0.2	1,659	4,876
1926-30	158,754	34.34	26.95	0.7	5,857	4,014
1931-35	164,676	32.08	33.58	0.8	6,971	9,773
1936-40	175,698	32.32	19.93	1.2	10,813	2,298
1941-45	183,381	32.08	16.44	1.3	12,438	4,927
1946-50	203,049	31.5	15.6	1.6	15,543	3,318
1950-53	219,028	32.8	14.1	1.9	12,205	904

[a] Source: Lord Simon of Wythenshawe, (report) *Population and Resources of Barbados*, 1955. Used by permission.

[13] G. W. Roberts, "Emigration From Barbados", *Social and Economic Studies*, (September, 1955), p. 281.

POPULATION INFLOW AND OUTFLOW, 1933-1956

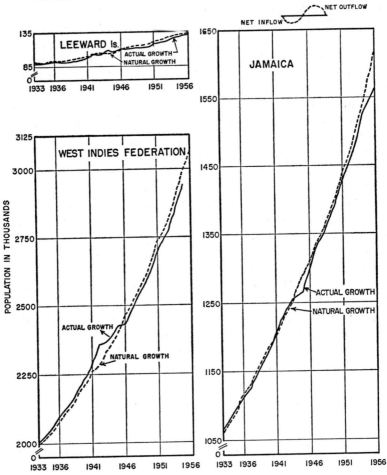

Figure 6

badians who had emigrated in the previous generation. It is thought, and hoped, he reports, that the period of heavy repatriation is ended; and the fact that there was an average net emigration of about three hundred annually during the years 1951-53 lends support to this view. Lord Simon is correct when he asserts that the problem of security during emigration on a substantial scale is very real: hardly any country is willing to accept Barbadians as permanent immigrants, and the prospects of emigration in the

POPULATION INFLOW AND OUTFLOW, 1933-1956 (continued)

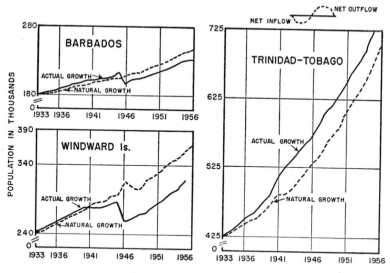

Figure 6 (continued)

coming decades, except for a few hundred each year seems to be remote. Lord Simon offers Table 3 on migration of 1921-1953 (page 41).

In appraising Table 3 it should first be noted that between 1904 and 1921 at least 70,000 residents left Barbados. This mass emigration was the result of large-scale hiring of contract labor to build the Panama Canal. Many of the emigrants were young people who were potentially parents. Consequently, the emigration caused the birth rates to decline. During the period between 1904 and 1921 the average decline in population was about 2.3 per cent per year. But we see from the table that the rate of increase soared from 0.2 per cent in 1921 to 1.9 per cent in 1953. During the fifteen years following 1921 much of the increase can be attributed to migration. But beginning around 1935 the increase in population is the result of the decline of death rates. Between 1935 and 1953 the average birth rate remained constant. During the same period the death rate declined from 33.58 to an all time low of 14.1.

Clarence Senior feels that while the immediate contributions made by large scale out-migration from the West Indies are real and apparent, most of the people will never have a chance to emigrate because first, they cannot overcome the racial barriers erected by the countries of possible immigration; second, they cannot compete in skills, education, industrial discipline, and cultural levels with the millions of prospective European emigrants; third, they do not have levels of living low enough to compete with Asians willing to accept "coolie" conditions in some Latin American countries; and fourth, their colonization on vacant farmland is too costly and the organization of productive farm colonies is so difficult that this way out is quite unlikely to develop a sizable stream of migration.[14]

Urbanization. Specialization of functions invites specialization of areas; it prompts a territorial division of labor both within and between islands. One might expect, as in the more advanced industrial societies, that West Indian cities would represent a mode of social organization which furthers efficiency in economic activity. Nothing can be further from the truth. Urbanization in the Islands is hardly synonymous with economic progress. The growth of cities is a result of lack of opportunities for a livelihood in the agricultural areas. Cities find that they must feed, clothe, house, and employ the newcomers. Unfortunately, they do not have the capital to accomplish these goals. Contrary to the pattern of urban development in the United States, where each outer residential area tends to be increasingly the abode of stable socio-economic populations, in the West Indian cities one is struck by outlying slums and blight. While economists and geographers have noted that economic advances in urban centers call for increases in the proportion of the labor force engaged in service activities, in the West Indian cities there is, with rare exceptions, insufficient economic advance. Each year there are more and more people in need of the services which the city needs to supply.

Urban theorists tell us that urbanization on any scale (with upwards of forty per cent of the country in cities of 2,500-plus) is closely bound up with greater specialization of functions in industry and agriculture. These theorists tell us that such an urban trend contributes to the overall rationality of the economy since these cities become dynamic centers for innovation and change. But in the West Indies, this observation apparently does not hold. Whatever rationality of the economy ensues from urbanism is overwhelmed by low incomes insufficient to carry the necessary services essential to a higher standard of living. In fact, the cities, like Topsy, just grow. Trinidad and Barbados, by census definition, are nearly forty per cent urban while Jamaica, the Windward and Leeward Islands are over twenty per cent urban (1946 enumeration). These islands suffer from a critical lack of those important economies which stem from the existence of a disciplined and skilled

---

[14] Clarence Senior, "Migration and Overpopulation," paper read at the First Western Hemisphere Conference on *Population Problems and Family Planning,* Puerto Rico, May 12-15, 1959.

labor force, a concentration of consumers, and the availability of essential commercial and service functions.

Accordingly, the presence of overly large cities in the West Indies (and, in fact, any pre-industrial society) serves to act as a curb rather than a stimulus to wider economic growth. In the words of Bert F. Hoselitz, the growth and maintenance of pre-industrial cities over the world "have been somewhat parasitical in the sense that profits of trade, capital accumulated in agricultural and other primary pursuits, have been dissipated in grandiose urban construction, servicing, and consumption by a colonial elite. The labor and enterprise which might otherwise have been invested in some form of light manufacture of material processed in the interior are drawn off to the great city by the attractive dazzle of a million lights. To that extent, the development of mercantile capitals retards development of other productive potentials."[15]

The West Indies, like Egypt, is far more urbanized than its industrial position would require. This condition is not of recent origin but has characterized the Islands for at least forty years. The over-urbanization is therefore real, and it has increased with time.

The pattern of urban growth shows parallels to that of Korea. T. O. Wilkinson has shown that in Korea after Japanese occupation in 1910, economic development lagged far behind urbanization.[16] He found that Korean city growth was more the result of the "push" from a hard-pressed rural economy than of the "pull" from expanding opportunities in urban areas, and the tendency was increased after the departure of the Japanese.

West Indian urban migration, as part of a world-wide trend, does not seem to be directly related to whether or not a particular city has anything to offer in the way of employment. In Bridgetown, Barbados, the population has increased by more than one-half since 1921, whereas the increase over the rest of the island has been only one-third. Bridgetown has no industry. The story is fundamentally the same for Kingston, Jamaica.

Even a casual visitor to the larger towns and cities recognizes that city growth is everywhere ahead of general modernization. One could take the classical *laissez-faire* position and insist that this urban growth will ultimately cease, that either the rate of urbanization will fall off sharply or industrialization will gain a new impetus. Levels of community living do not, however, rise and fall like a yo-yo. Things can (and frequently do) simply de-

[15] Bert F. Hoselitz (ed.), *Economic Development and Cultural Change* (Chicago: The University of Chicago Press, 1955), Vol. III, No. 2, p. 131. Copyright 1955 by the Univ. of Chicago.

[16] T. O. Wilkinson, "The Pattern of Korean Urban Growth," *Rural Sociology*, (March, 1954), pp. 32-38.

teriorate to chaos. Changes for better or worse will occur only when people decide to make the changes. Over-urbanization could serve as a catalyst in stimulating economic growth in the Islands. It could be argued that the cities are the fountainheads of leadership and new social movements. Yet, governments faced with idle, impoverished and rootless urban masses, are, for their own survival, compelled to take drastic action with regard to agitating leaders and movements. Of course, if governments are dilatory in effecting social and economic change for improvement of the lot of the masses, then they should be cast out. The point is: economic development is often hindered by outmoded institutions and political practices, hence the burgeoning city, as the source of new ideas and movements can be said to be potentially favorable to change.

These are all potentialities. Whether or not these potentialities are realized in fact depends on a multitude of forces in complex countervailing relationship. The fact remains that in the West Indies more people are moving off the land and backing into the cities—backing in the sense of being ill-prepared in skills and in urban life ways. It is here that the problem of overpopulation reveals its most depressing manifestations as well as revealing the areas of life where planned action can best be applied. The city will increasingly become the base of operations for demographic study. Every characteristic of human nature is not only visible here but magnified. In the freedom of their cities, West Indians, no matter how eccentric, find an environment where they can find some kind of self-expression. The city tolerates everybody and everything: the criminal, the beggar, the genius, the wealthy, the pervert, and the talented. Here all secret ambitions plus suppressed desires find expression. Here policies for population control can be launched, any innovation drawing an audience of obstructionists as well as supporters. The fact that the city magnifies, in fact advertises, human nature is what makes this arena of human life so interesting.

CONCLUSION

At the outset of this chapter economist Arthur Lewis was quoted as saying that in the West Indies the "problem of the land is usually the crux of the matter." While I believe he has oversimplified the causal complex, it is true that the land is the stage upon which men must pursue their ends and define their problems. If we assume, for the moment, that the land is indeed a significant first cause, it becomes so intermeshed with other forces that in the course of time it is no longer the "crux of the matter" but one among many conditioners (labor, technology, social and economic organization,

46

ideology), eventually supplying little more than the momentum in the process of change. In 1960, labor has become redundant because mechanization has entered the agricultural scene to intensify the problem of poverty and overpopulation. Furthermore, in the development of a nation-state, agricultural improvement and industrialization must be complementary, the latter taking up the slack in raising the income scale and absorbing those idle hands stilled by mechanical improvements on the land. Because, in the West Indies, industrialization has not kept pace with the agricultural revolution, it too becomes a "crux of the matter."

The interlocking problems are manifold, some of which are: balanced trade; the creation of inducements for industrial development; the re-routing of life-goals from those associated with sex and reproduction to those which will improve personal material well-being for a mechanized world; the establishment of a skilled labor pool; the creation of markets for industrial products; dedication by the masses to the new nation-state.

Because the West Indies has little capital, little fuel or skilled labor, the outlook is bleak. Yet the modernization of agriculture continues and cities inherit the redundant agrarian labor force. But the process can not be reversed, if for no other reason than that workers associate agricultural work with slavery. A formula of retreating to simple agricultural methods in a mechanized world is to invite the dead hand of the past to hasten the disintegration of a society made up principally of spiritually disinherited souls. An ever expanding and idle labor force will not wait for West Indian industrialization to catch up.

If the West Indies were truly an "underdeveloped" country in the sense of untapped natural resources, then energetic experimentation with the economic organization would serve as the safety valve for an exploding population. But the West Indies is already overdeveloped. Time will not permit an aping of the United States and the Soviet Union with their great land masses, leaving human reproduction to private interests and retreating to economics and technology to save the day. The agrarian land reform movement, led by Eric Williams, flies in the face of realistic techniques in modern agriculture: business agriculture is here to stay. Furthermore, the alliance of property-owning groups which controls the economic destiny of the Islands, cannot be expected to accept a set of measures running counter to each of its short-run vested interests. Any enforcement would be willfully sabotaged. A political platform tied to land reform can only serve as a palliative measure to appease a restive peasantry.

The land is no longer the "crux of the matter" because formulae for action-in-agriculture cannot reach fruition in time to cope with the problems attending a bursting population. Planners must now turn to the people themselves: their social organization, their life assessments and valuations as they affect human numbers. Economic, geographic and technological programs become routes of action which must yield to the more direct approach: population control.

Chapter III

Diet, Heredity and Sex Interest:
The Biogenic Dimension

The question of population quality raised by geneticists, nutritionists, physiologists, anthropologists, eugenicists, and others, has led directly to the consideration of the effects of differential diet and racial capacity upon sex activity, and population growth and decline.

In appraising these influences, two theories, one very recent and one quite old, invite analysis because of the stature of their proponents, the strength of the disciplines which they represent, and their possible importance to West Indian demography. The "new" is the fertility of hunger theory professed by the noted nutritionist Josue De Castro, who, in his book *The Geography of Hunger*, says that starvation stimulates sexual activity, resulting in more mouths to feed in the world's hungriest areas. The solution, according to De Castro: increased food production, wider distribution and greater variety in diets. The "old" is the "recapitulation theory," the idea that the extant primitive is a child as compared to the civilized "adult," that cultures and races must be understood in terms of fixed, successive biological stages of development. The idea of biological evolution of mankind is held fundamental in explaining physique, fecundity and fertility.

DIET AND FECUNDITY

As there is some relationship between nourishment and the standard of living, and because life is so completely dependent upon food, available food per person is sometimes used as a measure of man's sex interest, his capacity to reproduce. Nutritionists seem to be agreed that, on the average, a daily intake of food per person of 2250 calories is required for good health and efficiency. With this figure as the standard, the Food and Agricultural Organization of the United Nations, in its 1946 *World Food Survey*, made the following appraisal of the extent of malnutrition throughout the world: the high-calorie areas include most of the Western World, all of North America, and much of Europe. Oceania and the Soviet Union also belong to this group, but it includes only three countries in South America. The medium-calorie areas include most of Southern Europe, three countries in Asia, a part of the Middle East, a part of Africa, and a part of South America. The low-calorie areas include most of Asia, a part of the Middle East, all of Central America, and probably parts of South America and Africa.

49

The Organization's 1952 report stated that the picture had remained unchanged. Based upon available studies, I have found some West Indian islands enjoying "medium-calorie" consumption, and others suffering from low-calorie intake. To be specific, B. S. Platt[1] found in the three more "prosperous" islands the following average daily caloric consumption: Barbados, 2,413 (1944); Jamaica, 2,092 (1942); Trinidad, 2,582 (1944). K. H. Straw[2] supplies 1952 figures for Barbados and Trinidad respectively, as 2,590 and 2,577. A 1957 study of St. Kitts diets, conducted by Doctors Roland A. Schneckloth, Kenneth Stuart, A. C. Corcoran, and Felix Moore, found an average individual calorie intake of 1,639 for that island. Fitting the more recent of the above figures to the general world scene, a rough approximation of the place of these four islands in calorie consumption is gained (Table 4).

TABLE 4
Calories Consumed, Per Person, Selected World Areas, 1951-1952[a].

Country	Calories per person per day
Canada	3,237
Denmark	3,126
United Kingdom[b]	3,098
Barbados	2,590
Trinidad (1944)	2,582
Brazil (1948-49)	2,343
Japan	2,100
Jamaica (1942)	2,092
Ceylon	2,057
St. Kitts (1957)	1,639
India	1,572

[a] Sources: K. H. Straw, op. cit., p. 26. B. S. Platt, op. cit., p. 26. International Labour Office, Geneva, Year Book of Labour Statistics, 1951-1952. R. A. Schneckloth and associates, unpublished manuscript on St. Kitts.
[b] Excluding N. Ireland.

While Trinidad and Barbados appear to meet the dietary norm for good health, Jamaica and St. Kitts are short of accepted standards. However, B. S. Platt finds that Barbados, Jamaica and Trinidad are short of accepted standards for specific nutrient requirements (his study did not include St. Kitts). Trinidad is short on protein, while all three island peoples are short of calcium and the B_2 vitamins, especially riboflavin. Dr. Schneckloth and associates made some interesting findings in St. Kitts. Studying the diets of four

[1] B. S. Platt, Nutrition in the British West Indies, Colonial No. 195, H.M.S.O., 1946, p. 26.
[2] K. H. Straw, "Household Budgets and Nutritional Analysis of Food Consumption of Barbados," Social and Economic Studies, (June, 1954), p. 26. Used by permission.

families in each of three villages,[3] they found nutritional disease to be rare. While the calorie ration at the dinner table was low, it was supplemented by chewing sugar cane—as evidenced by the few adults with front teeth. These investigators reported a crude birth rate for the islands of fifty-two and a death rate of twelve per thousand. Thus the reader is given to believe that fecundity is not suppressed by the type of diet. Of equal importance, though given only passing attention by the investigators, was the discovery of considerable hypertension among the infertile women in the age bracket 30 to 49, as compared with women who had had children and had not suffered from toxemia of pregnancy. The reader is left with the inference that social psychological conditions are possibly influencing reproductive capacities in some St. Kitts women. Perhaps Schneckloth and his associates could throw additional light on this finding when their report is published.

This brief excursion into West Indian diet warrants the generalization that as the birth rates in the Islands remain at a high level, the nutritional value of food per person has, *on the average*, been sustained on a level deemed satisfactory by qualified experts. Of course, some populations need to improve their diets more than others. This assertion is made at this early point in the chapter in order that the reader might better evaluate the highly publicized "new theory" of Dr. Josue De Castro, which follows.

The Hunger-Fertility Hypothesis

Witnessing how some of the worst population pressures over the world are in areas where there is chronic hunger, Dr. Josue De Castro of Brazil has developed the challenging thesis that malnutrition actually breeds more babies. Obviously confusing fecundity, or the physiological capacity to bear full-term offspring, with fertility (the actual reproductive phenomenon), he presents the "fact" that the highest fertility is to be found in those groups with the lowest percentage of complete animal proteins in their diets.

To support his thesis, Castro makes two claims. First, the psychological effect of chronic hunger is to arouse the sex urge to the point of compensating emotionally for the shrunken nutritional appetite; the sex instinct, he insists, becomes dominant when chronic hunger—particularly hunger for proteins and certain vitamins—produces chronic lack of appetite. Second, sterility is the result of diets rich in proteins.

From the evidence at hand, Castro's claims seem not to fit West Indians.

---

[3] Cayon Village, Sandy Point Village, and Old Road Village. Each family was asked to put aside one extra adult serving at each meal for each of two weekdays and one Sunday. The meals of each day were combined, mixed with water in a Waring blender and frozen prior to analysis.

And one authority, Dr. Ancel Keys, Director of the Physiological Hygiene Laboratory, University of Minnesota, writes:

"I can assure you that chronic undernutrition of chronic subsistence on very small amounts of animal proteins does not produce a 'shrunken appetite' or 'loss of interest in food'." Furthermore, "I have seen no relationship between the sexual instinct and level of nutrition except. . . . in real starvation where the sex drive disappears."[4]

Castro, it seems, overlooked the fact that in some over-populated countries, sex activity, through generations of plenty and famine, has been more openly cultivated, a fact which fits the West Indies. To attribute patterns of sexual relations to the nutritional pattern verges on the ludicrous. Keys, in his studies of diet in Italy, Japan and the United States, found the percentage of calories supplied by proteins almost identical in the three countries yet the birth rate in Italy was, at the time of the studies, low, but high in the United States, and in Japan even higher. He found the proportion of calories from animal proteins high in the United States, low in Italy, and very low in Japan.[5]

The second claim of Castro, that sterility is the result of rich protein diets is not then defensible. In fact, the experiments on rats by Slonaker (on which Castro seems to rest most of his case), wherein a high percentage of rats were sterile by reason of rich protein diets, have been superceded by thousands of more recent experiments which fail to confirm the theory at all.

Physiologists explain that whereas in experimental animals (particularly in rats) vitamin E in the diet is necessary for proper development of the embryo this is not necessarily true for humans; mothers can supplement vitamin E deficiencies through manufacturing their own through synthesis, assuming adequate presence of amino acids. But this is of no particular help in explaining variations in either fecundity or fertility. Given a malnourished population with low sexual motivations envisaged by Castro, if the accessibility of the sexes to each other is comparatively unrestricted (there is a high level of promiscuity), when one sex union proves unproductive, then in time there will be a union which will indeed result in conception. Sex freedom can countervail in some degree low sex drives.

From the research summarized above, the dietary deficiencies in the West Indies are not extreme. How then, is the high birth rate to be explained? Negatively put, it is not to be explained by nutrition patterns.

---

[4] In Roy G. Francis, *The Population Ahead* (Minneapolis: University of Minnesota Press, 1958), p. 38. Copyright 1958 by the Univ. of Minnesota.
[5] *Ibid.*, pp. 38-39.

However a socio-physiological experimental study is needed, involving two cultural sub-groups in which the accessibility of males to females is known and the diets are controlled. The results would supply some clues as to the causal relationship between nourishment and reproduction. This is the only conclusive way to prove or disprove the Castro thesis.

There is a lack of scientific evidence to bear out the hypothesis that a protein-rich diet will have a fertility-suppressing effect. Whereas birth rates are generally lower in countries where protein diets are common, it does not necessarily follow that food volume, or even the composition of the food, is the controlling factor. Rather it is the mores.[6] At the extreme of undernutrition, human reproduction decreases and the sex urge ceases altogether. At substantially all other levels of nutrition there would appear to be no evidence for an important relationship between diet and the reproductive tendencies of man.

Mind and the Theory of Recapitulation

"West Indians are child-like people who breed like animals!" This, the claim of many white residents of the Federation, carries the implications that high fertility practices are a biological phenomenon rooted in heredity, and that mankind through its own efforts can accomplish nothing to change these reproductive proclivities. This is a claim conveniently tied to the old racial theory that a nation's progress is dependent on the presence of a particular stock in the population, variously noted as Aryan, Nordic, Teutonic, or the white race in general. More particularly the thesis reads:

". . . there has been one branch of the human family so distinctly superior to all others than it alone has been the creator and sustainer of civilization."[7]

---

[6] Harold F. Dorn: "The Effect of Public Health Developments upon Population Growth", *Ann. New York Acad. Sc.* 54:742-749, 1952. F. A. Southard, Jr.: "Famine" (1948), in *Encyclopaedia of the Social Sciences*, Vol. V-VI, New York, 1948, 85-89. K. E. Mason: "Differences in Testis Injury and Repair after Vitamin A-Deficiency, Vitamin E-Deficiency and Inanition", *Am. J. Anat.*, 52:153, 1933. Z. B. Ball, R. H. Barnes and M. B. Visscher: "The Effects of Caloric Restriction on Maturity, Senescence, with Particular Reference to Fertility and Longevity", *Am. J. Physiol.*, 150:511, 1947. Helen C. Griffin and G. St. J. Perrott: "Urban Differential Fertility during the Depression", *Millbank Mem. Fund Quart.*, 15:75-89, 1937. C. A. Smith: "The Effect of Wartime Starvation in Holland upon Pregnancy and its Product", *Am. J. Obst. & Gynec.*, 53:599, 1947. C. A. Smith: "Effects of Maternal Undernutrition upon the Newborn Infant in Holland", *J. Pediat.*, 30:229, 1947. F. G. Benedict, et al.: *A Study of Prolonged Fasting* (Washington: Carnegie Institution of Washington, 1915). A. Keys, et al.: *Human Starvation* (Minneapolis: University of Minnesota Press, 1950). A. J. Carlson and F. Heolzel: *Overnutrition: Its Causes and Consequences* (Springfield: Charles C. Thomas, 1950). A. J. Carlson and F. Heolzel: "Nutrition, Senescence and Rejuvenescence", *J. Gerontol.*, Vol. VI, 1951 (Program Abstracts), p. 69. H. M. Evans and M. M. Nelson, "Relation of Dietary Protein to Reproduction in the Rat", *Federation Proc.*, 11:45, 1952.

[7] N. L. Sims., *The Problem of Social Change* (New York: Crowell, 1939) p. 123.

The problem oriented demographer is often faced with resistance from West Indian whites when family planning for Negroes is proposed. These whites argue that the masses are aboriginal and their behavioral traits are part and parcel of a biological stage long since passed through by the superior race of men. It is an old scheme of mental evolution popularized in the phrase "ontogeny recapitulates phylogeny" which originated at the end of the nineteenth century prior to the development of modern genetics. The most representative exponent of the recapitulation theory, G. Stanley Hall, once wrote:

". . . we are influenced in our deeper more temperamental dispositions by the life-habits and codes of conduct of we know not what unnumbered hosts of ancestory, which like a cloud of witnesses are present throughout our lives, and our souls are echo-chambers in which their whispers reverberate . . . we have to deal with the archeology of mind, with zones or strata which precede consciousness, as we know it, compared to which even it, especially cultural intellect, is an upstart novelty."[8]

Hall, in presenting his stages of human development wrote: "The child comes from and harks back to a remoter past; the adolescent neo-atavistic, and in him the later acquisitions of the race slowly become prepotent. Development is less gradual and more saltatory, suggestive of some ancient period of storm and stress when old moorings were broken and a high level attained."[9] The belief in animal mentality and child mentality stems from Darwin's work on evolution, upon which were erected stages of evolutionary development postulated for biological, cultural, physical, and mental phenomena. All kinds of analogies, assumptions and auxiliary hypotheses were drawn up, among these being Haeckel's "biogenetic law." This law linked the early maturational stages of the human with former stages in the development of the species. Zoologists pushed the theory beyond the embryonic period calling attention to behavioral phenomena in the postnatal phase of development as evidence of recapitulation. Anthropologists of the late nineteenth century attempted to apply biological concepts of evolution to non-biological events and concluded that human culture had evolved through a unilinear series of steps culminating in occidental civilization. Our primitive contemporaries were represented as arrested cultural groups, backward peoples with limited mental capacities. Thus, with no direct evidence, the recapitulation theory of culture was arrived at by analogical reasoning and coordinated to a point of sheer beauty with a general scheme of mental evo-

---

[8] G. Stanley Hall, *Adolescence* (New York: D. Appleton and Co., 1904), II, p. 61.
[9] *Ibid.*, p. xiii.

lution, genetically conceptualized. The mental development paralleled the organic stages, beginning with the lower stages of animal mind and terminated with the adult "rational" mind of occidental man. The natural history of this theory was finished by genetically-oriented animal psychologists as they related the notion of cultural stages in the evolution of the race to maturational phases in the development of the individual concluding that savage mentality and child mentality were directly comparable. Using the clues supplied by zoologists, psychologists participated in extending the theory of recapitulation to the postnatal behavioral development of the child (to them, "behavior" and "conduct" were coterminous).

As could be expected, race-conscious whites eagerly embraced the doctrine and added the further implication that the culture of savages (which meant all disadvantaged races) is basically a reflection of, if not completely determined by, innate racial capacities.

As a theory of mind the recapitulation theory had no place for the influence of socio-cultural forces. More precisely, the doctrine insisted: first, human thought and action are basically functions of the biological structure. Second, societies pass through a sequence of cultural stages which, biologically based, are a function of an evolving mentality. Occidental man stands at the apex—biologically, mentally and culturally—of evolutionary development. Third, the occidental child condenses in prenatal and postnatal development, respectively, the phylogenetic stages of its prehuman ancestry and the mental and cultural stages in the history of mankind. Fourth, each generation assimilates to some degree the experience of past generations insofar as they have been absorbed into the biological heritage.

Although the theory is not supported by independent evidence, the "occidental whites" of the West Indies, as elsewhere, have held somewhat tenaciously to the theory as a doctrine of attack, justifying on "scientific grounds" race discrimination, mocking any attempts to control the "adolescent sex impulses" of Negroid "primitives." As a social (not scientific) fact, the theory is nevertheless a barrier to family planning in the Federation. With the whites "noble," and the Negro "sensual," these characteristics are acquired by nature, not by nurture. To remind these advocates that the stocks deemed "superior" are made up entirely of hybrids, is to invite deaf ears.

CONCLUSION

The ultimate reason for the failure of organic concepts and conditions to account adequately for changes in the socio-cultural realm is the recognition of a near complete division between these two conditions of existence. We are dealing with differences in kind. "Something new has been added," the culture or "superorganic," which itself becomes a determining factor in its own development. This is not to say that biological principles and factors are not relevant. Rather, they alone are insufficient for the analysis of the human problem of overpopulation. A biological theory of social process and emerging social problems fails for the following reasons:

1. The comparative variability of human societies and constancy of the biological factor.
2. The failure to appreciate the richness and variability of society as phenomena largely *sui generis*.
3. The simplistic and particularistic nature of a biological theory which would be too generalized in scope to be of use in the analysis of concrete social problems.
4. The fact that social process can be adequately explained on historical grounds.[10]

Man differs from lower orders of animal life in having created, outside of the biological context, a set of common understandings, including definitions of himself, embraced by tradition and established custom. Society is the triumph of man over nature. Within this province man defines his problems and seeks ways to resolve them. While the biological fact of reproduction is a denominator common to all groups, it is nevertheless affected very differently by different human settings. The student of society encounters highly variable definitions of offspring, different motives for paternity, in different groups, and different roles and statuses accorded to both parent and child. The only possible conclusion is that the desire for offspring is learned and that parenthood is subject to a wide range of interpretations. Witness, on the one hand, the native Australians and Trobriand Islanders who overtly deny physiological paternity and the paternalistic Chinese family, on the other hand, where the failure to produce offspring constitutes a sin. Then witness the number of West Indian women who look upon a child as an unfortunate accident, shoving the child off to the grandmother so as to avoid any interference with social affairs. The Marquesas Islanders have standardized this procedure even more than West Indians.

Robert F. Spencer has expressed himself succinctly on this subject, saying: ". . . while growth and expansion of population are concomitants of the biological phenomenon of fertility, man, far removed as a result of his self-domestication from mere biological cause and effect, creates patterns of thought and behavior which have the end result of controlling his own biology. It is recognized that various pathological conditions—hypertension,

---

[10] Cf. W. F. Ogburn, "The Historical Method in the Analysis of Social Phenomena", *Publications of the American Sociological Society*, (1921), pp. 70-81.

psychosomatic illness, incidence of virtually any pathological state—have a direct relation to the force of culture. So also it is apparent that the man made conditioning of culture has a direct bearing on human fertility."[11]

[11] Robert F. Spencer, "Cultural Aspects of the Population Problem," in *The Population Ahead,* ed. by Roy G. Francis (Minneapolis: University of Minnesota Press, 1958), pp. 106-107. Copyright 1958 by the University of Minnesota.

Chapter IV
The Economic Dimension

In the transition from slavery to freedom the West Indian social economy has been marked by a struggle between those who would maintain the plantation system and those who would encourage the dignity of free labor. This struggle, first centering in Jamaica in the 1860's, has diffused through the Islands, becoming an integral part of racial and political movements. Labor on the sugar estates has come to be associated with slavery. Political aspirants capitalize on this affinity at every opportunity.

This association between slavery and sugar work was not entirely of peasant origin, however. White planters had been inclined to treat free workers (before and after emancipation) little differently from their slaves. Yet, as free men, the blacks expected to be treated with dignity and a certain formality. Formal respect often meant more to them than economic gain. The failure of white planters to see (or at least to honor) this quest for respectability led to misunderstanding, confusion, and at times open conflict.

With freedom, the Negroes brought forward their African concept of land ownership, namely the right to occupy and cultivate idle land. No land, even if it were the property of the Queen, was to be kept vacant. Squatting on Crown Lands became commonplace, the squatter refusing on moral grounds to move. Missionary churches aided the cause of the liberated by exerting pressure on estates to sell tiny plots to individual free Negroes. However, those proprietors were unwilling to sell off their land in small pieces. With the missionaries supplying the needed organization and experience in European business tactics for the rapid development of land settlement, the "new tropical economy" soon had its bridgehead. This association of missionary churches with land reform and the dignity of man served as the catalytic agent for religious conversion and growth far into the twentieth century. As protectors of Negro freedom, religions were often attacked by the planters for distorting the cause of Christianity and undermining the economic future of the West Indies.[1] After all, the religious calling should be simply one of teaching and preaching to the people rather than guiding them out of the plantation social economy. Obviously, the planters disliked the role of the missionaries as champions of the oppressed.

As missionary leadership became less enchanting to the Negro populace, the new champion for the little man's tropical economy was the labor union

---

[1] Philip D. Curtin, *Two Jamaicas: The Role of Ideas in a Tropical Colony, 1830-1865* (Cambridge: Harvard University Press, 1955).

59

movement of the 1940's and 50's centering on the cities. Guided more usually than not by feverish, self-seeking, race-men rather than by constructive intellectuals, the labor movement lacked the necessary vision for a people's movement and the mace passed into the hands of educated colored men in Federation politics. The crusade to dignify the Negro peasant under a people's capitalism has been led by two intellectuals: Dr. Eric Williams and Sir Grantley Adams. Dr. Williams, an economist with a Ph.D. degree and one-time academician, is the argumentative Premier of Trinidad, a firebrand visionary of sorts, while Sir Grantley Adams, the Prime Minister of the Federation, is an Oxford-trained barrister shrewd in the ways of politics. On the shoulders of these political adversaries, together with Premier Manley (at this writing) of Jamaica, has fallen the job of spelling out the logic and the philosophy of a people's capitalism. While poorly coordinated, the over-all intent of their efforts is to erect an abounding grass-roots economy in competition with that of the planters and in this way to achieve the ultimate end: to bring down forever the "white man's burden." Skillfully vague, the ideology draws both cynics and advocates, arousing new political and socioeconomic problems, widening the gap between Negro and white, European and African. Williams and Adams are dedicated to the proposition that the standard of living of West Indians can be raised by changing the economic face of the Islands. It is the age-old formula for catching up with high birth rates.

Weakness of West Indian Economic Theory

In conventional fashion, Williams and Adams, together with intellectuals in Jamaica, have seized upon the notion that human beings respond everlastingly to monetary inducements. When a society, be it West Indian or any other, is undergoing change, economic values are first brought to bear upon the problems followed by technological values, then political values, and finally the non-material or ideological values. More broadly put: Williams and Adams argue that the material, economic and technological forces are always the most compatible to any change, while the religious, artistic, ethical, and other non-material values are invariably antagonistic or indifferent to change.

This kind of presupposition is fallacious for there is no logical *a priori* consonance between the economic and technological values as they penetrate an established way of life. Likewise, there is no reason for expecting disharmony between an established non-material set of values and a new scheme of values. The facts seem to point to instances where economic

60

values penetrate first, while in others the technological; in still other instances, religious and ethical values enjoy first acceptance. Usually several different categories of values enter the scene simultaneously.

Eric Williams in particular, dedicated to making the West Indies an oasis for non-whites, has made acquisitiveness (land reform) his symbol of the race struggle. He says nothing of the importance of changing demographic values. This is his blind spot, as it is for most classical economists bent on poverty reduction. As an intellectual and political leader, he has adopted the notions of practical men of action from advanced technological societies, proclaiming that an impoverished country must first ape the economic traits of these countries, then their political opinions, followed by their "better" philosophical traits. He fails to recognize that any society will absorb those aspects of the "intruder" which best fit the interests of the borrower. To sponsor a formula for action geared to the borrowing of demographic values seems to Williams out of the question—a case of putting the cart before the horse.

This matter of effecting change in a "backward" country calls forth the whole province of culture contacts. In the West Indies, we are witnessing a "nation in need" on the threshold of borrowing material and non-material traits. Sociologists, historians and anthropologists have supplied instances on how a nation in need borrows. The Mexicans of Tepotzlan borrowed chiefly the elements of the non-material culture of the Spanish. The Chinese, in contact with the West tended to absorb more in the realm of Western ideologies than material techniques. All this serves my point: that borrowing involves irrational as well as non-rational modes of behavior, but this behavior can be understood within the broader framework of the moral order. In other words, the incentives for borrowing are generally quite consistent with the ultimate values held within the society. Thus, material acquisitiveness, so characteristic of American industrial capitalism, is not a universal principal of human motivation in the West Indies and thus hardly an exclusive starting point in the "borrowing" process.

The intellectuals of the Federation seem to argue that economics must call the tune and that all other forces will tend to fall obediently in line. Social scientists have noted that economic behavior in peasant societies, however, is frequently oriented to non-economic goals and is limited by widely varying institutional contexts. Thus, economic incentives may not be equated with materialistic goals. Money in the hands of the poor does not buy food, shelter, and clothing alone. Financial incentives are effective only in proportion to the range in individual and group interests and values that can be satisfied through the use of money. Increased wealth for the little man of the West Indies is likely to increase the number of those who consume what it buys. Economists of the West Indies might dwell on Biblical advice (Ecclesiastes 5:11) which states, "When goods increase, they are increased that eat them."

Economics and human incentives find themselves mutually woven into the fabric of the normative order of Island society. Communities and institutions define the situation, for there is no guarantee that the broad community will uniformly harmonize individual and collective interests. Here, where reigns a cultural apathy toward abounding acquisitiveness, the building of an urban economy upon a consuming farm system will frustrate those planters, entrepreneurs, and economic competitors dedicated to the accumulation of wealth. It is a case of conflicting definitions of "ambition and success" and of "social responsibility."

Now a sociological analysis of the ends and motives of human beings does not completely destroy economic theory whether it be in demography or business, but sets the formal analysis of the economic aspects of human behavior within the context of what we know about human organization generally. It is unfortunate that the science of population has been built over a foundation of classical economics for the result is that migration and vital rates are explained in terms of impersonal competition. Economics is a viable, cognitive thing because it is an aspect of human behavior, present throughout all human experience. But even today, demographers infer that population is one side of the scales and food or natural resources line up on the opposite side. They fail to accept the fact that population is both a resource and a consumer of resources. Social ingenuity becomes a quality of material goods. In the West Indies, few raw materials are utilized in their free and native state. There is invariably some form of modification that goes far beyond the simple acts of picking and gathering.

Though the economic achievements of the Islanders are indeed manifest in their material baggage, those manifestations become significant, or functional, precisely because of what these people do with these products. Thus, economics is a mode of doing, running through the whole gamut of human activity. Accordingly, the demographer must try to avoid speaking of the "economics of this" or the "economics of that"; nevertheless, this is precisely what he, and political leaders, do in assessing the future of the Islands. In fact, what we see is congeries of social scientists and political leaders taking refuge in economic models (operating with very few variables)—a false start when the processes being studied are quite incomplete and have the potentiality of changing at a rapid and irregular rate. I have in mind the irregular spread of urbanization across Barbados, Trinidad and Jamaica, the spread of contraception in islands such as Grenada, the oscillations in the migration picture. We are observing an incomplete process of which past parallels may be quite inadequate; and we may expect to be continually surprised by new problems while still struggling to understand the old. Differently put, many behavioral scientists are trying to transfer comprehension of the old agrarian scheme of life to the new, without sufficient consideration of the different conditions and the changing face of what has occurred meanwhile.

POVERTY AND LEISURE ECONOMICS

Economic activity in the Islands cannot be concretely separated from "rights" and "duties" of persons. Thus the term "labor economics" becomes intermeshed with general sociological concepts of status and role. Furthermore, the entire province of economic productivity yields to the conditioning of time and place, as, for example, the variable definition of an "honest day's work" as it involves cane field workers over against urban clerks and civil servants. Similarly, the terms "occupation" and "labor" are far more complex in the West Indies than was ever assumed possible by classical economic theorists. Certain jobs are making their way into new status positions calling for modified worker stereotypes, expected modes of conduct, and effort put out. The term "economic man," as a rational, self-interested individual devoted to the efficient pursuit of ends quickly becomes useless because it denies the concept of the social group; it is an internally unstable concept.

The following facts presented by Siffleet and Rottenberg point to the slight utility of classical economic theory because of erroneous postulates about human motives and social organization. Economic terms as labor, enterprise, wealth, and income gained their meanings in terms of the old conceptual scheme of economics. The difficulty in the use of these tools of analysis when applied to West Indian agrarian life is that their "operational definition" is not the same as in a free market system. For example, sugar is fixed by governmental regulations. In fact, all the Islands depend upon a controlled economy.

The Antigua Labor Force

In Antigua, unfilled jobs in agriculture cannot be taken as a measure of full employment or for estimating total income-earning capacity of households. Nora M. Siffleet in her study of national income and national accounts[2] reports that in 1950 only 20 per cent of the unemployed were willing

---

[2] Nora M. Siffleet, "National Income and National Accounts", *Social and Economic Studies,* (July, 1953), pp. 5-135.

to accept any kind of work which might be offered to them, and the remainder had strong occupational reservations. She writes that although Antigua is almost entirely dependent upon cane cultivation, only 5 per cent of the unemployed were looking for jobs in agriculture. Of all the unemployed, 66 per cent said that they would refuse to accept work in the cane fields if it were offered. Furthermore, a substantial proportion of the working population worked for less than a full week: 30.6 per cent worked less than 29 hours during the week of the research. Poverty proved to be anything but an absolute economic term.

Oriented toward small communities, Antiguan workers order up their work load in terms of leisure *for the present*. This stands in some contrast to middle classes of the United States where leisure is for the future—for retirement. Because the Antiguan's income aspirations are weak and his desire for leisure strong, the economic structure is woven into the matrix of ideologies. Of course, the more detached the worker from his community controls, the more he fixes for himself his own maximum income aspirations. These aspirations vary with the work situation and season, and are as much influenced by co-workers and pressures from those he accepts as by his superiors. Thus incentives for income as well as for leisure are seldom uniform but ride above and below a median axis. Siffleet asserts that most agricultural workers feel no social stigma in living at a close-to-subsistence level and are somewhat inclined to offer less labor when income incentive programs are launched by employers.

Those interlocking forces which arouse and justify this leisure ethic, so characteristic of Antiguan agricultural labor in particular, and the West Indian labor force generally, are numerous, some of which may be mentioned:

First, the influence of the Roman Catholic Church must not be overlooked. Ranking second in membership to the Church of England (Figure 7), the Catholic Church looks upon work as a form of punishment for the sins at the Garden of Eden. It is the Church which has headed the Christian idea that Heaven is the place where no work shall be performed, where death, with all of its unpleasantries could have been circumvented if Eve had not eaten the apple. In fact, Catholic clergymen are disinclined to admonish the workers to put forth earnest effort on this earth. During the Ecclesiastical Year from November 30, 1958 to November 22, 1959, West Indian Catholic sermons were based on the general theme of *Christian Morals*.[3] With the Holy Trinity and the Ten Commandments receiving about equal

---

[3] Topics for Catholic sermons originate from a central source in Trinidad, and allow for slight modifications by island priests to suit local circumstances.

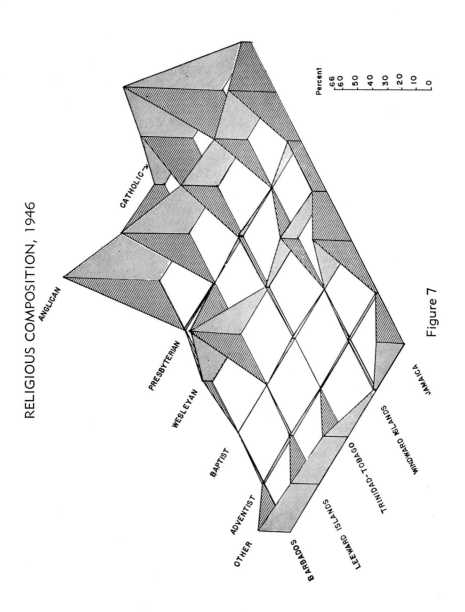

RELIGIOUS COMPOSITION, 1946

Figure 7

emphasis, there was but one sermon devoted to the concept of work, called "Duties of State: Sloth." One would deduce, by this title, that the concern of the Church was with irresponsibility and lazyness on the part of government officials rather than by the population generally.[4]

The Protestant ethic[5] has never profoundly influenced the motivations of the agricultural workers. They avoid an orientation toward ceaseless effort and rational conduct as an intrinsically moral form of behavior. While Protestantism in Europe successfully transplanted the ascetic devotion to disciplined hard work from monastic life (to which it was largely confined in the early period) to the mundane affairs of economic life, this way of life could not be transferred successfully to the West Indies by missionaries and planters. Catholic and Protestant peasantry would not embrace any strong condemnation of pleasure and emotions as exemplified by the Puritan "blue laws," or any sobriety and detachment conducive to rational conduct. To save wages through depriving the self of immediate pleasure and to practice sexual restraint are alien to a people who live for the moment. While the Negro listens solemnly to preachments concerning the "wickedness of the world," he interprets the admonitions of his clergyman to mean that he must adapt to this wicked world, or perhaps, withdraw from it, but hardly help transform it through methodical efforts in everyday life and regular work. He does not feel the European anxiety aroused by the doctrine that man cannot affect his predestined fate or even know whether he will be saved or damned, an anxiety to be relieved through immersing oneself in work. Collective resistance to the Puritan doctrine of asceticism and disciplined devotion to hard work and vocational pursuit is, of course, consonant with low morale. Thus the worker feels slight need to be absolved of his sins by either priests or bishops because his life organization is not structured around deep conscience, faith or self-imposed discipline.

I dwell at some length on this weak association of religion to work because I am convinced that any planning program in the Federation calculated to sharpen the aspirations of these backward people for the raising of their standard of living (to make income-earning a more powerful mover), to introduce the competitive spirit and to make them over in our Puritan-like image is fraught with danger, though, nevertheless, the impelling first course of action. Indeed, these folk may very well be socially more stoic than

---

[4] Other sermons were: "Superstitious Practices," "Oaths and Vows: The Sin of Perjury," "Respect for Our Neighbor's Soul: Scandal," "Self Respect and Temperance: The Evil of Over-Drinking," "Humility: The Root of All Virtues," "Charity: The Summary of the Law."

[5] See Max Weber, *Essays in Sociology* (New York: Oxford University Press, 1946), pp. 256-257.

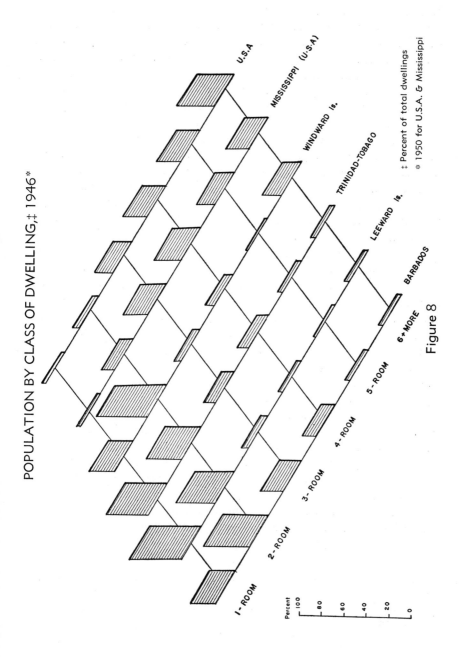

POPULATION BY CLASS OF DWELLING,‡ 1946*

‡ Percent of total dwellings

* 1950 for U.S.A. & Mississippi

U.S.A

MISSISSIPPI (U.S.A)

WINDWARD Is.

TRINIDAD-TOBAGO

LEEWARD Is.

BARBADOS

1-ROOM
2-ROOM
3-ROOM
4-ROOM
5-ROOM
6+MORE

Percent
100
80
60
40
20
0

Figure 8

67

Englishmen or Americans, but to provoke a spiritual revolution, to destroy the value systems which are gaining root, may produce chaos from which the society can never recover. But this is a risk to be run and, possibly, the price to be paid for gainful survival. These people live badly by any standard; they are often malnourished, badly housed (Figure 8) and somewhat diseased. To improve their standard of living, more of them must work and they must produce more in each hour of work, for the purpose of saving the foreign exchange expended in the purchase of food and so increase the wealth of the area.[6] They must reduce their numbers by means of developing interests competing with those of sex and reproduction; the only alternative is to become a hopeless charge of the technologically "developed" countries. Many of the traditions of these prosperous societies must become theirs or they must remain poverty-stricken. As a never ending flow of gifts to them will only promote current practices, there is no other way out but to concentrate on the incentives of West Indians.

"Religion in the underdeveloped countries," writes Chester L. Hunt,[7] "is far removed from any stress on the puritan virtues. The tradition-bound rigidity of Islam, the otherworldly emphasis of Buddhism, the ascetism of Hinduism and the fiesta-laden Catholicism of countries with a Spanish tradition may embody important teachings, but their emphasis is not calculated to produce industrious workers, thrifty capitalists or daring promoters. Since all religious groups claim that religion is the foundation of conduct, one might well raise the question as to how the traits of character essential to a business society may be developed when they are not supported by the dominant religious movements."

Second, in addition to the influence of the Catholic Church, the slave economy of a hundred years ago made its mark upon this leisure ethic. Men and women were driven to work against their collective will and the more effort expended brought on little or no additional income or reward from the plantation owners. Is it any wonder that upon freedom the Negro peasant should take the attitude that work is something to be avoided?

Third, the warm and humid climate is hardly conducive to energetic performance. The workers not only perform at a slow and rather indolent pace, but also are disinclined to engage in rigorous recreational forms—par-

---

[6] This is expressed as a possibility but not necessarily a fact. An increase in food production, particularly if it is stimulated with little regard to cost, is likely to be accompanied by a decrease in some of the existing production. The mere fact that increased food production consists of different products from export ones does not automatically ensure that more food will in fact represent greater total production.

[7] Chester L. Hunt, "Cultural Barriers to Point Four", *The Antioch Review*, (Summer, 1954), p. 162. By permission.

ticularly group play. Hence the word "leisure" is more appropriate than the word "recreation."

Fourth, the nature of the diet may be influencing human effort. In some communities, the diet is low in animal protein and heavy in starch. Such a diet is hardly conducive to energetic activity.

It is interesting to note how sugar dominates the agricultural scene. Sugar is the chief agricultural export of six of the ten units and provides more than three-fourths of the export earnings of Barbados, St. Kitts and Antigua. A near monopoly of the world output of four crops is held by West Indian islands—arrowroot in St. Vincent, Sea Island long-staple cotton in the Leewards and nutmegs and mace in Grenada. Unfortunately, the world market for such products is very restricted, and the prices fluctuate greatly. In addition, there is always the threat that alternative products will completely replace them on the market. The catastrophic effect that this would have can be seen by observing that arrowroot accounts for 52 per cent of the total export from St. Vincent, and nutmegs account for 72 per cent of all exports from Grenada.

Trinidad is the only island which is not dominated by agricultural exports. Trinidad's petroleum products account for 45 per cent of the West Indies' exports by value. But Trinidad's place in the world market of petroleum is diminishing. In 1933 Trinidad ranked eleventh in world production of crude petroleum. Today, her oil production is barely one-half of one per cent of world output. Furthermore, the productivity per well is low, and opportunities for expansion are extremely limited by the cost of underwater drilling.

With agricultural exports accounting for 70 per cent or more of the world trade for each island, except for Trinidad, large land holdings by a few individuals coupled with the distaste for agricultural work by the labor force, means perennial poverty for the masses. Antigua is a good case in point. Simon Rottenberg,[8] in his 1947 study of that island, found the people living in extreme poverty, the per capita income being less than 100 dollars (U.S.) per annum. They were consuming things which were not produced locally; the economy depending almost completely upon the export of sugar and Sea Island cotton.

Rottenberg insisted that the Antigua working force was voluntarily under-employed because it preferred leisure to income at low living levels. The planters, he reported, complained of being unable to find sufficient

---

[8] Simon Rottenberg, "Income and Leisure in an Underdeveloped Economy", *The Journal of Political Economy*, (April, 1952), p. 96.

workers to take the cane crop from the fields within an optimum time because of the unwillingness of laborers to perform certain classes of tasks whatsoever. Moreover, interviewed planters complained that those workers accepting employment refused to work full weeks. They liked to bind themselves to the work situations as in a contract. This suggests to them a temporary obligation to the employer. Thus as they entered the work scene they performed by the task rather than by the hour, often reporting to the job when they pleased. Preferring jobs for which wages were low, they put in the number of hours which suited their convenience and worked at a pace set by themselves and their co-workers. During one week, almost forty per cent of all wage earners in the cane field worked less than thirty hours. Rottenberg contends that workers frequently rejected high-earning trades in favor of others of less earning power. In 1950 only 6 per cent of the unemployed surveyed said they were seeking work in agriculture, this in the face of the fact that approximately 45 per cent of all those gainfully employed were in agriculture.[9]

The Urban Labor Force

My own observations of the incentives of the urban labor force throughout the Islands reveal apathy equivalent to agricultural labor. This is more true of skilled and unskilled occupations, although it does reach into mulatto groups engaged in civil service. The shirt industry in Trinidad, using skilled workers, suffers from occupational apathy. The *Trinidad Guardian* printed the following bylined article in August, 1959:

WORKERS' INDIFFERENCE HITS SHIRT INDUSTRY
Guardian Industrial Reporter

Productivity efficiency in Trinidad's garment manufacturing industry is only 70 per cent of that of the United States. According to one prominent representative of the industry, "an average of 25 to 40 dozen shirts are produced on each assembly line, per day in his territory, as compared with the American figure of 40 to 60 dozen."

Reason for the gap, is what he called "indifference to incentives." Unlike the U.S., the stimulus of money has so far failed to coax greater effort from the Trinidad worker.

Despite the territory's rapid strides in the field of industrialization, the novelty of this phase of national production and the absence of an industrial background

---

[9] Calling 1947 a typical recent year, Rottenberg stated that one corporation had amalgamated most of the private estates engaged in cultivating sugar cane. This one firm delivered 110 thousand tons of cane; other estates (private unincorporated), 15 thousand tons; and peasants, 45 thousand tons.

and character of factory workers, have resulted in mentalities that, because of limited education, do not realize the need for truly hard work and for increased productivity.

Prevailing conditions have produced a large number of unskilled persons who drift with the economic tide. And the 1,000 (approximately) who have settled in the garment industry have come to look on increased productivity as the same thing that should not be invited into the factory lest it create redundancy and a percentage of dismissals.

BONUS PLANS

Bonus plans offering more money for more work, have drawn blanks, and in fact, so negative are attitudes, that many workers prefer to do the minimum work in the minimum time and idle for the rest of the time. This, the representatives called, "ways to beat the boss."

He showed that the workers' methods of sharing the wealth, work and employment, gets official support from the trade union. Any attempt to remove less efficient employees by way of streamlining staff to meet greater productivity, is quickly challenged by union authority.

In one respect, this is a natural reaction on the part of those who are pledged to defend the workers. As well, redundancy is much more of a problem to the unskilled.

But then, the representative pointed out, there are also serious problems on the part of employees. In his own words, "I do not know of any other business in the West Indies that is so competitive." Garment manufacture does not require a great deal of capital to start—a factor that has fostered a comparatively large community of big and small manufacturers. This, plus accompanying over-production has kept prices down.

CUSTOMS UNION

Secondly, although world trends show profits of three to four per cent (three to five turnovers per year) it is less in Trinidad. Low prices and small profits he said are difficult to reconcile with demands for higher wages by workers who refuse to step-up productivity.

As well, there is the problem of restricted foreign markets. Both in and outside the West Indies, high protective tariffs are levied. It is hoped that the Federal discussions in next month—with federal tariffs as their theme—will hasten the advent of customs union, which will be a godsend to the industry—and at least will set the pace for further protection in December when the present protection lapses.

The representative added that although the total employment is low, it is high by comparison with the five per cent of population in the territory's oil industry, and deserves every sympathy from government, and every possible help from the appropriate trade union.

71

The supply of labor offered by a seamstress in a Port-of-Spain shirt factory, a clerk in a Kingston department store, or a government vital statistician in Castries, is not simply the function of wages. Where the element of prestige (high or low) countervails the wage schedule, new wage changes and economic inducements have slight affect on labor supply and labor output. To speak of labor supply as a mere function of wages, therefore, is to pose a superficial, sterile analytical tool obscuring the realities of the wage-labor equation.

What is unproductive in the Islands is not so much the land as the labor. Negro merchants participate in making labor redundant, joining the coercive efforts of the labor force. These entrepreneurs carefully define the duties and prerogatives of every subordinate (suitably refined in time by the worker and his peers), his maximum work load and minimal wage. While these employers are outwardly annoyed at the "inefficiency" of their staff, they are usually loved by their subordinates because they "spread the work around" and are more troubled by the employee who works too hard and encroaches on the work-radius of another, than the man who works too little. Thus to "spread the work around" is to "spread the wages around," a procedure expected by all. An American tourist in a Port-of-Spain department store will be struck by the army of supervisors, floor walkers, department heads, and subdepartment heads and runners. I recall in particular the summer of 1959, when I entered the largest department store in Castries, St. Lucia, for the purpose of buying an American weekly news magazine. Five individuals handled my purchase, as follows: (a) the floor walker approached me jauntily, inquired of my needs, and clapped his hands for (b) a runner—a school boy of about twelve. The lad escorted me twenty feet to the correct counter where (c) the stationery clerk graciously gave me my magazine but summoned (d) a runner (of higher station than the first) who took my money to (e) the distant cashier's cage for change and receipt. While the runner was allowed to carry money only a counter clerk could return the change to the customer. Now to be a part of such a situation was great for my ego but hard on my American conception of sound business practice. Nevertheless, a native born shopper expects such gyrations as natural and in the order of market-place procedure. For an employer to place a cash register on each counter would be tantamount to encouraging technological unemployment.

The Contract and the Civil Servant. In the United States, an employment contract is a master status-determining device. And in the Islands, to work by the contract, rather than by the day, is to stand high among one's peers. The use of this formal bond indicates a recognition by administrators that it is not the only group in the institution, that another group is operating

72

under a separate set of interests. The interests of Island public administrators are outwardly, at least, those of efficiency, increased productive effort and competition between all members of the organization. The interests of the workers, however, are generally those of job security, pleasant, unfatiguing work, cooperation, and fellowship between colleagues. In the presence of this situation, the employment contract is adopted by government and quasi-government agencies for one or both of the following two reasons: first, to rid the organization of undesirables who remain too long in the service, and second, to protect the organization from losing desirable workers prematurely. Thus the contract becomes a weapon to counteract any employee "aggressiveness."

To the uncritical mind, the contract represents harmonizing the wishes of both sides concerning the same object when it becomes evident that the interests of one party are not identical with those of the other. This formal agreement is usually drawn up in the universally accepted manner representing the culmination of earlier conferences, offers, and perhaps, counter-offers, by both prospective worker and employer. In this manner the contract is made to appear as a compromising instrument between two respective interests who will work together in an accommodative relationship for the purpose of rendering mutual service. It is a bond of indebtedness of trust by which the agency, as debtor, is obliged to furnish the worker, its creditor, an appraised payment of money, and perhaps food, shelter and insurance, in return for the worker's skilled services. In this form, however, the contract is in contradiction to the ideology of the agency. While the contract rests upon the supposed equality between the parties, the governmental agency rests traditionally upon the inequality between the parties. Traditionally, the agency (like a business firm) is designed to subordinate the employee. Any appearance of equality is either an ideal abstraction or a temporary arrangement. Neither party recognizes the situation as one of equality. In fact, neither party wants equality. The realism of the relationship is one of workers constantly seeking to dominate management (and vice versa) and to make its own interests those of the agency.[10]

Government and quasi-governmental agencies, through their adminis-

[10] This statement must be qualified only to the extent of noting that the informal organization, in the course of its pressure relations with supervisory personnel, rarely rejects entirely the established authority, as in a ship's mutiny. Certain of the agency's "rights" are accepted as "natural" and "proper." Only those agency innovations which transgress those hard-won rights of the workers are resisted and branded as "wrong" and "undemocratic." For traditionally the West Indian civil servant exhibits the kind of fear and respect for the agency its administrators expect. There is a tacit recognition by both parties that the agency is to enjoy the manifest "right" of dominance. The informal organization, however, claims the "right" to challenge any new rule which modifies the precedents of the past.

trators, control at the outset the definitions of those key words and phrases in the contract such as: "duty," "faithful performance," "negligence" and "reasonable." However, through time a "reasonable interpretation" of the contract becomes a license for both parties to challenge, break, and redefine the instrument to suit their respective objectives.

Some West Indians may enter willingly into a contractual arrangement because it represents a subjection to some rule or organization, but most do so because it offers freedom for passive activity, freedom from restraint. They enjoy telling their peers that they work by the contract, often speaking of the postcontract period when they will return to a voluntary unemployed state of leisure before seeking a new binding relationship. They are inviting the envy of others not only because of a temporary and easy-going relationship with an employer but, in addition, because of the conventional liberties which attend such a status, such as long annual leaves with pay.[11]

The civil service worker in the cities embraces much of the cane-worker's economics-for-leisure. He aspires to a government "position" where he can find security with a minimal output of energy. He is often the object of derision by less fortunate workers who, with mixed feelings of envy and hate, call his kind a privileged "social class" of dignified ne'er-do-wells.

Of course, I must avoid over-generalization. A sweeping statement that *all* West Indians are indolent, lazy and unmotivated is dangerous. My intent is solely to bring into strong relief the disinclination of a goodly proportion of the Negro labor force (centering first on plantation workers) to define work as a virtuous and stimulating activity; that by reason of this satisfaction with a very low income, the likelihood of early expansion of the nation's economy is small. The more money that is poured into the Islands, the more these folk will use their added incomes to be greater consumers rather than investors in economic enterprise. Easy living hardly serves as a catalyst for economic self-improvement.

THE QUICKSANDS OF CAPITAL FORMATION THEORY

High Fertility and Pervasive Poverty

High human fertility is an all-pervading force which will condition the Islands' economic destiny throughout the next generation. But should births miraculously start to decline and continue downward to half their present

---

[11] Civil service leaves, with pay, have a colonial background designed to expatriate civil servants, a practice which may soon be stopped. One letter to the *Trinidad Guardian* editor reads in part: ". . . I am totally opposed to taxpayers paying leave passages for civil servants and members of their families, and I think it is fully time that the people of the West Indies as a whole should oppose this waste of public funds. . ."

level by 1985, the government's high hopes for economic development could well be realized. The urgent necessity for a rapid reduction in the birth rate is supported by considerable socio-economic evidence. Prominent is the fact that in this impoverished country it is difficult to maintain a healthy balance between the need to save for investment in productive facilities on the one hand, and, on the other, to meet the urgent necessity to spend for welfare and consumer goods and services, such as housing, education, health, food, clothing, etc. While outlays for productive facilities contribute directly to economic growth, expenditures for welfare and consumers goods and services contribute only indirectly, if at all. Ultimate success in economic development is contingent upon a sharp reduction in the birth rate. Rarely in the course of history has the road to a nation's survival been so clearly defined.

Projecting the Islands' national income from 1955 to 1985, on the basis of current population trends, the high fertility invites a smaller total product divided among many more consumers than would be the case under low fertility. A more rapid increase in the number of consumers (mostly children) is the ultimate cause of the slower rise in total output with the higher population trend.

In this era of death control, with its sanitation and public health programs, population explosions happen in poor countries when high death rates are cut quickly and cheaply. Birth rates tend to remain at traditionally high levels so population growth surges upward. This endangers any plans to achieve an economic break-through to higher levels of living. Since 1921, population growth has accelerated rapidly, due mainly to the changing pattern of death. Famine and plagues have been controlled. Transportation has improved so that food can be shipped rapidly into stricken areas. But like most underdeveloped areas, the Islands are unable to raise enough food for their rapidly growing population. By modern standards, West Indian agriculture is overcrowded with workers, unproductive, inefficient, and primitive. The country has relatively few industrial opportunities with which to siphon workers off the land. Furthermore, there has been a sustained high working population directly dependent on agriculture, without any substantial increase in cultivated land.

It is this sustained pressure of population upon the soil that has contributed to movements to the cities and the emergence of a class of landless laborers and tenants. As agrarians in economic abandonment they are receptive to any political philosophy that offers them hope. They are pawns in the hands of all kinds of demagogues.

I have called attention to the catastrophe that can accompany plantation land reform, a program for the development of tiny "self-sustaining" agricultural plots. On the other hand, the mechanization of plantation agriculture is becoming anything but a panacea for the ills of the West Indies. Mechanization results in producing a higher yield per man employed, not an appreciably higher yield per acre cultivated. Mechanization is essential in such countries as the United States where labor is relatively scarce and expensive. But in the West Indies, the conditions are just the reverse. There is a plethora of labor and a lack of full employment. The great majority of agricultural workers are unemployed or under-employed for three or four months out of the year. Application of even the simplest mechanical methods tends to produce idle hands. And to find alternative work for such a mass of people is beyond the power of any government.

The Islands' limited industrialization helps to keep her per capita income among the world's lowest. While national figures are unavailable, Barbados posts a figure in 1953 of $197 (U.S.) and Jamaica $191. In 1955, the per capita income in Jamaica was $234 (U.S.) resting between India with $59 and the United States' rate of $2,000. So long as the population of the Islands increases at about two per cent per annum a real national income increment of at least two per cent per annum is required to provide for the bigger population. And this growth of national income would not permit any rise in living standards if the present factors of population growth remained constant, or fairly so. From the sketchy data available, the trend of national income in the last decade gives little reason for optimism. So heavily dependent upon one crop economies, most of the islands are at the mercy of the capriciousness of rainfall. Accordingly, there is no means by which to ensure automatic development, or even stability, in their economics. Of course, methods of cultivation, varying yields and market prices interplay with rainfall to generate income. Also tourism influences income in the larger islands, but it is everlastingly dependent upon availability of risk capital, and partly on attractive opportunities for investment.

The most carefully marshalled economic accounts of the selected islands leave most investigators with the impression that economic policy-making is the only route away from collapse. Regardless of these programs, continued high fertility will lead the society to economic suicide. With a slow growth of national income and a growing burden of population, the standard of living of the masses will still be low, despite any considerable increase in wages, because of an inequitable distribution of total income (Figure 9, Table 5). If there is any cure-all for a poor country's problem, it rests in the development of a transcendent drive to improve its lot, to take positive steps to overcome high birth rates with the speed that the urgency of the situation demands and allows. A possible course of action is proposed in Chapter VIII.

TOTAL PRIVATE INCOME BEFORE TAXATION, 1949

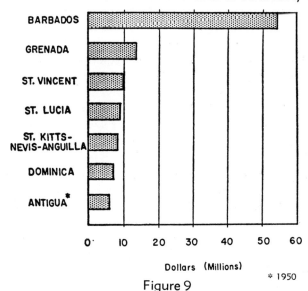

Dollars (Millions)

Figure 9

* 1950

TABLE 5

Total Private Income Before Taxation, 1949

Island	Population[a]	Amount (mil. B.W.I. $)	Per Capita Income
Barbados	205,000	54.14	264
Grenada	75,000	14.356	191.1
St. Vincent	66,000	9.715	247.1
St. Lucia	76,000	9.192	120.7
St. Kitts, Nevis & Anguilla	47,000	9.481	201.7
Dominica	52,000	7.835	150.7
Antigua[b]	45,000	6.100	136.1

[a] Source: Nora M. Siffleet, "National Income and National Accounts," *Social and Economic Studies*, I, (1953), pp. 5-139. Used by permission.
[b] 1950.

Capital Formation

Income and Expenditure Patterns. Private individuals and groups carry the bulk of the responsibility for capital accumulation in free societies. If for the moment, we argue that in order to raise the standard of living of West Indians, there must be tremendous increase in capital, the building up of this capital through private initiative requires (a) thousands of peasants, skilled and unskilled artisans and workmen, accumulating savings from their own labor; (b) large capitalistic efforts that draw heavily on the savings of other people; and (c) cooperative effort by enterprising persons who create capital assets for mutual use. Of these requirements, the first is most fundamental yet the least promising because of several countervailing tendencies.

On the supply side, the islanders have a small capacity and incentive to save, resulting from a low level of income. The low real income is a reflection of low incentives for productivity, the low productivity in turn is hampered by lack of capital. Now the lack of capital is the result of small capacity to save. So the circle is complete. Turning to the demand side, the incentives to invest may be low because of the weak buying power of the labor force, which is due to their small real income, which, again, is due to low productive incentives. The consequent low level of productivity, however, is a result of the small amount of capital used in production, which may be caused at least partly by the small inducement to invest.

The masses of West Indian Negroes will not lay aside savings so long as a high proportion of their numbers feel half-nourished, and are highly illiterate, suspicious of governments and unschooled on what a savings program could (given a decline in fertility) do for them. To launch a program of savings is to invite disappointment if it is assumed that such a program must succeed on a broad scale. Even if the present savings programs of laborers were expanded successfully it would take such a long time to reach fruition that chaos (arising from an expanding redundant population) would already have set in. And some economists insist that a higher rate of investment (regardless of its source) is almost inevitably attended by currency inflation.[12] Others play down this tendency insisting that the only solution or apparent solution for the West Indies, is to borrow from abroad, that in this manner it can finance the local currency expenditures entailed by its development programs. However, there has been considerable controversy over the wisdom of this latter approach by reason of its short term servicing of local capital requirements, that the domestic economy has not been appropriately developed to the point that economic pump-priming through borrowing can overcome in the foreseeable future the net losses from international trade.[13]

---

[12] The basic reasons for ensuing inflation are discussed in Lyle W. Shannon, *Underdeveloped Areas* (New York: Harper and Brothers, 1957), pp. 274-275.

[13] E. F. Nash, "The Problem of Overseas Markets", *Social and Economic Studies*, September, 1958, pp. 132-34.

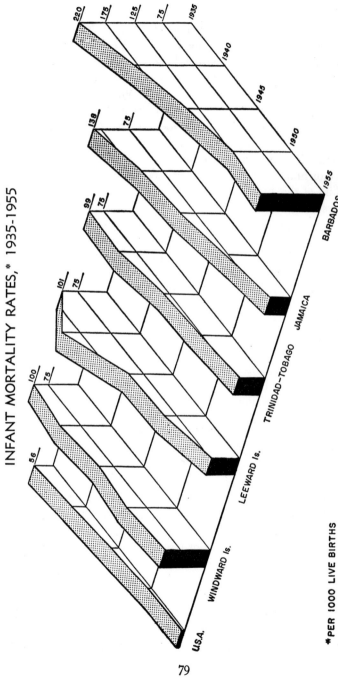

INFANT MORTALITY RATES, * 1935-1955

Figure 10

*PER 1000 LIVE BIRTHS

79

There is such a high level of economic consumption in the Islands that any advantage gained on the production side of the ledger is quickly wiped out by consuming forces. Furthermore, any economic surplus, whether it goes by the name of capital investments, grants, loans, or food, this surplus is eventually checkmated by high human reproduction. The bulk of the family income is devoted to expenditure on food, K. H. Straw, finding in Barbados (1951-52) that 53 per cent of the "typical family's expenditures" were so channeled. In the United Kingdom, only 39.9 per cent were spent in that fashion.

Recognizing how the rate of consumption must increase in proportion to the pressure of human numbers upon the available resource equipment, the compounding of this human pressure serves to accelerate the pace at which the resources will be used up. High costs make for scarcity. Runaway inflation is the scourge of the people. High fertility, coupled with low mortality is depressing the rate at which capital can be accumulated thus accentuating capital decline by the very responsibility of maintaining for a few years children who eventually die before they reach a productive age. Figure 10 above, traces the high (but declining) infant mortality rate in selected islands. Any implication that infants rescued from early death will become self-sustaining members of the labor force is incorrect—their premature deaths are uneconomically postponed by medical technology. The drawings in Figure 11 show the high proportion of deaths of children under nineteen to total deaths for Trinidad, Barbados and Jamaica, respectively, this being most pronounced for Barbados. The general picture is one of high unrecoverable costs of maintaining this unproductive cohort destined for premature death. In contrast with Barbados, where in 1955, 44 per cent of the total deaths involved youth under 19, the United States in 1956 had only 9.6 per cent of the total deaths made up of children in this age group.

Taxation and Income Inbalance. The capital formation picture through taxation is a picture of uneven income distribution in which the wealthy few enjoy a heavy proportion of the total income. In 1942, of those Barbadians subject to income tax, earners with incomes under £600 (comprising 81.2 per cent of the taxpayers) amassed only 41.7 per cent of the island aggregate for that year. The income of Grenada in 1942 was in the neighborhood of £2,078,000, equal to £24 per head. Of this, £362,000 was received by 802 individuals paying income tax. The gap between the income of professional and semi-professional individuals, on the one hand, and the mass of the workers, on the other hand, appears appreciably wider in the West Indies than in more prosperous countries. Within the urban labor force there seems to be a greater wage discrepancy between skilled and unskilled

TOTAL DEATHS UNDER 19 YEARS, SELECTED ISLANDS, 1920-1955

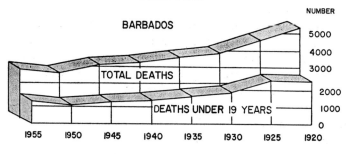

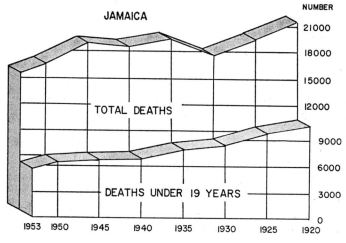

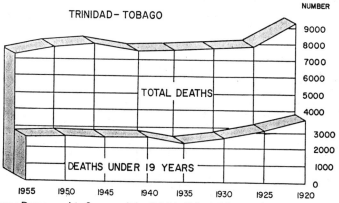

Source: Demographic Survey of the British Colonial Empire by R. R. Kuczynski. Demographic Yearbook, 1957.

Figure 11

workers.[14] The West Indian disparity in incomes can be explained by (1) extreme educational and ethnic differences, marked by a small well-educated minority following one set of work standards, and a comparatively illiterate peasantry living in a quite different world; (2) a large labor force of cheap unskilled workers, often including child labor; (3) concentration of land ownership in the hands of small upperclass minorities.

The "progressive" taxes in vogue serve to finance government and such social services as education, health and housing, and thus help in reducing some of the inequalities in standards of living. But the "regressive" taxes (taxes on basic commodities) tend to increase these inequalities, with inflation intensifying the disparity in standards of living. While in the economically advanced nations as much as one-half of the central government's revenue originates from progressive and direct taxes on income and wealth, in the Islands regressive taxes (sales taxes, import duties, etc.) supply the bulk of the revenue. This accounts for the political tension between poor and wealthier islands over a "Customs Union." Also, many government services are of a general nature, and their benefit is difficult to apportion among income groups. Public health and educational programs, for example, benefit both the poor and the rich. Yet some programs, particularly tourism, hardly reach the poor at all. For practical purposes, however, social services can be regarded generally as rendering more benefit to the poor.

In her study of national income, Nora Siffleet[15] summarizes, for selected islands, the proportion of direct taxes paid by individuals in contrast with companies before taxation in 1949 (Figure 12), revealing how in Dominica 99 per cent of the direct taxes originate from individuals while in Barbados 45 per cent derive from this source. The study, based upon a sample, supplies

---

[14] In technically advanced United States, there is not, however, the general leveling process going on with respect to incomes as popularly believed. The ideologically-fostered myth of the increasing equalization of income is largely based on the statistical work of Simon Kuznets, who concerned himself with only the richest five per cent of the population and its share of the nation's income. Kuznets found that the income-share of the top one per cent and the top five per cent of the population had dropped sharply and fairly consistently. However, the wages of skilled workers in the United States, many of whose wives also work, plus the rise of installment credit since World War II, account to a large extent for the improvement in the nation's standard of living that has induced the mistaken notion of a more democratic income distribution. Recent statistical evidence supplied by Gabriel Kolko (*Wealth and Power in America: An Analysis of Social Class and Income Distribution*, Praeger, 1962) shows that the basic distribution of income and wealth is essentially the same now as it was in 1939, or even in 1910. While low income groups live substantially better today by reason of mounting real wages, their percentage of the national income has not changed. Through the 1950's, the income of the top tenth of our population was larger than the total for the bottom five income-tenths. The only significant rises in income distribution have occurred in the second and third-richest income tenths. Taxation, according to Kolko, has not served as a major instrument for a more equitable income distribution.

[15] Nora M. Siffleet, *op. cit.*

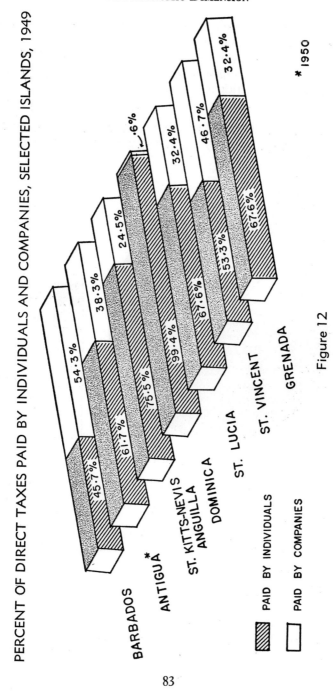

PERCENT OF DIRECT TAXES PAID BY INDIVIDUALS AND COMPANIES, SELECTED ISLANDS, 1949

BARBADOS

ANTIGUA*

ST. KITTS-NEVIS
ANGUILLA

DOMINICA

ST. LUCIA

ST. VINCENT

GRENADA

45.7%   54.3%

61.7%   38.3%

75.5%   24.5%

99.4%   .6%

67.6%   32.4%

53.3%   46.7%

67.6%   32.4%

* 1950

PAID BY INDIVIDUALS

PAID BY COMPANIES

Figure 12

83

ample clues of the heavy burden placed upon individuals in direct taxes. In the same study, three revealing tables of statistics on Antigua (without doubt the poorest of all the principal federated islands) are included to substantiate the conclusion that fresh capital can hardly be drawn via direct taxation from an already poverty-stricken labor force.

Figure 13 shows that 68 per cent of wage-employed persons in Antigua

WAGE-EMPLOYED PERSONS BY ANNUAL INCOME FROM WAGES DURING YEAR JULY 15, 1949-JULY 15, 1950, ANTIGUA

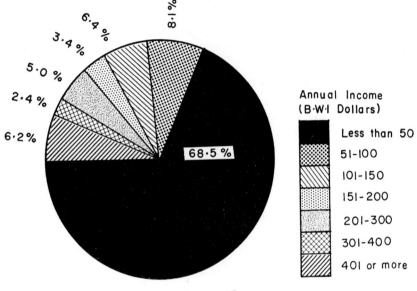

Figure 13

claim to have earned less than 50 dollars in 1950. Thus the pattern of incomes is one of small wages distributed among the high proportion of adults in the labor pool.

In Figure 14, Siffleet supplies statistics on annual income of self-employed Antiguans, in which 80.3 per cent of these persons are shown to earn less than 50 dollars (B.W.I.) per annum.

CONCLUSION

Proposals in economic tinkering. Students of overpopulated and poverty stricken countries have profferred numerous economic formulae by which these nations might improve their lot. Three of these are discussed here.

84

OWN ACCOUNT EMPLOYED PERSONS BY ANNUAL INCOME
FROM OWN ACCOUNT EMPLOYMENT IN 1949-1950, ANTIGUA

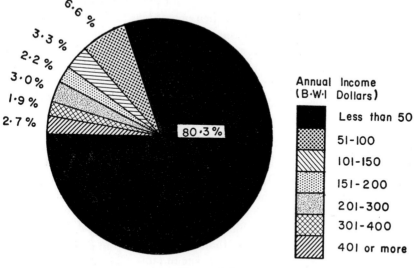

Annual Income
(B·W·I Dollars)

Less than 50
51-100
101-150
151-200
201-300
301-400
401 or more

Figure 14

1. By curtailing the consumption of the higher income groups, the amounts of savings available for investment purposes could be markedly increased. Anthropologist Sol Tax[16] believes that by the elimination of production of the nonessential goods and services and of investment in facilities that are to produce nonessential goods, scarce resources could be freed for investment projects. He scolds private interests that are socially necessary but do not promise rich returns in the short run, asserting that the "squandering of limited supplies of foreign exchange on capital flight or on importation of redundant foreign goods and services could be prevented and the foreign funds thus saved could be used for the acquisition of foreign made machinery needed for economic development."[17] Proponents of this formula feel that machines should be made the prime agency of work-tempo rather than the operator himself, that output per man hour can be increased despite the lackadaisacal attitude of the labor force. The proposal suffers, however, from the failure to consider the necessity of putting increasing number of idle hands to work, and that efficient machinery in agriculture or

[16] Sol Tax, "Selective Culture Change", *American Economic Review*, (May, 1951), p. 357.
[17] *Ibid.*

industry invites technological unemployment in areas where natural resources are limited, compounding the redundancy of labor.

2. Launch a program of peasant savings for the purpose of accumulating working capital. Such a formula is often opposed, as in the West Indies, by aversions toward savings. Furthermore, the program would have to succeed on such a broad scale that an expanding population could absorb the net gains in such a long-pull enterprise. Also, suspicion of governments and government-sponsored programs can stifle a peasant-savings program. Most important, economic "bootstrap" formulae are based upon faulty reasoning when fertility-control programs are left unattended.

3. Industrialize the population. Countries log-jammed by overpopulation have been turning to programs of attracting industry through tax exemptions. As a comparatively recent technique, there has not been ample time to show its possible effect on changing the economic life of the population. However, to change the economic life is not necessarily to improve it. The basic task is to find those symbolic values associated with industrialization and urbanization within which lie the ultimate solution of the problems of overpopulation.[18] In the West Indies, the resources are either so few or those than can be exploited (such as bauxite in Jamaica) require such a small labor force for its extraction and refining that, given the necessary capital, these efforts would have small impact on the level of living of the masses.

The basic reason for the low level of living in poor countries, according to many economists, "is the primitive condition of the tools and techniques used by the thousands of self-employed peasants and artisans who account for the largest share of production."[19] The blind spot in this assertion is the failure to recognize that any change in the technology or economics of a country without concurrently changing the social organization would gain nothing. While there is some truth that in the planning process the change in one facet of human activity all interlocking conditions of existence will often fall in line, it does not work in social settings where a competing component of human existence is master-determining and can countervail the force intended to spring a desirable chain of events.

So long as the economically advanced nations of the world enjoy a one to two per cent annual increase in per capita income, the material conditions of people in the Islands must advance both absolutely and relatively to that of high income populations. In fact, the percentage increase must be more than two per cent per year for many decades to come. With a market

---

[18] Leonard Broom, "Urban Research in the British Caribbean: A Prospectus", *Social and Economic Studies*, (February, 1953), pp. 113-119.
[19] Lyle Shannon, *Underdeveloped Areas* (New York: Harper and Brothers, 1953), p. 212.

structure of low capital and low natural resources per capita, the West Indies, in order to resolve its social-economic dilemmas and contradictions, must put first things first and boldly reduce its population through fertility control programs. Then, and only then, can the deterrent values to economic growth be made vulnerable to redefinition and economic formulae be put to work. The success of a desired economic system is contingent upon the aspirations of those who would prosper by it.

Chapter V

The Technological Dimension

Technology is the hero of our piece. This is a world of rocks and rivers, sticks and steel, of sun and starlight, of galaxies, atoms and molecules. . . . The means of adjustment and control of security and survival are, of course, technological.

LESLIE A. WHITE[1]

Intrigued by the realization that man can increase the present effective supply of depletable and non-replenishable resources by reducing the waste involved in their use, demographers often become technological determinists of sorts. Man, they argue, can increase the supply of resources by bringing within the "circuit" of human use things which otherwise would be valueless. With motivations held constant, and from seeing how economically prosperous countries have embraced technology,[2] they would rearrange the available foods and fibers, harness solar energy, make ocean water potable, find minerals in the sea, impose machinery and contraceptive devices upon agrarian, redundant population. All of this would be done on the assumption that men are adaptive creatures and that social change responds mechanically and inevitably to technology. Technological change and progress thus become coterminous—a teleological theory of change. The cycle becomes one of harnessing the material world, which in turn changes communal patterns of tastes and income distribution, which in turn transmutes tastes into effective demand for goods, technologically brought forward.[3]

Of course, some technologists are less rigid than others. William F. Ogburn, whose name is almost interchangeable with "machine," qualified his position with the statement: "Man appears to be the master in the particular use he makes of the machine, but we seem not to be able to control all the derivative results of its creation and manufacture."[4] Social anthropologist W. Lloyd Warner, equally impressed with the compelling force of technology, has said:

Assuming that societies undergo a form of social evolution from simple to complex (and accepting the fact that they retrogress too), we can say that the

---

[1] *The Science of Culture* (New York: Grove Press, Inc., 1949, Published by arrangement with Farrar, Straus and Cudahy) p. 390. By permission.

[2] "Technology" is used in this chapter in the restricted sense to mean the physical world and its supporting sciences and industrial arts.

[3] See Joseph J. Spengler, "Population Movements, Employment and Income", *The Southern Economic Journal*, (October, 1938), pp. 129-157.

[4] William F. Ogburn with the assistance of Jean L. Adams and S. C. Gilfillan, *The Social Effects of Aviation* (New York: Houghton Mifflin Company, 1946), p. 9.

more complex the technology the more complex is the society.

As technology increases in complexity, the economic institutions likewise increase in variety, complexity and power.

As technology increases in complexity and modern control over the physical environment develops, the sacred systems of the society tend to decrease in importance to the society and its members.

As technological, economic and political hierarchies become more complex, the area covered by kinship and family relations decreases in importance.[5]

THE TRAP OF EFFICIENCY

The key word in technological enterprise is "efficiency." Paul S. Henshaw, enraptured by the efficiency powers of technology in the improvement of man's lot, presents the following statement of its potentialities:

With respect to the physiology of reproduction, it is evident that man has entered an Alice-in-Wonderland type of world and has passed little beyond the portal. Today's formulas with tomorrow's improvements offer prospects for advancing human efficiency and expanding human capacities the same as did the discovery of various wonder drugs some decades ago. Increasingly, the span of life is being extended and the body maintained at higher levels of well-being and working efficiency. In effect, ways are being found to suspend or even to reverse physiologic time, permitting us to live again with the conditions and vigor of earlier years. Just as modern physics brought realization of the alchemist's dream of transmuting the elements, it may be that modern biochemistry will bring realization of the Fountain of Youth.[6]

The impact of new technology upon West Indian death rates has been indeed profound. Table 6 traces the movements in crude death rates from 1921 to 1954, showing declines up to 66 per cent.

The drop in infant mortality has been equally striking (Table 7), with Barbados, the most densely populated island enjoying a 65 per cent decline in a generation.

With these inroads into mortality experience, the average length of life in thirty years has increased in Barbados 26 years. In another two generations, life expectation for West Indians may match that of the United States by age and sex. Unless birth rates begin to fall soon, the population will climb steadily higher.

The steady reduction of mortality since 1930, has been achieved by the discovery of new methods of disease treatment applicable at reasonable cost.

---

[5] From lectures on comparative institutions, University of Chicago, 1945.

[6] Paul S. Henshaw, *Adaptive Human Fertility* (New York: McGraw-Hill Book Company, Inc., 1955), p. 217. Used by permission.

TABLE 6

Movements in Crude Death Rates[a]

Territory	Crude Death Rates for			% Decline 1921-25 to 1954
	1921-25	1945-46	1954	
Barbados	32.9	16.7	11.2	66.0
Jamaica	23.5	14.1	10.7	54.5
Antigua	27.2	15.8	10.6	61.0
Montserrat	18.6	13.5	12.9	30.6
St. Kitts-Nevis	27.6	17.4	11.1	59.8
Trinidad	21.7	14.0	9.7	55.3
Dominica	23.3	19.6	12.6	45.9
Grenada	18.4	16.4	9.3	49.5
St. Lucia	22.2	15.4	12.0	45.9
St. Vincent	18.8	15.9	15.2	19.1

[a] Table courtesy of G. W. Roberts.

TABLE 7

Movements in Infant Mortality Rates[a]

Territory	Infant Mortality Rates for			% Decline 1921-25 to 1954
	1921-25	1945-46	1954	
Barbados	313.5	157.4	109.4	65.1
Jamaica	175.8	94.7	66.1	62.4
Antigua	215.9	96.4	88.0	59.2
Montserrat	166.0	103.6	123.5	25.6
St. Kitts-Nevis	228.4	123.5	69.6	69.5
Trinidad	133.1	81.3	60.6	54.5
Dominica	162.3	130.0	99.4	38.8
Grenada	106.1	107.1	47.0	55.7
St. Lucia	125.1	100.5	101.3	19.0
St. Vincent	115.3	100.9	117.4	......

[a] Table courtesy of G. W. Roberts.

Death control is rapid because it does not depend on general economic improvement or changes in the motivations of people. This cannot be said for birth control. Now the Pan American Sanitary Bureau, with its Institute of Nutrition of Central America and Panama, has developed a palatable baby food known as Incaparina which may arrest even more the heavy death toll among infants. In the best traditions of science, this new food, composed of a blend of corn, sorghum and cotton seed flour, with torula yeast and vitamin A added, will sell for about 3 cents (U.S.) a packet and still allow a 28 per cent profit for the manufacturer. With adequate protein, this innocuous enough mixture can compound the population explosion not only in the Islands but throughout Central America. The chances are good that thousands of babies, destined for early death from malnutrition, will soon receive a daily ration of food containing the equivalent of three glasses of milk in nutritional value. And where science ends, the economic and political strains will assuredly increase by reason of population growth and declining job opportunities—an ominous potential. While the perversities of "progress" are painfully evident to the scientists of INCAP, apparently they rebel, as do those who will respond to their genius, more against death than against birth, proclaiming how unbearable it is to stand by with indifference while children needlessly die. Perhaps this example of technological ingenuity may lend stimulus to comparable social ingenuity in resolving the problems which Incaparina seems destined to compound.

Efficiency can thus be both a boon and a bane. If this seems too extreme a viewpoint, there can be no doubt that efficiency constitutes a challenge to institutional practices. That is, to administer a social organization according to purely technical criteria of rationality is irrational, because it ignores the nonrational aspects of social conduct. Foreign technical assistance programs reflect this blind spot. The expert, assigned to improving housing, building factories or improving agricultural technology, is charged with the job of giving expert advice on particular problems without regard to the by-products of the improvement he is working for. Accordingly, technical aid for the improvement of health tends to increase the population at a rate about as rapid as the increase in production or at times even more rapidly. When the program is in full operation, the native population is frequently no better off, in standard of living, than it was at the beginning. Well known is the impact of the industrial revolution, begun about 200 years ago, upon population growth, a spark that led to initially improved levels of living. About the middle of the eighteenth century the death rate began to fall chiefly as a result of the improvement in food production. And health work was still of little significance. The birth rate declined but slightly after a sharp drop in the death rate had set in. This led to popular S-curve theories. To proceed on the basis of this experience in an already saturated group of islands such as the West Indies, is to invite disaster. The hoped-for decline in births would come too late.

In 1954-56, as a consultant on housing in the Lesser Antilles, I was surprised that my associates in the field, as well as those in Washington, D.C., gave so little heed to the fact that what they were doing might have repercussions on the life of the people beyond increasing the efficiency, comforts and goods available for their use. And insofar as improved housing was concerned, each new dwelling meant far greater survival chances for each infant, what with improved cooking, sanitation and sleeping facilities.

When I sought to introduce social workers and educational films to modify the incentives and routines of householders, Washington called this "busy work" reminding me that my job was to "get those houses up" and everything would work out for the better. Bad habits would melt away. It was assumed that we were involved in a cause-and-effect mechanism, that there was a simple relationship between them. As evidenced by the number of failures in the do-it-yourself housing program, the motivations of these natives were not appropriately measured prior to launching the projects. And motivations are complex. Not often can a single specific cause for an individual's action toward house construction be found. While a man's action can be influenced by passing him a bit of information or propaganda, it is frequently not enduring because this influence has not been meaningfully intermingled with the matrix of his interests.

In looking at the American technical aid efforts, I am struck by the apparent assumption that all we need to do is export the tools and know-how of efficiency production leaving other aspects of the local culture to mend for themselves. The bias of cultural anthropologists that the local patterns should be left alone because they are endogeneous (thus good and to be defended) has had its impact on our policymakers. We are admonished to refrain from insisting that the moral systems abroad mimic our own. This, I believe, is an unrealistic approach. If a country is to be impregnated with our materials and skills then assuredly there will be some response, a response which might prove more disastrous to the inhabitants than curative if left unattended by those who introduce the new methods and materials. There would seem to be some obligation on our part to be equally concerned with the social effects. If the people of overpopulated areas desire the tools and products of American technical ingenuity they must be prepared to see some of their cultural traits change. Accordingly, Americans are obliged to help them work out those conflicts and anxieties which emerge from new technology. The internal aspects of technical cooperation have been ignored by Americans as being "none of our business." Witness, for example, the value conflict emerging from technical aid as involving the values of efficiency versus friendship. West Indians, while respecting and coveting our technology, argue that "you people think only about efficiency while we place a higher value on friendship." They are confused by the contradictions between the friendly intent of our projects and our hard-working experts dedicated to technical competence. They are not sure whether we are being helpful when we push for, say, complementary crops, with all the accompanying complexities, when the recipients of our efforts prefer a simple work procedure rooted in sentiment and intimacy with others. They are somewhat frightened by the way our overseas missions think of the problems in terms of scientific laboratories rather than farms.[7] Arthur T. Mosher speaks of our experts and their policymakers as having "insufficient appreciation of the importance of the self-generating resources for agricultural development," of "Failing to give adequate value to the germinal concept of technical cooperation: the real value of technical cooperation is less in its immediate impact on production than in the increasing capacity of people in each country to solve their own future problems."[8]

In my own adventures in technical assistance, I have seen signs of delight when an American designed project aborts. The bystander was looking upon the disappointed experts as agents of change and hence a menace to many of the established values. The foreign expert is, more often than not, a "suspicious character," looked upon apprehensively by the recipients who were in fear he would do something that would upset the routines of life. The technician, unfortunately, forgets that he must play the role of salesman as well as technician as he builds houses, factories, or designs a community. More directly, the expert (as well as the local folk who would profit by his efforts) must anticipate being caught in the inevitable collision between the wish for stability, on the one hand, and the wish for progress and efficiency on the other. I found most West Indians reasonably dedicated to new housing but wanting no disorder in the work-play balance, and certainly none in the tax structure.

In the day-to-day routine of meeting people and working out answers to problems, the adviser is assisting the community in its search for an idealism that will reconcile conflicting philosophies. And this is a complex undertaking by reason of the obscure nature of the values themselves. Nevertheless, the technician and those who supervise his work must recognize that the most important thing to know about any group is what it takes for granted and what values are held sacred and inviolable. In the measure in which these values are regarded as ultimate imperatives, they are neither discussed or debated, often not even explicitly stated.[9] I have seen sound improvements sabotaged through evasion of responsibility. I have in mind mono-pitched roofs, inside kitchens and bathrooms, and even birth control clinics. New housing with unshuttered large windows will invite few occupants in Barba-

---

[7] See Arthur T. Mosher, *Technical Cooperation in Latin-American Agriculture* (The University of Chicago Press, 1957), pp. 310-415. Copyright 1957 by the Univ. of Chicago.

[8] *Ibid.,* p. 412.

[9] After Louis Wirth, "Ideological Aspects of Social Disorganization", *American Sociological Review* (August, 1940), p. 477.

dos because they let the "duppies" in—tiny creatures that creep into the home at night and allegedly choke those persons who are asleep. Technological changes will be adopted only if they are compatible with local superstitions and doctrines, in short the cultural heritage. Thus new technology must move with the human stream. Frontal attacks seldom work.

While local people may speak admiringly of the efficiency and "split-second" timing of American technical assistance, they have seen the comings and goings of foreign influence, the rise and fall of "schemes." Their mind-set is oriented more to cycles or rhythms than impatient change. The expert cannot afford to be branded as a "meddler," "hasty," or "pushy." Those who would introduce new tools and techniques into the West Indies must keep in mind that social objectives as "truth, beauty, and goodness" do not necessarily follow from technical efficiency. This calls for intelligent provision by the planners and knowledge concerning the nature of social change in democracy. In Asia as in the West Indies, response to birth control devices and propaganda has been so mixed that sponsors have become discouraged.[10] They are unable to find receptive audiences. They recognize that the transmission of new techniques is always incomplete unless persons can be found who clearly understand the long-range implications of such changes as new educational services, irrigation installations, sewage disposal systems, clinics for sterilization, child care or abortion. The successful application of new techniques is dependent upon the discovery of the community power structure, sometimes through the strengthening of an emerging elite, and sometimes upon altering social values to provide the necessary rewards for those persons who would cooperate and ultimately supervise the projects. Family planning programs will reveal success with contraception by some segments of the population but disappointing indifference or even hostility by others. From my research in Grenada and St. Lucia (Chapter VII), I know that the introduction of contraception as a wide scale attack will invite resistance by the males and variable response by females, the latter reactions ranging from timid, verbal acceptance to eager support.

CONTRACEPTIVES

The consequences of rapidly declining mortality in the West Indies, made possible through congenial new technology, can be understood only in conjunction with knowledge of what is happening to fertility. Scientific gadgets and chemical formulae raise fertility by lowering morbidity and correcting faulty reproductive systems. And when fear, indifference and

---

[10] Kingsley Davis, "Population and Spread of Industrial Society," *op. cit.*, p. 17-18.

hostility toward contraception are added to the successes of science, population soars. Mothers, embryos and helpless infants, once destined for premature death, now contribute to a rising tide of physical beings moving toward the bursting reproductive age groups.

Standard mechanical methods for withholding the human sperm from union with the egg involve diaphragms, creams, jellies, and condoms, but only the last is of any general use in the West Indian population. While the manufacture of these materials have created a $200 million annual business in the United States, the failure to fit these inventions to the cultural and psychological variations of West Indian sex practices has meant a stymied planned parenthood program. That is, the job for those who would control population growth is to first understand these practices and then fit the mechanical aids to them.

In this adaptation, one task is to develop concurrence within the populace on when human life physiologically begins. To fail in this effort is to arouse a boomerang reaction by some institutional leaders and their followers with respect to the place of contraception in sex education. Those who think nothing of the destruction and loss of millions of sperm cells through copulatory and extra-copulatory means, or the prevention of hundreds of ova from maturing in the ovary, react vigorously against the idea of destroying one sperm and one ovum after they have united. This stems from uncertainties, myths and pre-judgments about the time at which a new human being can be said to be in existence. By informing the public and its leaders that a new organism, as an early embryo, has few of the characteristics of a human being, that in the early days it behaves not unlike a parasite moving through the mother's body, and that it is almost impossible to distinguish between a human embryo and one of higher mammals at this stage, one stancheon will have been erected for more adequate programs in fertility control.

Thus the fertility control program becomes legal and ethical in character before it becomes technological. Even in the United States, research on contragestion (prevention of development of the embryo) and contranidation (preventative action prior to implantation of sperm) has been delayed because of vague laws and views pertaining to feticide. With increasing awareness of population pressure in the United States, and abroad, most laws and views will likely be clarified thus opening the door for drugs and mechanical procedures to prevent unwanted pregnancies.

In Japan, feticide in the form of induced abortion has been made compatible with Japanese values and incentives with a direct impact upon the birth rate. With the existing prejudices against induced abortion in Occidental countries, however, it has not been sponsored as a technique in family planning with the result that it has moved underground, subject to all sorts of clandestine influences. Whether induced abortion could be better controlled or managed if brought into the open is worthy of study by the defenders of public rights and private rights on reproduction.

Newer contraceptives, some still in the laboratory stage, that might receive acceptance in the West Indies should be mentioned. For those who object to genital contraception techniques, a "pill" for temporary suspension of fertility (physiologic control) is appearing on the market. Introduced as a public health measure, this simple (and potentially inexpensive) oral contraceptive will prevent ovulation. The two which have been subjected to the most experimentation carry the trade names of Enovid and Norlutin. The pills work directly on the pituitary inhibiting its normal output of gonadtropic hormone, the hormone which stimulates egg production in the ovary. While the laboratory tests of these pills have thus far proved their safety, there have been instances of side-effects.

Other research involves immunology for wives against sperm. When rabbit sperm was injected into the blood stream of a female rabbit an antibody to the sperm was created. This anti-body can be extracted and injected into other female rabbits to protect them against the sperm, much as Salk vaccine protects against polio. Also, a vaginal aerosol foaming jelly has been found apparently efficacious and harmless by the Margaret Sanger Research Bureau, as has a non-foaming vaginal tablet. Both are still in the testing stages however.

Perhaps not to be overlooked insofar as its possible transference to human requirements is concerned, is the research by a Yale pathologist, Leon F. Whitney on dogs. He has developed a simple drug known as malucidin, which reverses pregnancy.[11] When injected, the drug causes the pregnant female dog to reabsorb the embryo into her blood stream.

Suffice it to say, the technology of contraception may be improved for West Indian use. Until recently, little medical research has been devoted to contraception. But with appropriate attention, a revolution in contraceptive technique might be achieved which would ease the task of spreading birth control in the West Indies and backward areas generally. It is possible, though doubtful, that the future rate of natural increase in the Islands will be less than at present under the influence of two possible conditions: (a) fertility may decline through a shift in attitudes toward child-bearing, as it has in industrial countries; (b) with continuing emigration, the effective

---

[11] Another book could be written on the redundancy of dogs in the West Indies, their fertility and control problems. Needless to say, their appetites are making some inroads into the standard of living of the natives.

fertility of the remaining population may be reduced. Minus these events, techniques for population reduction must be both simple and subtle—subtle in the sense of appeasing the expectations of human communities. A program must be initiated that will appeal to a West Indian's own hedonistic self-interest.[12] It must be ordered up to move with the social tide rather than against it. Indirect methods are always more effective in a relatively illiterate population than an appeal to facts and rational procedures. Cultural inertia is the profound obstacle to the rational ordering of personal behavior influencing population trends.

INDUSTRIALIZATION AND URBANIZATION

Kingsley Davis, noted international demographer, conceiving of industrialization ("modernization") as a self-generating, master-determining force that can draw all associated components of change into line, offers the following solution to overpopulation in economically depressed countries:

The faster the rate of modernization, other things equal, the quicker will be the response of fertility, the earlier the end of population growth, the smaller the ultimate population reached, and the higher the eventual level of living.[13]

Convinced that reduction of fertility must "wait upon the growth of industry," Davis takes a dim view of campaigns, political, educational or technical, to diffuse contraceptives because adults are indifferent and insist upon the latent private desire to limit their off-spring.[14] Fertility-depressing industries must be introduced rapidly! He says:

. . . The hope is that industrial growth can be made so quickly that it will get ahead of the population problem not only by providing a higher standard of living for the population and the inevitable growth of numbers during the process of economic development, but also by bringing those new social conditions that will cause people voluntarily to limit their offspring. In short, it is hoped to repeat the experience of the now industrialized countries, but more rapidly.[15]

Like Davis, Binay Ranjan Sen, Director General of the United Nation's Food and Agricultural Organization, proposes a catch-up program through industrialization. Noting how agricultural technology by itself will not

---

[12] For a contrasting view see Frank Lorimer, *Culture and Human Fertility* (Zurich: Berichthaus, 1954), pp. 247-251.

[13] Kingsley Davis, "Population and Spread of Industrial Society", *Proceedings of the American Philosophical Society*, Vol. 96, No. 1, 1951, p. 16.

[14] *Ibid.*, p. 18.

[15] Kingsley Davis, "Population and Change in Backward Areas", *Columbia Journal of International Affairs* (Spring, 1950), p. 46.

solve the problem of food scarcity, Sen suggests fighting hunger through industrializing the poor agrarian countries so that a market would be created for increased farm production.[16] Poor countries, he observes, simply eat the increased food that agricultural technology affords and either cut down on their agricultural exports or may, in fact, import food. This cycle of poverty can only be broken, he says, through the income derived from processing what added food is produced and selling it abroad. Sen has come to the conclusion, then, that a poor agrarian country cannot, with the help of agricultural technology, feed itself into prosperity, thus his formula is to bring about a transition for these countries with the implantation of food-processing machinery. He proposes balanced industrial-agricultural economies leaving the matter of high fertility unattended. The implication of this formula is that, all things being equal (birth and death rates held constant), a catch-up program of industrialization will bring prosperity to overpopulated agricultural-based nations. People would not be permitted to devour the farm surpluses by this means.

Industrial determinists appear to base their claims upon two assumptions: (1) the material, external world supplies the significant tools by which man obtains food, shelter and protection; and (2) the inner resources, of which ideologies and myth-making are illustrations, satisfy human needs in such a constant fashion that in the development of human societies these inner ideational conditions may be omitted as important considerations. This is a modern form of the old conception that mind is a *tabula rasa*, a clean slate, until the impressions of the outer world are recorded on it. The environment (energy, inventions or any other "external" element) calls the tune and the organism plays it. Such a view fails to comprehend the interactivity of the multiple factors within the causal complex.

Defenders of industrialization must be asked: What is this interstitial stuff that passes between the physical and the social that causes a reduction in family size, in more urbanization, in more class mobility, recreation, women in the labor force? Must it originate in the technological matrix and behave in a quite fixed way? Indeed not, it derives out of the exchanges of experiences, from felt gain and loss, from fear and hopeful anticipation, and is identified as incentive. As an internal force it becomes the "plan of action" (to use a term of George H. Mead) fused to physical things permitting men to accept or reject new energy forms. Variations in the response to material innovations by different societies comprise ample evidence that incentives are initiating forces for change in their own right.

---

[16] *Time*, (November 30, 1959), pp. 20-21.

To industrialize, "modernize" or urbanize is to succeed in most instances in raising total production; but whether we will raise per capita production (what is available for per capita consumption) is another question. There is every likelihood that the increase (either in the form of food or cash gained from its sale) will be used to a large extent merely to keep additional children alive, allowing little or nothing for improvement of the level of living. In the West Indies, as in China and India, the birth rate is very high, although no higher than it was in the United States in its early days. Given no change in incentive, in self-image or life style, I insist that when people who are accustomed to living fairly close to the subsistence level get more to live on, their incentives will dictate that they use the new income to keep alive the babies they have. And from what I have seen in the Islands, in Puerto Rico and South American countries, there is no indication yet of any significant decline in the birth rate. But there is evidence in all of them of a decline in the death rate. Fear of death pre-empts the fear of birth and this is manifest in action. I have serious doubts that "modernizaton" programs planned to increase the productivity of labor can increase per capita consumption very much in the foreseeable future unless this effort is accompanied by a subtle value-restructuring program. Otherwise new industry, while increasing production, can also swell the residue of idle hands. Furthermore, the use of "urbanized" technology, involves large concentrations of capital, creating a need in a poor economy for large amounts of overhead *social* capital in the form of housing and sanitation facilities. In the West Indies, this need for overhead capital facilities could perhaps be avoided if, for example, technology were adopted which permitted decentralization of production. In short, efforts to encourage the West Indies to retrace the technological evolution of England and the United States in order to maximize the return from new capital formations is complex.[17]

If fertility control at any price is the goal, then urbanization is one possible way out. That is, the social shock which accompanies crowded and unsanitary city slums may eventually constitute the brutal force to detonate a social revolution concerning family organization and reproductive practices. Minus this social shock, urbanization is no boon to government planning for the reduction of fertility in the West Indies. Fertility is not proving to be a dependent variable, or precipitate, to urban industrialization. The introduction of mechanical industries into this non-industrial society can not be expected to automatically bring about a trend toward increased con-

---

[17] See Charles Wolfe, Jr. and Sidney C. Sufrin, *Capital Formation and Foreign Investment in Underdeveloped Areas* (New York: Syracuse University Press, 1955), Chapter 2.

trol of reproduction rates. The following statement by Margaret Hagood, in her book *Mothers of the South*, fits the problem of the West Indies:

Attitudes toward childbearing are the core of interest in the study of fertility, for it is the psychological reaction to external factors, such as traditional and economic pressures, which finally translates these societal forces into effect on the birth rates. These attitudes are difficult to state summarily. Undoubtedly there is ambivalence. The traditional pattern of the glory and the actual or imagined value of a large number of children pull in one direction, while the desire to avoid the suffering of childbearing, the trouble of caring for another child, and the responsibility of another mouth to be fed and body to be clothed pull in the other. An approximate balance of these forces means that the former wins out because children keep arriving when a laissez-faire policy is adopted. . .[18]

CONCLUSION

Some economists would insist that the direction taken by technological change may be analyzed and the direction predicted if such change is conceived as an endogenous variable—endogenous, that is, to the economic system. Professor Yale Brozen takes this view that technological change moves in directions determined by economic forces, writing,

Technology may be treated as a short-run given or perhaps an intermediate long-run given, since it changes slowly, just as we take the amount of plant capacity in an industry as a short-run given. In the long run, however, it changes in directions determined by economic forces just as the amount of investment in different industries changes in directions determined by economic forces. Just as we can say that the investment in one industry is going to grow more rapidly than in another when we know the relative costs and demand conditions, so we should learn how to determine when technological change will be more rapid in one industry than another, or more rapid in one direction than another.[19]

It is demonstrable that the adoption or development of technology is in direct relationship to the inclinations of men. Witness in the United States the development of penicillin and contraceptives in the drugs field in response to human fears of death, disease and general socio-economic discomfort. And while we have no way of telling whether the West Indies response to technological innovations will be creative or adaptive, certainly the economic variable of a complex change cannot tell the entire story. It is not enough to say that technological change is an endogenous variable and the

---

[18] Margaret Hagood, *Mothers of the South* (Chapel Hill: University of North Carolina Press, 1939), pp. 120-121.
[19] Yale Brozen, "Determinants of the Direction of Technological Change", *The American Economic Review* (May, 1953), p. 301.

direction is determined by economic forces. Knowing that the future emerges from the matrix of past history and present circumstances, this knowledge may not give a nation complete power to prevent all events, their timing, and their consequences. But they can try, and sometimes do so successfully.

Technologically oriented demographers often fall into the trap of failing to take into account the important notion of a time horizon, logically justifying a technology by its ultimate payoff. They ignore the idea of a "premature" invention, be it a new contraceptive, an industry to desalt sea water or newly discovered forms of energy. The time horizon imparts sense to West Indian development programs because it permits the avoiding of mistakes in aping the capital-intensive techniques of technologically advanced nations. While agrarian societies do seem to move toward imitation of these nations, the relationship between technology on the one hand, and the intervening, countervailing propensities to save, invest, spend, work, or seek leisure on the other, is a matter of first importance to be investigated by the behavioral scientist.

Chapter VI
The Dimension of Ideas, Beliefs, and Incentives

The purpose of this chapter is to explore the place of ideational forces in the demographic life of West Indians. Beginning with the recognition that interests generate the ends of practical activity, I have already remarked how students of population must concern themselves seriously with the social ethos—the set of collective understandings—before a meaningful and usable body of demographic facts can be marshalled. Because ideas, as expressions of human striving, are not always subject to rigorous experimental analysis, one is tempted to pass them off as "superfluous" in research work, cutting out thereby the very foundations of our problem before giving them a chance to show their importance. For if anything is clear about expectations, fears or myths, it is that men who have adhered to them believe them to be real. They cannot be ignored.

The various elements of West Indian social organization must be viewed as being intermeshed with the material conditions of existence. Ideas, dogmas and doctrines are social facts and must be assessed in terms of their influence upon population change. Those elements in human ideas and beliefs must be sifted out which are of motivational consequence to the actors.

Now, the theorem that ideas are powerful movers in human demography does not rest on any proposition as to the origin of ideas. We need only to maintain that at any given time the direction of demographic change is influenced by ideas in some way that is not identical with the influence of antecedent material conditions.

I am speaking not only about the configuration of hopes and values that together make up each West Indian's unique life organization, but of ideologies: beliefs, doctrines, notions, that exercise influence on group behavior. The latter are weapons of offensive or defensive nature or of escape and carry a body of principles, losing their significance when taken out of context. They not only furnish the direction to a group but offer attraction, inspiration and hope, maintaining discipline as well as morale. Furthermore, they function best when they are sufficiently ambiguous to enlist widespread support, but have enough explicitness to attract attention and induce active identification. Thus ideologies help human beings to get their bearings and to sustain their capacity for collective action.[1] However, many West Indian editorial writers, like intellectuals in public service, love to refer to ideologies

---

[1] Louis Wirth, "Ideological Aspects of Social Disorganization", *American Sociological Review*, (August, 1940), p. 477.

as being *mere* ideologies—as if they were irrelevant epiphenomena having no substantial roots in, and relation to, the realities of existence. Alexis De Tocqueville wrote a century ago that "a society can exist only when a great number of men consider a great number of things in the same point of view; when they hold the same opinions upon many subjects, and when the same occurrences suggest the same thoughts and impressions to their minds."[2] If a society can be regarded as such only after people work out a set of common understandings, i.e., a set of reciprocally acknowledged claims and expectations expressed in action, the people of the West Indies are a society only in its early phase.

The data which support the generalizations found in this chapter are based upon (a) personal observations while living in the Islands—participating in the life of the people as they went about constructing new villages under my supervision, (b) published and unpublished cases, (c) the impressions of writers livings in the Islands, (d) the results of open-ended interviews.

In the West Indies, the social scientist will find sundry competing ideologies ranging between idealist and realist poles. However, these polar frameworks are the most worthy of attention because of the clarity with which they are spelled out, and because of their vital affect on population problems. The idealistic perspective is borne chiefly by the mixed-blood group, the more action centered portion of the population. It expresses disgust with the apathy, hopelessness and indifference which permeates the Islands, contending that the proponents of such a mental state can see only those elements in existence which support their negativistic point of view. They would contend that these economically downtrodden folk, together with colonial and propertied whites, are incapable of correctly diagnosing future possibilities. The latter group, called "realists" for lack of any better label, hold that the idealists are guided either by wishful thinking or a premeditated plan for the disguise of possible improvements—this for personal gain. The bulk of the Negroes, with apathy concerning the destiny of their country, have turned to the defense of life organizations which bear no regard to problems of the commonweal.

The individuals at the top of the political ladder, mixed-bloods such as Grantley Adams and Eric Williams, pose as constructive revolutionists, proclaiming how they would mold a productive social economy for the newly founded Negro nation. Intensely interest-bound to their new situation, they

---

[2] Alexis De Tocqueville, *Democracy in America* (Cambridge: Sever and Francis, 1863), p. 398.

would lock horns with the forces of inertia. Leader-nihilists—revolutionists without much revolutionary vision—ride on the coat-tails of Adams and Williams, and with their negativism attack all British and American aid programs, clergymen, the press, and all other political aspirants. Ruthlessness and cynicism are combined with a kind of innocence.[3]

Into this innocence one can read an absence of ideological conviction to the degree that hatred conveys pretense. With generally good training in elocution and debate, the leader-nihilists lack the most necessary and awesome of demogogic gifts: a belief in the sacredness of their mission. However, it is possible that this form of leadership can prove beneficient, by arousing other leaders toward the weaving of a fabric composed of free and positive institutions. In any event, this nihilism can serve in the development of a collective self-consciousness.

As institutions, communities, and life styles align themselves behind these ideological streams, issues of religion, morality, economics, and overpopulation are amenable to open discussion. When the social demographer explores these ideologies he finds himself in an advantageous predictive setting. That is, if he knows what a man believes in politics, in religion and economics, he is led to know a man's "rights" on work, play and reproduction.

In relatively simple and static societies, the problem of how to achieve consensus is not a serious one, since consensus rests upon tradition and authority, reinforced by sacred sanctions, and, if need be, by force. In the Islands, however, where mores are weak, consensus, and laws and ordinances are

---

[3] Trinidad Premier Eric Williams has been accused of leader-nihilism, as suggested by the following letter to the editor of the *Trinidad Guardian:*

Editor, "Trinidad Guardian"

As a member of the Police Force I observe that Dr. Williams is now called Premier and he and his Cabinet will have a ninth Ministry which is expected to control the Police.

The whole of Trinidad and Tobago should wear black on June 26 as they insist that Dr. Williams is only looking for power and more power for himself, and himself alone. He has shown himself very clearly to be a dictator.

What good, in the name of God and humanity can this power which he has created for himself do for the police and the poorer classes of people throughout Trinidad and Tobago? I say none whatsoever.

I regret very much that I ever voted for Eric Williams and his government as I can only see more and more taxes, rising cost of living, more unemployment, quarrels between Williams and the Americans over the Chaguramas issue, more stealing, killing, raping and larceny.

Are our people any better off than in the past? I say they are one million times worse. Dr. Eric Williams and his government in my opinion are, without knowing it, going to cause destruction to the people of Trinidad and Tobago. We are all chocking with taxes and more taxes.

I supported the PNM in the hope that the Police, and our people in general, would be benefited, but I have made the greatest mistake by putting power into the wrong man's hands. We the Police have to do what Eric Williams wants us to do, whether we like it or not. Some of us will have to shine his shoes and some will definitely have to be stooges.

May God send another leader to deliver us out of bondage. The PNM must go.

Sufferer,

San Fernando.

built upon conventions which, although occasionally disregarded, are generally respected even though their violation does not entail serious sanction. In short, to study the relationship of West Indian society to population, one can dig only as deep as the existing conventions, weak as they may be. The institutions of home, school and church are hardly institutions at all, i.e., the custodians of sacred sanctions, but the places where conventions are reiterated and a foundation for the achievement of a unity is fostered. They may be the spawning grounds for new beliefs and practices. The leaders of these institutions will, of course, insist that the norms they promulgate are intrinsically valid, while the "followers" are apt to keep their judgments in abeyance. Hence, the generalization: any West Indian who would *literally* follow the exhortations of the Christian religion as set forth in his denomination, for even as short a period as twenty four hours, would find himself in conflict with his fellows who ostensibly profess the same doctrines and creeds but interpret them less literally. The more precise the definition of values becomes, the more likely it is that fewer West Indians will share them. I say this because the rigidity of institutional definitions tends to reduce elasticity in the face of changing situations and multiple group values. Cynicism and skepticism are increasingly the expected reactions to those definitions of things and ideals as sponsored by "outside groups" such as white men or those who would exert influence from the top downward.

Summarizing, the difficulty in ferreting out the motivations of West Indians insofar as they involve human procreation is complicated by several tendencies.

1. They do not express their ends clearly; they are usually implicit or inferred in action. They rarely are explicitly stated.

2. They state their ends in general terms—they comprise a general plan and the investigator has to spell out the meaning. For example, West Indian Negroid women will often say that their goal is to "sit up like a lady." This requires considerable investigation to find out what "sitting up like a lady" involves in concrete action.

3. They confuse means and ends. And ends are always moving further and further away from the group. Actually means and ends are intelligible only when viewed in the light of one another.

4. The same values do not have the same attraction to all people. This makes prediction most difficult.

5. There are contradictions between the values themselves. For example, the mixed-bloods say they desire progress, i.e., they want to enjoy new technology and opportunity, but they also want order. While many people speak out for progress they also must be made to recognize that this calls for a

certain amount of disorder—a degree of maladjustment. Indeed, all West Indians like their freedom but the more of it they pursue, the more they sacrifice certain securities; one must be bargained off on the other.

FERTILITY AND RELIGIOUS VALUES

Perhaps borne of necessity, the Roman Catholic clergy is morally tolerant yet intellectually intolerant of "living in sin." And their followers know it. Officially, the Church assails consensual marriage, the production of children outside of wedlock, as well as the distribution of information on artificial contraceptives by either public health nurses or doctors.[4] But for the sake of holding their parishioners there is more barking than biting. Some observers have said that the power of the Catholic Church, as a pressure group opposed to artificial birth control, is greater on the political level in the Protestant islands than in those heavy in Catholic membership. This may be true in Methodist St. Vincent, but hardly the case in Anglican Barbados. In Jamaica, where the Roman Catholics do not number more than 10 per cent of the population, the government hesitates to carry out a program of birth control instruction because of Catholic pressure. The leading newspaper, *The Daily Gleaner*, has periodically challenged the Catholic attitude on birth control and has waged a campaign in favor of family limitation as the only means of national salvation.

But in Barbados, the Church of England, its activities and concepts, are closely tied to the colonial government thus enjoying the status and security of a government department. In its efforts to please the government, it has become so watered down as an institution that to many West Indians it has lost most of its spiritual meaning. Letters to the local newspapers by the clergy still oppose abortions and birth control "except in cases of dire medical necessity." But in everyday religious activities the clergymen, by their silence, tacitly approve of the moral standards as they now stand. "God will take care of us all" is the familiar pronouncement. A rather scathing denouncement of Anglican clergymen in Barbados was contained in an editorial of the *Barbados Advocate* on April 5, 1955; actually the editor was challenging only the formalism of the Church:

---

[4] Anglican officialdom appear more tolerant on birth control matters each passing year. In 1958, the Archbishop of Canterbury sponsored a committee of nineteen theologians and sociologists to study "The Family in Contemporary Society." The 220 page report recommended that the Church of England cease opposing birth control. "The more we understand of our procreative powers," it said, "the more responsible we are for the way in which we use them." If our conscience will not tolerate, when we know how to prevent it, a torrent of infant deaths, no more should we, with the knowledge we have, encourage an ungoverned spate of unwanted births."

ILLEGITIMACY

. . . The Churches of Barbados have for too long sought to regard illegitimacy as something for which they can blame the child. For example up to now the Anglican Church of this Island baptises illegitimate children on a different day from that on which legitimate children are baptised. The reason for this barbarous custom must be ascribed to a belief held by the Clergy that the illegitimate will somehow contaminate the legitimate. It would certainly be interesting to hear the reasons by which the Clergy would seek to justify this practice.

In Barbados too many Anglican Clergymen will not give Communion to divorced persons but we have not heard of their refusal to give communion to the mothers and fathers of illegitimate children. The disturbing feature of illegitimacy in Barbados is the attitude adopted by such organisations as the Churches which attach a greater stigma to the illegitimate child than to the couple who have produced the illegitimate child. . . .

People who try to improve the lot of the less fortunate members of the community must beware lest they apply rigid moral doctrines and standards to people who have been moulded by a system which they neither created nor sought. A more rewarding endeavor would be to protect the women and child who associate in, and is the product of, such "common law" marriages. . . .

In all attempts to solve the problems of illegitimacy the Churches of Barbados have an important part to play. Unfortunately, the Churches have adopted such attitudes in the past and still continue to take up such impossible positions that they seem incapable of the mental approach which the problem requires. . . .

Throughout the Islands are scattered a great number of evangelistic, revivalist churches and missions. These feverish groups are relatively ineffective as agencies of social control because the enthusiasm of their members quickly dissipates when the services conclude. Little more can be said of the Catholic and Anglican Churches as agencies for the promotion of grassroots sentiments for the control of common law marriage, concubinage, illegitimacy or infanticide.

If there is one tradition in the Islands, it is the belief that somehow a mother (or grandmother, as it often turns out) should support her own children. While church leaders preach father-responsibility and inveigh against sex relationship outside of marriage, they have accomplished little. The fundamental weakness of the churches as instruments of fertility control is pin-pointed in this failure. There is some evidence that congregations have deserted priests and preachers who have insisted upon the rigid observance of monogamous standards. As mentioned, the more visible disparity between preachments and practice as found in the Roman Catholic Church perhaps explains why priests hold their congregations.

108

The Dimension of Ideas, Beliefs and Incentives

Protestant versus Leisure-Ethics

The Protestant ethic, characterized by such concepts as "hard work," "competition," "force," "climb," and "survival of the fittest," runs counter to the leisure ethics. As discussed in Chapter IV, to the West Indian, life is first for leisure, interrupted occasionally with work so that leisure itself is possible. This hedonism countervails the development of a capitalism as we know it in more technologically advanced nations. Max Weber, in his *The Protestant Ethic and the Spirit of Capitalism*, insisted that the development of capitalism would not have been possible without the Protestant ethic. The Reformation apparently never invaded the West Indies. The Protestant ethic explains that the wealthy ("elect") have the forces of history on their side—that their wealth is a symbol of Godliness. The implication of this attitude is that the masses must also turn their thoughts to becoming economically successful. If the symbol of being God's elect is material, then more and more people in the West Indies would long ago have turned their efforts and aspirations toward acquiring these symbols.

The point is that any development of capitalism for West Indians must be geared to a change in attitude toward work. Work must be made acceptable as a necessary and desirable way to invest one's time. Reflecting on the traditional Christian attitude toward work, the reader will recall how the Lord drove Adam and Eve from the Garden of Eden because they had eaten fruit from the Tree of Knowledge of Good and Evil, commanding them to earn their bread by the sweat of their brows. Leisure, relaxation and play had been life symbols in Paradise. The Lord's command to work was a sentence to life-long punishment. Thus, as we search in the Judeo-Christian tradition prior to the Reformation, we find that leisure is a symbol of Godliness, while work is the burden and price which must be paid for sin. By this logic, West Indians are the closest to God.

Whereas the traditional notion of Paradise or Heaven was a place where life's punishing work was finished, where a man could rest and relax unto eternity, work on earth was made eventually into a virtue. Through the centuries, man's definition of his life situation changed. From the new ethic of Protestantism, grew the notion that work is a deed which contributes to the glory of God. But for the concept of the "calling," the changed attitude toward work and the redefining of usury, Max Weber tells us that the occidental world would never have had the essential ingredients for modern capitalism.

While life in the West Indies is not the exact opposite of life in Europe or the United States, one would be hard put to describe West Indian life styles in terms of the Protestant ethic. Indeed, a small portion of the population, namely the white and certain middle-class mulattoes, has shaped its norms and values after the tradition of occidental civilization, but the great mass of the Islands lives by life styles rooted to the leisure ethic. This majority is, generally speaking, colding indifferent as to how it obtains its material goods. Modern Epicureans, these West Indians live by the day; life is a series of detached acts in which a man calculates the sum of happiness or misery by different courses. Each act is not regarded as directly bearing upon the structure of society. There is no general awareness that relatively free sex relations, for example, have their impact upon the general welfare, that an illegitimate child involves a new burden upon the group. Group play is almost completely absent. Cooperation between geographic neighbors takes place hardly more than on those occasions where coffin-building and midwifery are the orders of the day. Otherwise a person is on his own to exploit or be exploited. The criterion of good and evil becomes one of sensation; feeling is the cannon by which a person judges all objects, including people.

Slavery, Work, and Sex Play. Inasmuch as most West Indians are Negro or mulatto with African heritage, we cannot hope to understand their hedonism without examining the impress of slavery. Since several good accounts of slavery conditions are available, there is no need to go into great detail. Sociologically speaking, what slavery did to the African culture was to strip it of all its formal aspects. Families were split up and the slaves were thrown into heterogeneous units. Attempts to carry on traditions and customs were nearly impossible because of the stern suppressing hand of the slave masters. In brief, the broader institutional structure, the principal mechanisms of control were smashed. The means whereby individuals and groups could achieve and maintain their pre-established composure were gone. The hardships of life imposed by the masters required that the slave devote most of his energy to maintaining his own existence. Except in those circumstances where the family unit or clan remained together, the slave soon adopted an attitude of "aloneness." He learned to live from day to day concerned about nothing but his own general welfare.

It was under such circumstances that a free attitude toward sex developed. The only time that the African slave could afford any pleasure was at night when the masters had retired. Sexual promiscuity was a means whereby the slave could experience a moment of pleasure as well as defy the authority and wishes of his master. Because men greatly outnumbered women there was no opportunity for them to pair off in a "natural" manner. Thus sex became a heightened form of recreation and play. M. G. Smith writes:

110

As a consequence of these various factors, mating of slaves was typically unstable. But their offspring were not regarded as either legitimate or illegitimate; the children of a slave woman were the lawful property of her owner, who could alienate them at will. The legitimacy-illegitimacy dichotomy only applied to persons born free and was never applied to slaves, as it was meaningless in that context. If, therefore, after Emancipation for various reasons the majority of slaves and their descendants continued to mate in unstable associations lacking legal recognition, the "illegitimate" status of the children had no significance among them.[5]

Although promiscuous sex play is not uncommon among Negroes in the Southern United States today, there has been a steady decline in such activity since the abolishment of slavery. The explanation of this is apparent. As the Negro has gradually been emancipated from his status of slave, he has taken on, to a greater extent, the values and mores of his former master. He "learned" that sexual promiscuity was "immoral." But with the abolishment of slavery in the West Indies, there was a rapid decline of European masters. Thus, for the West Indian Negro who had come to accept promiscuous sex activity as a game, there was no dominant culture to teach him that such a notion was "immoral." His attitude of promiscuity had become perfectly meaningful to him and there were no conflicting variables introduced into his life which would contradict his existing values. Of course, with the increasing over-crowding, there is the inconvenience which attends more babies. But in the light of immediate pleasure, West Indian males prefer to see only as far as the pleasures, ignoring the resulting discomforts to others.

The West Indian's attitude toward work is to a certain degree traceable to the tradition of slavery. He was forced to work long and hard and received only subsistence for his labor. It is quite logical that to the extent he resented this treatment he would develop an attitude of indifference toward work. Or let us look at his situation from another point of view. Minus the incentive of the Protestant ethic and the hope of material gain under capitalistic free enterprise, what reason was there for him to work? Three overwhelming conditions remain today that stand as barriers to these islanders changing their attitude toward the value of work. First, the great proportion of land as well as other economic resources remain in the hands of only a few. Second, the population density of the West Indies is so great that if all the economic opportunities available on the Islands were equally divided there would be so little for each person that there would be little incentive for work. This second assumption rests on a third: the West Indians might

---

[5] M. G. Smith, "Some Aspects of Social Structure in the British Caribbean about 1820," *Social and Economic Studies*, Vol. 1, No. 4, (August, 1953), pp. 71-72. Used by permission.

eventually adopt a philosophy of hard work, climbing and competing if they had the opportunity. However, this is only a possibility. Life for leisure has come to be as meaningful for them as work is for the bulk of Americans. They are indeed fascinated by the gadgets and luxuries of Western culture and would gladly accept them if they were gifts. But they are far from being obsessed with the desire to have them. They are not yet ready to give up a life style of leisure in order to obtain the gadgets and luxuries of the Western world.

Fertility and Kinship Values

Family and kin are important the world over, forming the foundation of social organization. Some kinship organizations, of course, are weaker than others.

The family in these British islands might be interpreted as highly sophisticated or "civilized" when viewed from the standpoint of an urban sociologist —a way of life marked by a high degree of individuation and responsibility geared to situations. Anthropologists have noted that family relations in primitive societies[6] can range from highly permissive and equalitarian to rigid authoritarian. Those primitive societies which are agrarian in character are often found to be marked by families with well defined rights and obligations plus a high respect for traditionally recognized roles and statuses. Rather than "from each according to his ability and to each according to his need" anthropologists find family life based upon the adage, "from each according to his status obligations in the social system, to each according to his rights in that system."

More often than not the father in the West Indian working class family is little more than a transient temporarily attached to the family. This has meant very high rates of nominal illegitimacy, up to 70 per cent in some islands. This loose family organization is based considerably upon the belief that marriage is pointless unless it can be celebrated with the proper amount of conspicuous consumption. This delays the marriage of a couple living together until middle age or later. And failure of mates to make good on their pre-marriage promises accounts for considerable unhappiness. Social intercourse between legal spouses is minimal. That is, the husbands and wives do not readily share their leisure time. Moreover, there seems to be

---

[6] Certainly it is impossible to characterize the organization of one institution or society as being more "primitive" than another. "Primitive," like the words "agrarian" and "industrial," often carries false implications—that one way of life is more sophisticated and, perhaps, more satisfying than the other. By the word "primitive" I simply mean a way of life marked by a noted absence of written records and mechanization.

112

slight emotional interdependence as a foundation for family integration. There are few terms or overt expressions of endearment between husband and wife or between fathers and children. As children leave the home to establish themselves independently, whatever unity was present in the family quickly dissipates. This tendency varys from group to group. In some areas, sons rarely, if ever, visit their parents after they have left home, although daughters will visit their mothers periodically. Brothers and sisters seldom visit with each other after they have established separate households.

In the Islands, one finds highly unorganized to organized neighborhoods, with corresponding degrees of family integration. But there is one constant: men enjoy greater latitude than women in exercising family responsibilities, the females, more usual than not, inherit the chores of child rearing through the abdication of the husband. Descent can be matrilineal or patrilineal. Patrilineal descent is preferred if the father recognizes his child, is willing to have the fact officially recorded, and renders financial support. When the father is unknown or somehow dishonored, the child will take the mother's name. Thus the family frequently takes on matrifocal and matrilineal characteristics outside of "mother-right." Mothers derive their rights and burdens quite reluctantly but philosophically. These maternal responsibilities may be circumvented through infanticide, abandonment, or leaving the child with the grandmother. Thus we are in the presence of a residual category of intermediate and complex kinship systems that deviates significantly from any of the theoretically simpler types described in anthropological literature.

Family and Fertility Incentives

Anthropological evidence tends to support the thesis that emphasis on continuing kinship groups provides powerful motivation for high fertility.[7] We are told how, in pre-technological societies, with emphasis upon unilineal descent and corporate kinship groups, children are valued as fortifying the continuing lineage. After all, individual security and prestige are enriched by projecting the family life into the future. But in the Islands, the thesis does not hold; the family characteristics described above are significantly absent although fertility remains on a very high plain.

High birth rates are less associated with island-wide social organization

---

[7] Bronislaw Malinowski, *The Sexual Life of Savages in Northwestern Melanesia*, (London: 1929); ———, *Argonauts of the Western Pacific*, (London: 1922); Sophia B. Aberle, "Frequency of Pregnancies and Birth Interval Among Pueblo Indians," *American Journal of Physical Anthropology*, (July-September, 1931); Meyer Fortes, "A Note on Fertility Among the Tallensi of the Gold Coast", *American Sociological Review*, (July-October, 1943); ———, "Kinship and Marriage Among the Ashanti," in Radcliffe-Brown and Forde, *African Systems of Kinship and Marriage*, (London: 1950).

and tradition than they are with community value systems. In many instances (particularly with respect to the hedonistic life style) motivation for fertility is aimed at live births and not toward children particularly. That is, a baby lying neglected on the ground can give as much legitimation to a mother as a baby at the breast. Accordingly, in facing up to the task of reducing a population's size, the first step is that of recognizing that fertility is brewed in the pot of self-interest. A unilineal system of descent, for instance, is not necessarily appropriate to the individual's needs. The separate individual hardly has a definite place in the larger community and his place in a neighborhood is often not enduring. Furthermore, men generally do not want children for the sake of parenthood (middle class Negroes somewhat excepted). They crave for evidence of virility. Children restrict a man's radius of motion, economically, spatially and sexually. When a girl tells her boy friend or husband that she is pregnant, he is pleased in learning of his virility, but hardly happy that he is about to take on an economic burden. Responsible fatherhood makes him a marked man.

Bear in mind that the social disorganization following the abolition of slavery resulted in social psychological disturbances. But the *laissez-faire* attitude which accompanied the release persists today. *Laissez-faire* is one of the few common denominators of West Indian "structure." Sex ethics are strongly geared to individuation. While there is a varying degree of emphasis upon small community affiliation, the organization of activities and interests is very different from that in a clan-structured society. In many districts, boys and girls are taught by the time they are twelve to seek intimate relations with their counterparts. I recall my Negro cook telling me that she hoped her daughter (illegitimate) would have "experience" before she married. Furthermore, she hoped that the husband would have had experience. In the relationships between young males and females (the word "courtship" is not appropriate) there are not only few words, songs, and promises of long-lasting endearments, but in actual practice there is little fidelity. Marriage, itself, like the precursive consensual unions, is essentially one of convenience for the male; suitability and expediency are the deciding factors. For the female, marriage is a more consecrated idea.

These islanders then, are "permissive" to fertility. The slavery and plantation organizations which founded the initial structure of the Negro world having undergone "cultural shock." The disintegration of slavery and encouragement of individual farms have led to fertility based upon a philosophy of individuation and hedonism. Thus an objective demographer can see nothing but dangers ahead in an indefinite continuation of the present high level of fertility accompanied as it is with a declining mortality rate.

The gradual breakup of traditional plantation organizations, in the absence of fresh forces making for the emergence of new positive social goals, has led to persistent population increase.

What urbanization has done to the American agrarian family is what slavery, and subsequent emancipation, has done to the West Indian family. Slavery was a heavy instrument for *Kulturfall*, to use an anthropological term. It succeeded in stripping the Negro of his kinsmen, Gods, language, and ideals, subjecting him to economic production and sexual satisfactions as called for by his master. With the disappearance of slavery, the routines of life that had emerged out of the period were thrown into confusion, promoting even greater personal and inter-racial disturbances. It meant the release of a relatively undisciplined individualism. Accordingly, there may be found communities and nuclear families marked by low levels of fertility as well as those with high fertility. There is a noticeable resignation toward social and economic circumstances—an inevitable component of social disorganization. This attitude is served by a history of colonial discipline from the top-down rather than dedication to grassroots self-help. Indifference toward public problems is partly explained by inexperience in arousing collective action.

The Institution of the Keepers

Because of the cultural diversity and the emphasis on individuation, it is difficult to give a simple pattern of consensual unions or "keepership"[8] so vital in the demography of the Islands. The following description is, therefore, an admittedly forced one, serving only to give the reader a general conception of the relationship of the sexes and the predicaments of their by-products—children. Realizing that I cannot portray the individual variations or even the "average cases," I rely on the well-known "pure-type" conceptualization— a deliberate exaggeration of keepership. By employing this procedure, I am *creating* a complex referent in West Indian society, profferring thereby a useful hypothesis for future empirical analysis. That is, my construct, verifiable under *certain conditions*, serves as a tool for use in further research and hypothesizing in this very complex area of investigation (Chapter VII is an illustration of generalizing from the relation of analytic empirical variables).

---

[8] This form of marriage, writes Melville J. Herskovitz and Frances S. Herskovitz, resembles extra-legal matings in most of the new world, marking a reconciliation of European monogamic institutions and African relationship groupings based on broader definitions of kinship and plural marriage. *Trinidad Village* (New York: Alfred A. Knopf, 1947), p. vi.

Sexual experimentation, or promiscuity, begins between boys and girls before puberty; the majority of girls become pregnant at an early age, many with their first boy-friends. The first pregnancy is resented by the mother of the girl. In most cases the girl is not rejected by her household but is impressed with the necessity of trying to find "someone to be responsible for her." Then follows a period of experimentation with trial and error unions, at shorter or longer intervals, which last from a few months to many years and that are accompanied by a number of pregnancies. As faithful concubinage, these unions frequently eventuate in marriage. When they do not, they may endure until death severs the union. Sexual promiscuity is considered right and natural for everyone, particularly the male, but this does not, however, preclude the expectancy of faithfulness in concubinage and marriage. In areas where unemployment and underemployment are high, as in sugar districts which provide employment for only six months in a year, the transient workers who invade the areas at crop time take a "housekeeper," with usually no intent that the arrangement, though satisfactory, shall be permanent.

Faithful concubinage is a near necessity for many girls with their first babies. The possibility of women cultivating a garden is uncommon because of the nature of land tenure, the nature of land-use and sheer ignorance. These girls, therefore, have to buy their food. Since opportunities for employment are limited, and the conditions for female labor poor, the pregnant girl is very likely to turn to a keeper relationship. Failing a man, the mother and grandmother usually support the home as best they can.

By reason of apparent conflict between official law and the Negro's unwritten constitution, the terms "illegitimate child" and "illegal marriage" are fuzzy by definition. The bastardy cases in the law courts are amusing and bear out this moral and legal confusion. The majority of such cases are brought by women who have been deserted by their menfolk soon after the birth of the child. Some, however, are concubines of some years standing. In such cases a woman may have been only temporarily deserted. But the fact that she does not allow the customary interval to elapse, as happens with married couples, and appeals for a maintenance order is sufficient. The courts will give legal recognition of concubinage as common law marriage by decreeing that the father pay for the child's support. On many islands such as Dominica, the mere declaration of the mother than a certain man is the father, is adequate "evidence" of paternity.

If an unwed girl can somehow compel a man to contribute to the support of her child, she gains some recognition in the eyes of her peers—although this motive does not discount the economic incentive. For if a girl is not employed, she will bring about the necessary pressures more quickly. In general, money and prestige operate together.

West Indians do not enter into marriage for companionship. After all, every male has his "best friend" (male), and the same goes for the female. Marriage is a status-giving agency, particularly for women. Witness the constant reference in the literature to the claim that a "wedding is not a cheap affair for the average couple." And food and drink cost a great deal. Automobiles must be provided to convey the chief guests from the house to the church, and so on. Musicians must be paid, bridal gowns purchased. In the eyes of a black man or woman, to be married without this paraphernalia would be no marriage at all. Most neighborhoods and communities prefer it this way, as a mark of ultimate status achievement for aspiring youth, and as a means for a good time by all.

Upon marriage, the bride's expectations change. She wants a house, one or more servants, expects to handle money and to "sit up like a lady." Some communities do make exceptions to this pattern, with a heavier emphasis upon religious belief, particularly in those areas where church leadership is strong and where the population is more stable and able to maintain itself without the members moving constantly to find employment.

Faithful Concubinage and Illegitimacy. Possibly one-half of the technically illegitimate children in the Islands are born into enduring consensual marriage sanctified without benefit of clergy. Unfortunately, it is the children of the more promiscuous and financially irresponsible unions that crowd the urban slums and detention houses. They are the youthful offenders who steal vegetables and fruit, who live without support except by their own wits. They generally refuse to attend school regularly and often end their careers in the venereal disease clinics, poor houses and prisons. They are without homes, education or employment, and constitute a great threat to the future of West Indian society.

The weak bond found in promiscuous unions is well illustrated in the following interview with a Dominica taxi driver:

Q. You say that you are unmarried but have a nine month baby daughter living in Barbados with its mother. Would you tell me the story about your acquaintance with the mother?

A. Well, sir, I live with my father here in Roseau. And when Margie was 13 (and I being 15) we started playing together. She was a virgin and after about three months we had our first sport. But she miscarried the baby about three months later. Then she got very fat. Oh, we prefer slim girls but her getting fat didn't bother me.

Q. Where would you go for this "sport?"

117

A. I would call on her at her house. And if I wanted it, as soon as her mother left the house for, say, an hour, well we did it. If we didn't do it in her house we would go, like most other young folk, up along the rivers. You see, the best bathing in Dominica is in the rivers. We would go swimming together and then have it afterwards.

Q. What do your friends think about your having a child but not being married?

A. Oh, they all think it is fine. Nobody thinks I have done anything bad. You see, that is the way most people have their children. They don't have enough money to marry. Margie never asked me to sport but never turned me down. We would do it about three or four times a week ever since I knew her. Yes, sir, I had other girl friends, but Margie was my special. No I wouldn't tell the other girls about the women I knew—they get pretty jealous. But all the girls knew I was the father of the little girl—but it didn't matter any.

Q. Weren't you afraid the other girls would have babies too?

A. Yes, it worried me some. But some girls are pretty smart. They know how to stop it if they want to. Boys who can afford it buy rubbers; they cost about 2/5 but most buy the pills for the girls to put in themselves. But I want you to know that Margie and I liked each other very much. She writes me very often from Barbados. But I couldn't go to Barbados because I would only have to loaf around. At least here I can drive a taxi once in a while. But I wanta go to Canada.

Q. Was Margie's mother angry when she found out what you two had done?

A. She made a little scene but got over it in a hurry when she found that Margie was making a baby. You see, Margie was her only child. She was very happy about the baby because she could help bring it up. She took Margie and the baby to Barbados where the old house is.

Q. How did your father feel?

A. He felt the same way. I gave Margie a little money when I started to work. I still send her money.

Q. Do most young couples live with the girl's mother when they marry or decide to live together?

A. Yes, sir.

Q. Do most boys have "special" girls like your Margie?

A. Yes they do. Many of them have enough money to marry but they want their liberty. But the girls want to marry though. When a boy doesn't run around with girls then his friends call him "cheap"—he doesn't want to spend any money. They will call him an "anti-man" [homosexual] even tho' they know he isn't. Men and women in the West Indies are very jealous of who they run around with. If you want to make a man very angry then you say to him in front of a group that you have been "draggin his girl" around—the boy will be very angry, even if he knows it isn't true—might even kill the man for sayin it. Girls carry-on the same way.

Q. Well, I suppose there wouldn't be any prostitutes in Dominica.

A. Oh there are prostitutes—but no going price—from 2 shillings to 2 or 3

118

dollars. But most boys have special women, giving them five or ten dollars once in a while when the girls want a dress or something. In fact, I now have another special girl who lives alone in town. I just call on her when I want to. I give her money at different times. I like her company for the cinemas, dances and parties.

RATIOS OF ILLEGITIMATE TO LEGITIMATE BIRTHS BY PARISH, GRENADA, 1949-1953

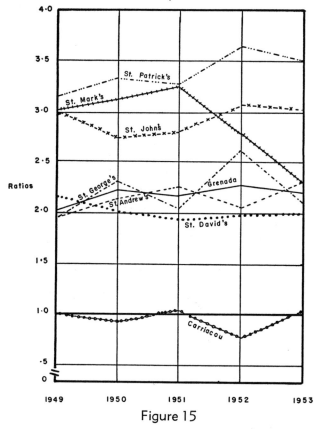

Figure 15

Figure 15 suggests that there is more illegitimacy in rural areas (Carriacou excepted) than in the urban parish (county) of St. George's, Grenada. Only in 1952 did the latter parish approach the high illegitimacy rates of the rural parishes of St. Patrick's, St. Mark's and St. John's.

By reason of the sketchiness of data, one cannot claim a striking contrast between rural and urban illegitimacy rates. Considerable capriciousness is evident.

119

Plotted in Figure 16 are legitimate to illegitimate ratios, using 1949 as the base year. Observe the great oscillation of illegitimate rates over the period 1949-53, around the somewhat stable trend line for Grenada as a whole. The parishes of St. Andrew's and St. Patrick's reveal the highest ratios, with the tiny island parish of Carriacou under strict Catholic control, enjoying the lowest ratios. Here is added evidence of cultural pluralism.

ILLEGITIMATE TO LEGITIMATE RATIOS
(1949 AS BASE YEAR), 1949-1953

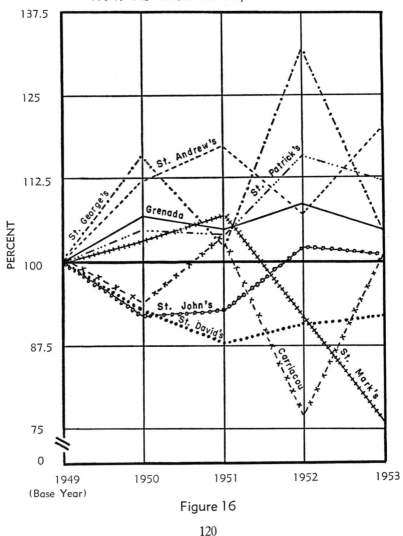

Figure 16

Infanticide as "Birth Control." The pre-meditated destruction of infants through neglect and starvation is one West Indian method of controlling the size of the family, thus it may be interpreted as postnatal "birth control." Infanticide not only plays a vital part in infant mortality rates, but the practice is as variable as meanings incorporated into the child-object by the mothers. This assertion parries the position of neo-classical demographers that changes in fertility and mortality are simply functions of changes in demand for labor; that this demand governs the supply of human beings.[9] Labor incentive is not the all determining causative force in determining family size in the West Indies.

Relying on Jamaica infant mortality figures, the first observation is that illegitimate infants tend to suffer a higher death rate than legitimate babies, exposed as they are, to greater survival hazards during the first few months of life (Table 8).

TABLE 8

Ratio of Illegitimate to Legitimate Infant Deaths, Jamaica, 1951

	Males			Females		
	per 1000[a] Death-rates		Ratio of Illegitimate to Legitimate death rates	Death-rates per 1000[a]		Ratio of Illegitimate to Legitimate death rates
Months Ages in	Legitimate	Illegitimate		Legitimate	Illegitimate	
0	25.25	37.80	1.4970	22.06	30.47	1.3812
1-2	7.18	14.29	1.9902	6.42	12.51	1.9485
3-5	10.64	17.52	1.6466	7.47	15.08	2.0187
6-8	9.89	16.64	1.6825	7.96	15.37	1.9309
9-11	9.56	14.88	1.5564	7.44	14.85	1.9959

[a] G. W. Roberts, *Population of Jamaica* (London: Cambridge Univ. Press, 1957), p. 190.

The second observation is that illegitimate males experience the highest infant mortality rates but when the ratio of illegitimate to legitimate males is placed alongside the female ratios, the latter assumes a higher plateau commencing after the first month. The male ratio, after an initial sharp rise, undergoes an irregular decline. Unfortunately, data are unavailable for carrying these ratios into the second year of life. I can only postulate that we have here important clues to the presence of "unnatural" environmental forces working to the detriment of female infants, "unnatural," that is, when compared with infant mortality experience, by sex, for technologically ad-

---

[9] Sydney H. Coontz, *Population Theories and the Economic Interpretation* (London: Rutledge and K. Paul, 1957), p. 97.

vanced countries. Stated in another way, male babies, by conjugal status of the mothers, do indeed die in greater proportion to their counterparts (Figure 17). I suggest that most of these deaths are from "natural" causes derived from weaker physiques. But from the last column in Table 8, the female babies, with their superior constitutions, fail in Jamaica to maintain their superior survival pattern.

NUMBER OF CUMULATIVE LEGITIMATE AND ILLEGITIMATE INFANT DEATHS, JAMAICA, 1951, BY SEX

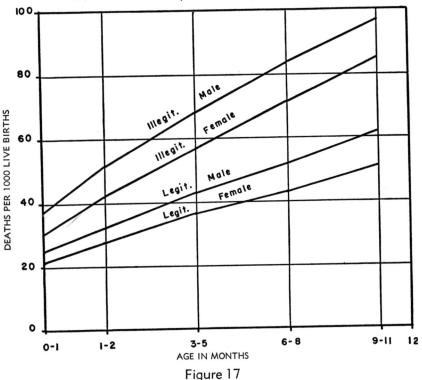

Figure 17

Third, the reluctance of Caribbean demographers to acknowledge that economic and physiological causes of infant deaths are either false-starts, at best, or partial approaches, when viewed in the light of female life style systems, signifies faulty analysis. When the play of social interaction, with its meanings and expectations, is given attention by these investigators, it is usually incidental, detached and secondary. That economic, physiological and ideological variables, among others, interlock and countervail, seem not to impress these demographers, particularly if they are oriented to vital statistics. G. W. Roberts,[10] for example, explains infant death rates in Jamaica as follows: the incidence declined as economic rent increased (correlation coefficient of –0.63; t of 2.79). He found also a correlation coefficient of –0.18 between rent and legitimate deaths; –0.36 for rent and illegitimate deaths. Then from these calculations he gives the impression that the difference in infant mortality rates of these legitimate and illegitimate cohorts is the result of economic conditions of existence. His correlations do not support his interpretation. What he did uncover was that (a) illegitimate infant mortality in high rent areas was likely to be the same as the illegitimate infant mortality for the low rent areas, and (b) that in high rent areas the legitimate infant mortality rate was apt to be lower than the illegitimate infant mortality for the same area: but that this is also true in low rent areas. Stated in another way:

> If A=Illegitimate infant mortality rate
> B=Legitimate infant mortality rate
> C=Rental value
> D=Rate of illegitimate births
> Then rCD was found statistically significant (–0.63)
> But rCA was found non-significant (–0.36)
> Also rCB was found non-significant (–0.18)

Economic rent is not a variable that throws causal light on the differential rates. The real operating elements were glossed over. Some "unnatural" force (at least to orthodox demographers) is at work—some force of a social nature that is not readily amenable to quantitative measurement. The range of income between groups and individuals among the Negro population is not sufficiently great to account for the great disparity between legitimate and illegitimate infant death rates. When the plurality of unmarried mothers with their smaller families give birth to 70 per cent of all infants, yet yield a 97 per 1,000 infant mortality rate (this in contrast with a death rate of 59.2 for legitimate infants), to attribute the difference to economic conditions is too strict, and is an oversimplification in the light of recognizable subjective forces.

Feeling that they have emancipated themselves in good measure from the exigencies arising from economic scarcity, many islanders have built life styles upon philosophic hedonism. Rational or not, these people believe their interpretations of life and order their goals accordingly.

Women will defend their concubinage life style as moral and distinguish

---

[10] G. W. Roberts, "A Note on Mortality in Jamaica", *Population Studies*, (June, 1950), pp. 64-85.

it from promiscuity with a remark such as: "I don't live like no animal. I have my six children from John—they're all from him one." To be sure they would like to avoid the economic responsibility of large families. And some accomplish it through child abandonment and infanticide. The following case of infanticide copied from an annual report of the Barbados Social Welfare Department portrays the life style of a promiscuite:

CASE #1
Barbados
Boy, Mickey died January 1, aged 18 months

Mother's Family History—Margaret aged 19 is Mickey's mother and the third of twelve children, three are illegitimate and children of different fathers. Eleven people in this family live in a house measuring 20' x 9', partitioned into two bedrooms and a shed roof for kitchen.

Margaret herself, illegitimate, shared this accomodation with her mother (49); her mother's husband (51); three girls aged 16, 7 and 6 and five boys aged 10, 8, 7, 5 and ten months (this baby the illegitimate child of the sixteen year old girl.)

The adult man and woman and the two girls, including Margaret, worked as agricultural labourers and supported the household when employed. Margaret illiterate but not subnormal in intelligence. Flippant in character and showily dressed (e.g., wearing earrings in canefield while heading out canes).

Family income and expenditures.—Not ascertainable and doubtful if they knew. No pooling of wages by the workers. The man drinks heavily and gives the woman very grudgingly from time to time as he says he objects to supporting other people's children.

There is a small plot of land and chickens are kept but the eggs are sold to buy rice which will "share better" and make the children feel more satisfied.

Margaret and the sixteen year old girl traveled frequently to Bridgetown. During Margaret's pregnancy she spent much time away from home looking for work as the expected child's father, known as "Gay Boy," would not give her any support and her foster father would not have her at home.

After Mickey's birth his grandmother took him from time to time into the home but the boy was always sickly and Margaret took him to the General Hospital.

Hospitalization.—June 30 to July 6   Diagnosis: Bronchial pneumonia and Bronchitis

July 13 to Feb. 2   Diagnosis: Bronchial pneumonia and Bronchitis

Sept. 10 to Sept. 11   Diagnosis: Malnutrition
Oct. 6 to Oct. 10   Diagnosis: Malnutrition
Nov. 30 to Dec. 12   Diagnosis: Malnutrition

The Doctor in charge of the case reported—

"In each case the basic underlying condition was malnutrition, the pneumonia and bronchitis being merely due to lowered resistance infection."

The Hospital staff was not impressed by Margaret's attitude towards the child; her impatience and annoyance when sent for (on one occasion the Police had to be called in to find her) and her remark when told on the last occasion she should give the child cod liver oil and milk, "What you worrying me for? I have to work and have no time with him and he is too much trouble to me."

Mickey died the following January some three weeks after leaving hospital. "Gay Boy"—the father, who had contributed nothing to his support, arranged a good "Turn-out" and paid all funeral expenses.

Margaret now states she has no further use for "Gay Boy" as she is now in love with another man.

Recognizing that poverty was involved in this case of child neglect, it was a proximate cause, rooted in turn to the quest for irresponsible pleasure.

In case #2, below, an infant death from "Marasmus" is described. This "disease," of "Voodoo" origin, purports to mysteriously "dry up" babies and kill them.

CASE #2

Boy Born 1st November, 195.., Died 5th July, 195..

November 1st 195.. Male child delivered in country Almshouse. Weight at Birth: 7 lbs. 3 ozs. Healthy.

Mother. Aged 18 at time of the death; unmarried. One of 4 children. Never knew her parents; brought up by a grandmother now dead.

First child born in same Almshouse prematurely when mother was 14. Died at birth.

During pregnancy of second child mother lived for a time with putative father of expected child. He however doubted his paternity and expectant mother went to live with a sister. Subsequently the sisters quarrelled and she left to live in a rented house furnished with a bench, two stuffed bags for mattresses and a few pots.

Income and Expenditure

$3 to $4 weekly (hard times); $5 (crop)

Rent $1.00 per week
Woman who looked after child while mother worked $1.00 per week

Early February 195.. Child taken to a private doctor because lumps appeared in its side. Child given two injections and sent to Hospital to have an abscess cut. Doctor's fee: $3.00

February 26th—Child admitted to Hospital—diagnosis: Marasmus.

March 20th—Child discharged from Hospital—"Condition relieved."

Early May—Child developed carbuncles in its back and head.

Middle May—Child again seen by private doctor. Diagnosis: Marasmus. Hospitalization recommended. Doctor's fee: $1.00 Child taken to Out Patient's Department; given injections and medicine.

July 5th—Boy died during night.

July 6th—Body taken to Mortuary at Police station and post mortem held. Cause of death on certificate: "Starvation."

Other relevant information taken from report of Officer who visited. Mother seems below average intelligence. She stated child was always thin and sickly and very difficult to feed. (Half pint sheep's milk was delivered daily but it would not take it. Occasionally the diet was supplemented by cereals and eggs.) After the death of the child a tin of proprietary milk food and another of Glucose was found in the house. Some of the contents had been used but it could not be established that the baby had taken any.

At time of visit in July after the baby's death it was evident the mother was pregnant again. Mother advised to have blood test.

September—Mother visited again. She had not been for the test. Was then awaiting the birth of third child. Earnings diminished further by "hard times" and pregnancy.

In these Islands, where competition for economic gain explains, indeed, some of the infanticide, the grim economic facts of life are frequently supervened by life styles that can provide a minimal degree of satisfactions. These life styles embrace definitions of economic gain, ambition and success, of marriage, infants, as well as the accessibility of males to females. Thus the weight of economic poverty is made to diminish or accelerate under the weight of social assessments. Here, economic and non-economic things and ideals can, if need be, mutually "cause" each other. Like the snake biting its tail, the internal system of a person's life style involves components, each of which nourishes or starves the other. The apparent cause produces an effect, but the effect reacts upon the cause, the very first cause serving as a crude catalyst when we assess the final event. A newborn infant, doomed to destruction, is frequently the byproduct of the gnarled causal chain.

Figure 18, below, is a pure-type conceptualization of female life styles. From this sketch, a legitimate child is usually born into a family where the mother has selected the life style of familism as her social choice, thus the infant is expected to survive. A mother's choice of hedonistic consumption signals probable infanticide, assuming the mother is not basically marriage-prone, i.e., where the initial social choice is temporary. A choice of vertical mobility makes infanticide probable, with the same qualification. When a woman changes her life expectations, children are frequently abandoned, having survived past that age at which infanticide is deemed permissible.

This crude portrayal of female life styles permits one generalization: the high infant mortality rate in the West Indies, augmented by infanticide, in-

126

THE PLACE OF INFANTICIDE IN WEST INDIAN FEMALE LIFE STYLES:
A PURE-TYPE CONCEPTUALIZATION

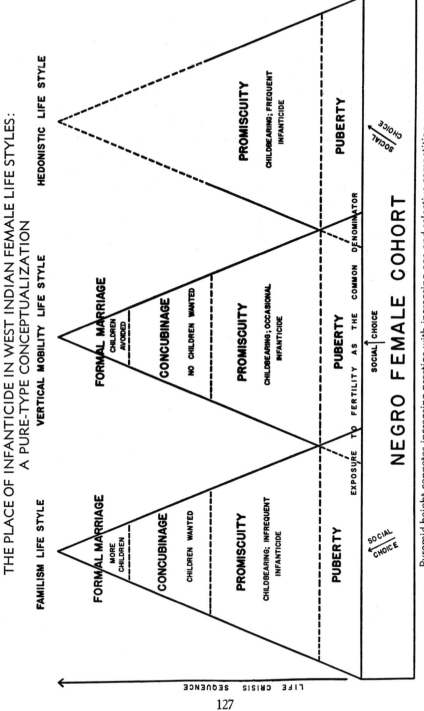

Pyramid height connotes increasing prestige with increasing age and selective competition.

Figure 18

volves a portion of infants never ordained for membership in the social arena in which their parents circulate.

The public health centers, the baby clinics, are the battlegrounds between the European official morality and the social moralities of native communities. As prenatal and post-natal clinics, supervised by white personnel (including lay women who serve as nurses aids or sponsors with "pet charity" attitudes), the contrasts in infant-definition are brought into sharp focus. The visiting promiscuites and faithful concubines, leaning toward hedonistic consumption or vertical mobility, with babes in arms, philosophically slough off the inevitable "tongue lashings" of the staff with visible apathy. They would hope that the greater community might keep their babies thus saving them from death through planned starvation or exposure. This is but another version of the ancient European practice of leaving unwanted children before the doors of the city council houses.[11]

---

[11] See Karl Winshold, *Deutsche Frauen in Mittelalter*, Wien, 1882.

Chapter VII

Fertility Expectations: St. Lucia and Grenada

The West Indies are inherently self-destructive in the sense that they do not provide, by most standards, demographic conditions and life styles that are appropriate for improved levels of living. This is clearly the case among the broad lower classes in both rural and urban areas. With a gross reproduction rate close to two,[1] more deprivation is ahead. The provision of favorable opportunities for children in this and the next generation will be doubly difficult.

Whereas involuntary causes affecting the birth rate (sterility, stillbirths, spontaneous abortions) are of importance in their total effect, such factors are relatively unimportant in explaining intergroup variations in reproduction. Such voluntary causes as infanticide, the adoption of contraceptives and continence, are only the mechanics or means of bringing about family limitation; in back of these controls are the intricate incentive factors which lead some communities more than others, to encourage such means. Hence, this chapter is concerned with the motivations of females, the pin-pointing of those areas of the population where vigorous programs for family planning might conceivably bring quick results. Obviously, drawing firm conclusions from a sample of verbal utterances is risky business, because people do not always transfer their expectations into action. But because there exists some relationship between what people say and what they do, this chapter seeks answers to the following question: who are the young women most likely to be receptive to family planning programs? To answer this question, pertinent fertility conditions of today must be summarized followed by an analysis of sex practices and fertility expectations of adolescent girls—the mothers of tomorrow.

The Mothers and the Mores

If there is any all-pervading cultural value in this pluralistic society, it is the belief that the human male is vastly superior to the female. Verging on near idolatry, young women, particularly of lower strata, are prone to accept the sexual advances of young men as being in the very nature of things; a male following is the prerequisite for respectability.[2] While the first child

---

[1] 1945-47. The rate is based on the number of female births to women aged 15-44.

[2] The women of Carriacou would seem to be one among other exceptions. See M. G. Smith, "Kinship and Household in Carriacou", *Social and Economic Studies*, (December, 1961), pp 455-477.

resulting from consensual unions legitimizes the mother among her peers, it is not likely to be held as dear as subsequent children born of wedlock. The actual amount of stigma suffered by the illegitimate child is not great, however.[3] Subsequent entry into a marriage-based family can mar the child's status on the occasion of later legitimate births. Nonetheless, he is protected by the plurality of his kind within the community.

While a young woman will admit preferences as to sire, often she exercises little selection, recognizing the slim chance of being married at all unless she is willing to expose herself to fertility. Thus she enters the consensual union without public pronouncement or prior ritual.[4] In most communities there is some importance attached to gaining sex experience. And the high proportion of females to males (Appendix table A2) must assuredly add to the incentive. The lower survival chances of male infants, coupled with the migratory inclinations of young men as they enter the labor pool, intensifies the game of sex, sabotaging family stability. A girl might enter and re-enter several conjugal-type families in a life-time, the parties to these unions bargaining off their attributes (wealth, beauty, power, prestige, color) as in the marketplace. Professor T. S. Simey[5] offers four broad types of domestic groups in Jamaica:

(a) *The Christian Family* based on marriage and a patriarchal order approximating that of Christian families in other parts of the world;
(b) *Faithful Concubinage,* based on a patriarchal order, possessing no legal status, but well established and enduring for at least three years;
(c) *The Companionate Family,* in which the members live together for pleasure and convenience, and for less than three years; and
(d) *The Disintegrate Family,* consisting of women and children only, in which men merely visit the women from time to time, no pattern of conduct being established.

This classification is not rigid, since over the years a person can experience all these forms, and there will certainly be groups which exhibit the characteristics of more than one type.[6]

Marriage, to the West Indian girl, is something to be hoped for. While the decision to marry is the boy's, the girl gains most from the legal union. Meanwhile, a woman may have children by several men. This is her "right."

---

[3] William J. Goode, "Illegitimacy in the Caribbean Social Structure", *American Sociological Review*, (February, 1960), p. 27.

[4] *Ibid.*, p. 29.

[5] T. S. Simey, *Welfare and Planning in the West Indies* (Oxford: Oxford University Press, 1946), pp. 82-83.

[6] William J. Goode seems to place all conjugal groups under the "matrifocal" type, i.e., an unstable family pattern in which the mother or grandmother is often in power because no father is there. *Op. cit.*, p. 30.

Of the 48,700 mothers reported in the Barbados Census of 1946, 42 per cent were married, 34 per cent were single, 13 per cent widowed or divorced and 11 per cent were classified as "common-law." The majority of mothers eventually marry.

But the marriage institution is not well entrenched in the West Indies because so many men avoid it. The ages at marriage, according to census figures, are among the highest in the world (for Jamaican males, 34.1; Barbadians, 31.7; Grenadians, 33.0). Figures 19, 20 and 21 represent comparisons of conjugal status of Americans (USA) and West Indians of Barbados and Trinidad.

From the above observations, the reader should sense a hard core of individualism residing at the center of the West Indian ethos, the value that each individual must act in accordance with what he conceives to be to his own self-interest. It is a condition of opportunism converted into a principle of action. Some individuals build their life organizations upon the principle of hard work and "Christian ideals," while others carve out self-images geared to living-for-the-day. For the most part, fertility practices are rooted

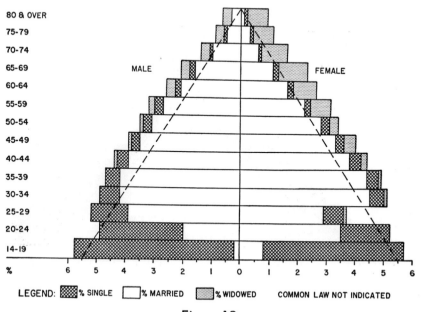

CONJUGAL STATUS, UNITED STATES, 1950
Based on 3 1/3% sample. Under 0.1% not shown. Source: U.S. Census.

LEGEND: % SINGLE   % MARRIED   % WIDOWED   COMMON LAW NOT INDICATED

Figure 19

131

CONJUGAL STATUS, BARBADOS, 1946

Under 0.1% not shown. Source: Census of West Indies.

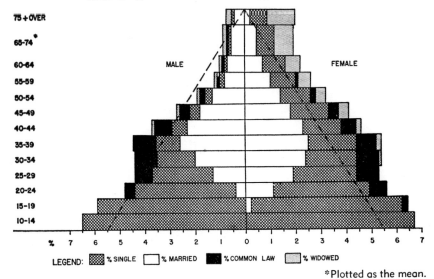

LEGEND: ▨ % SINGLE   ☐ % MARRIED   ■ % COMMON LAW   ▨ % WIDOWED

*Plotted as the mean.

Figure 20

CONJUGAL STATUS, TRINIDAD-TOBAGO, 1946

Under 0.1% not shown. Source: Census of West Indies.

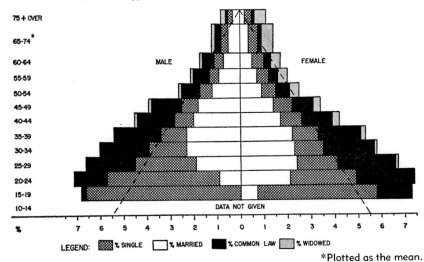

LEGEND: ▨ % SINGLE   ☐ % MARRIED   ■ % COMMON LAW   ▨ % WIDOWED

*Plotted as the mean.

Figure 21

132

to self-interest, the public interest given little license to intercede. With the crude birth rates high and the death rate low, this means an annual increment near three per cent. Judging by past experience for other high growth potential nations, and abstracting from the possibility that a cheap contraceptive could be widely diffused, the population of the Islands may increase by 100 or more per cent before it acquires (if ever) a 1940-50 Western age-structure. The task is to find those human groupings wherein fertility control procedures could be taught, then disseminated to others by the cooperating agents.

Tomorrow's Mothers

In the summer of 1959, I returned to the Islands to conduct a field survey of fertility expectations among adolescent girls in St. Lucia and Grenada. Several difficulties attended this inquiry, the first being the limited time and resources, and the second, stemming from the first: too small a field staff to "storm" the islands during the period at my disposal. Third, I knew from earlier experience that it would be impossible to go personally into the field and administer a schedule of this kind because young women are easily disturbed when encountering a white man armed with intimate questions, often suspecting that he is a government official bent on ferreting out information to be used against them. They would be overly cautious to the point of falsifying their answers. Thus if I were to obtain honest responses from these young women, I knew that I must secure the help of acceptable West Indians. This was not an easy task.

But mature social workers and "community organizers" connected with my earlier work under the International Cooperation Administration helped in building a small staff. Upon seeing the questions, two St. Lucians refused to cooperate at the last moment on the grounds that the island Administrator would disapprove of their conduct. A letter of authorization from the Administrator was to no avail. Fear of punishing sanctions from friends and superiors was apparently too great.

There was at the onset a question as to whether it would be possible to draw a random sample that would allow me to make an inductive statement about the universe. To do so would require that I draw a sample in a manner which would give every respondent an equal chance of being selected. This was impossible because the size of the universe was unknown.

The purpose of taking a random sample is to assure oneself that the respondents within certain probabilistic limits resemble the population. Several techniques have been developed to facilitate this. For example, where population directories are available, one can quickly select all the population which meets the necessary criteria for a sample and then by use of a random technique select the desired population for sampling. However, no directory exists in Grenada or St. Lucia which could be depended upon for my purpose. Another possible method of sampling was to interview by fixed position, a procedure used by census enumerators. That is, every nth house or area would be selected for the sample. This procedure also had certain limitations for my ends. First of all, the houses in the villages and towns in the Islands are not neatly arranged in blocks. Second, I was looking for respondents who met specific requirements, namely females who were in their adolescent years. If I chose to interview the respondents in every nth house who met my criteria, then I must make the assumption that those who do indeed meet them are randomly distributed among the houses in the area selected. There was no basis upon which I could make this assumption. In short, I would be unable to treat data gathered in this fashion as though they were randomly drawn because the manner in which the respondents were distributed in the houses would remain an uncontrolled variable and would thus represent an undeterminable bias.

As a matter of expediency, I chose to gather my sample by using the "snowball technique." That is, when interviewing respondent A, I would secure from her the name of another girl who would become respondent B; and she in turn would lead me to respondent C, etc. Now, in a small homogeneous population, every respondent would probably know every other respondent and thus the sample would constitute a peer group with some greater degree of homogeneity of attitude toward fertility and fertility control. It turned out this way in small villages. The girls were more similar to each other in social characteristics, this arising not only from the fact that they shared a common environment but that, to a considerable degree, they formed a sociometric unit. But in the two cities, the sample took on a different form. The girls included in these samples probably had greater variability in attitudes and background. Thus urban respondent A would know respondent B, by virtue of the fact that she had sent the interviewer to her. It follows that respondent B would know respondent A, who had recommended her, as well as respondent C whom she, in turn, recommended. There was, however, no assurance that respondent A knew respondent C. In fact, by the time the sample is increased to ten, it becomes probable that any one respondent does not know more than three or four in the sample. It is possible, therefore, that the urban sample was more heterogeneous in attitude toward fertility and fertility control.

The apparent limitations resulting from the method of sample selection dictate analysis of internal qualities of the samples only. Accordingly, I am committed to non-parametric tests of significance, i.e., tests which do not specify conditions about the parameters of the population from which the sample was drawn, only the internal characteristics.[7] Fortunately, there has been developed a statistical measure, known as *chi square*, to fit my needs, usually designated by its Greek lower-case letter, χ^2. The smaller the chi square becomes, the smaller are the differences between the sub-populations in the sample, the more homogeneous the sample, and the less willing we are to rule out chance as an explanatory factor.

The precise interpretation of chi square can be done by means of statistical tables that have already been prepared. The only additional information needed to "read" such tables is the concept of *degrees of freedom*, symbolized by "df." The degrees of freedom are directly proportional to the number of entries or cells in the statistical table that is used to compute chi square. The more items under investigation, the greater the number of cells in the chi square table and the more degrees of freedom appear. More important, as the degrees of freedom are increased, the numbers assigned to chi squares *of the same value* tend to increase. Thus, a chi square of 3.84 with one degree of freedom is equivalent to a chi square of 5.99 with two degrees of freedom which is equivalent to a chi square of 9.84 with three degrees of freedom, etc.

For many readers, this information is all that is needed: degrees of freedom (df) are used in reading the interpretation of chi square from a special table. In fact, degrees of freedom are only given in the following pages for the benefit of the statistically oriented. More accurate explanation is not needed, since the interpretation of each chi square is provided with the tables. This interpretation is referred to as the *probability* (represented by the letter "p") of an event occurring by chance. The closer p is to zero, the less chance is likely to explain the observed differences and, consequently, the more "significant" are any differences which occur. *In terms of the objectives of this analysis, when p is greater than .05 the two sub populations are similar to each other in terms of the traits that are being measured. When p is smaller than .05, the two sub populations are different.* This rule is arbitrary, designed to guard against letting one's personal prejudices influence his judgment. By accepting a fixed standard of homogeneity, we lessen the risk of changing our judgment to fit our preconceived "needs."

---

[7] See Sidney Siegal, *Non-parametric Statistics for the Behavioral Sciences* (New York: McGraw-Hill, 1956), p. 31.

The Schedule

The schedule of questions was logically related to the central problem of fertility expectations and was of the "closed-ended" type, i.e., calling for precise responses. Care was taken to begin with neutral items, that is, questions of a non-controversial nature for the purpose of gaining cooperation of girls who might be negatively oriented to the basic issue. In short, the beginning questions were aimed at evoking interest without arousing a strong controversial response. None of the girls approached refused to cooperate or demonstrated any noticeable hostility toward the schedule. In fact, the problem was just the reverse—a difficulty in breaking off the relationship with many girls seeking advice from the interviewers concerning sex and conjugal difficulties.

The survey was to include 100 young women in St. Lucia and Grenada. Their mean age turned out to be 17.85.[8] Six communities made up the study, three in Grenada and three in St. Lucia. Each island included samples from two villages and the central city. The villages ranged in total population from 90 (Ciceron) to 500 (Labaye). The responses to the schedule are given in Appendix Table A3. Twenty-three of the 100 girls were mothers; 5 were pregnant and 5 were legally married. Two of the married women had no children. Twenty mothers were not married. Of the pregnant girls, only one was married and the remainder were pregnant with their first child.

The influence of the island-place. In the Preface and elsewhere, I pointed out that the islands of the West Indies are culturally pluralistic. By this I mean that each of the islands has an ethos that differentiates it from every other. An analysis of the replies of the girls to the following ten key questions in the interview schedule substantiated this conclusion. If we consider, for example, the factor of church attendance on the different islands we get the following data. The question used in the schedule asked: "How often do you attend church?" The respondent could reply either, "Once or more a week," "Almost once a week," or "Almost never." Eighteen of the 29 St. Lucians reported that they attended church once or more a week. In Grenada, 16 out of 71 replied that they attended church this often. Using chi-square analysis, the statistician can establish how many girls would have been expected to say this if there had been *no* relationship between island residence and church attendance. In the table below, the observed responses are first listed, followed by the expected responses in parentheses. To this

---

[8] The median age was 18, the mode, 19 years. Respondents from the two cities were found to be slightly under one-year older than their village counterparts.

tabulation have been added the chi-square (χ^2), the degrees of freedom (df), and the probability (p).

Q. 19. How often do you attend church?

	St. Lucia	Grenada
Once or more a week	18 (10)	16 (24)
Almost once a week	9 (14)	38 (33)
Almost never	2 (5)	17 (14)

$\chi^2 = 14.826$ df=2   p<.001

In this instance, a chi-square of 14.826 was obtained, indicating that the tendency for the St. Lucians to attend church more regularly could not have occurred by chance more than once out of a thousand times. I must conclude, therefore, that the relationship is probably not due to chance, and tentatively conclude that there is some relationship between island residence and attendance at religious service. For the responses to this question, the expected number of St. Lucians replying that they attended church once or more a week was ten. Actually, 18 replied they attended church this often. Thus, the observed value deviated considerably from what I would have expected had there been no relationship between island residence and church attendance. More St. Lucians go to church regularly than we would anticipate if the social milieu of the island were having no effect. The Grenadian girls, however, were less diligent as church-goers than expected; 16 of the 71 girls said they attended church once or more a week, while 24 were expected to make such an assertion. Also, 17 Grenadians reported that they "almost never" attended church while I expected only 13 to answer this way.

Another question dealing with religious activity, was one asking the respondent, "Are you very religious, just average, or not very religious?" The replies to this question are set forth in the table below.

Q. 24. Are you very religious, just average, or not very?

	St. Lucia	Grenada
Very	10 (6)	10 (14)
Just Average	17 (16)	38 (39)
Not very	2 (7)	23 (18)

$\chi^2 = 9.733$ df=2   p<.01

Responses to this question also reveal significant differences between the islands with respect to religious conduct. The St. Lucians are significantly more inclined to consider themselves very religious. The respondents from the island of Grenada were more inclined to consider themselves not very religious. The table shows, for example, that had there been no relationship between island residence and religious attitude I would have expected 18 of

137

the Grenadan respondents to have stated they were not very religious. As a matter of fact, 23 of the respondents from this island said they were not very religious. The difference between the observed distribution of responses and what we might have expected under the conditions of no relationship is sufficiently great to enable me to discount the possibility that it happened by accident.

With respect to religious conduct and attitude, I am led to the conclusion that the islands do produce a significantly different ethos or significantly different pattern of social conduct. Now the problem becomes how the sex and fertility patterns have been affected by the different island milieus. On the basis of the above tables, I might be led to consider the hypothesis that the Grenadians will be more liberal with respect to their sexual attitudes and conduct than the St. Lucians. This follows from the expectation that people who attend church more regularly and consider themselves more religious would adhere more closely to the sexual morality set forth by the active churches.

The girls were asked a number of questions centering on attitudes toward sex, marriage and the use of contraceptive devices. The following table presents their responses to the question: "Doctors are making a pill which will keep you from having babies for a short time. These pills will not make you sick or permanently sterile. If doctors gave you these pills without their costing you anything, would you want to take them once in a while?"

Q. 28. Doctors are making a pill which will keep you from having babies for a short time. These pills will not make you sick or permanently sterile. If doctors gave you these pills without their costing you anything, would you want to take them once in a while?

	St. Lucia	Grenada
Yes	10 (15)	51 (46)
No	10 (5)	13 (18)

$$\chi^2=6.740 \quad df=1 \quad p<.01$$

From the data in this table, St. Lucians were less inclined to take the pill than the girls on the island of Grenada. If there had been no relationship between island residence and response to this question, 15 of the St. Lucians should have said they would take the pill. Actually, only 10 indicated a willingness to use such a device. On the other hand, had there been no island effect, 46 of the Grenadians should have indicated a willingness to take the pill. As a matter of fact, 51 were willing to make use of it. The difference between the actual pattern of responses and what I would have obtained, assuming no island influence, is sufficiently great to enable us to conclude that it did not happen by chance. The St. Lucians appear to be more resistant to the idea of using oral contraceptives. This is consistent with the already observed greater religious inclinations of the St. Lucians. However, the following tables demonstrate that many other aspects of sexual attitude and conduct are not consistent with what we might expect on the basis of known differences between the islands in religiousity.

The girls in this sample were asked the question: "When having sport with your lover, have you ever tried to keep from getting pregnant?" The girls from St. Lucia were significantly less inclined to take such steps. The girls from Grenada were more inclined to do so. The table below reveals that if the island milieu had been without influence, I would have expected 16 St. Lucians to have said that they attempted to avoid pregnancy. Actual-

Q. 25. When having sport with your lover, have you ever tried to keep from getting pregnant?

	St. Lucia	Grenada
Yes	10 (16)	48 (42)
No	13 (7)	10 (16)

$$\chi^2 = 12.50 \quad df = 1 \quad p < .001$$

ly, only 10 St. Lucians indicated that they do so. Among the Grenadians, 48 indicated that they take steps to avoid pregnancy. Had there been no island influence, we would have expected 42 to have stated that they attempted to avoid pregnancy. Again, the observed responses deviate quite significantly from what I would have expected had there been no island influence. The difference is sufficiently great to enable us to conclude that it did not happen by chance.

These data are in one sense consistent with the differences between the islands in religious attitude. I would expect the St. Lucians to be more conservative toward the idea of using mechanical means of preventing pregnancy. The data showed that this is the case. I can speculate that the policy of the Catholic Church with respect to contraceptive devices is in conflict with the position that it takes toward having children out of wedlock. For example, presuming that a girl in the West Indies will have premarital sex experiences, she must balance the morality of using contraceptive devices against the morality of having children out of wedlock. In St. Lucia, the decision is in favor of having children out of wedlock; in Grenada, the decision is in favor of contraception.

The above speculations are further reinforced by the responses that were given to the question: "If you knew of a very easy way to keep from having babies, which did not stop you from having a good time (sport), do you think you might use it?" Again, the St. Lucians are significantly less inclined to make use of devices for the prevention of pregnancy than are the Grenadians. This question attempts to get at whether or not resistance to

Q. 27. If you knew of a very easy way to keep from having babies, which did not stop you from having a good time (sport), do you think you might use it?

	St. Lucia	Grenada
Yes	15 (20)	56 (51)
No	13 (8)	13 (18)

$$\chi^2=7.709 \quad df=1 \quad p<.01$$

the use of contraceptives is a result of certain difficulties that some mechanical devices impose on the user. Evidently, even if there were a very easy way of preventing pregnancy, the St. Lucians would still be more resistant to the use of such devices. Had there been no island differences I would have expected 20 of the St. Lucians to say that they would make use of such a device. Actually, only 15 said they would take such a step. Once again, the St. Lucians seem to be more inclined to run the risk of pregnancy either in or out of wedlock than make use of easy preventatives. The differences between the islands are sufficiently great that I can reject the possibility that they happened by chance.

The next question reads: "Do you think a girl should have a baby as early in life as possible, or do you think she should wait a while?" Out of the 98 girls who responded to this question, 83 were in favor of waiting and only 15 believed that one should have a child as soon as possible. The two undecided responses were not included in the table.

Q. 22. Do you think a girl should have a baby as early in life as possible, or do you think she should wait a while?

	St. Lucia	Grenada
Soon as possible	7 (4)	8 (11)
Wait a while	21 (24)	62 (59)

$$\chi^2=2.828 \quad df=1 \quad p<.10$$

Differences between the islands were such that the St. Lucians were slightly more inclined to feel that a girl should have a baby as soon as possible. However, the differences were such as to enable me to conclude that they could not have happened by chance. These data suggest that there are moral and possibly religious factors which lead a girl to feel that having children immediately and perhaps indiscriminately is not a good thing. Despite these pressures to delay having children, the previous tables have already shown that there are countervailing forces which lead many of these girls to refrain from using means for preventing pregnancy.

Responses to the next item lend further support to the speculations above.

140

The girls were asked, "Do you think it is all right for a girl to have a baby before she is married?" Again, the preponderance of responses is that it is not all right for a girl to have a baby before she is married.

Q. 21. Do you think it is all right for a girl to have a baby before she is married?

	St. Lucia	Grenada
All right	9 (6)	11 (14)
Not all right	19 (22)	59 (56)

$$\chi^2=3.331 \quad df=1 \quad p<.10$$

Seventy-eight of the 98 respondents (omitting the two undecided cases) said that this is "not all right." However, it is worth noting that slightly over one-fifth believed that it is "all right" for a girl to have a baby before she is married. When we look at the differences between the islands we see that the St. Lucians were more inclined to think that it is "all right" for a girl to have a baby before she is married than was the case of the Grenadians. However, the difference is not sufficiently great to enable us to conclude that it could not have happened by chance. From this table and the previous table, we gain the impression that these West Indies girls are motivated to delay having children and, furthermore, that they are desirous of having their babies in wedlock. The moral and religious climate of the two islands is one of preference for marriage.

Despite the fact that this preference for marriage exists, the majority of respondents believed that it is all right to have sexual intercourse outside of the marriage state. The next table reveals the pattern of responses to the question: "Do you think it is all right for a girl to have experience (sport) before she is married?" Sixty-six out of 98 girls who made definite responses to this question indicated that they thought sex outside of marriage is "all right."

Q. 26. Do you think it is all right for a girl to have experience (sport) before she is married?

	St. Lucia	Grenada
All right	21 (18)	45 (48)
Not all right	6 (9)	26 (23)

$$\chi^2=1.847 \quad df=1 \quad p<.20$$

The differences between the islands are insignificant. The St. Lucians are just as inclined as the Grenadians to feel that sex outside of marriage is permissible. We see, then, that although religious differences between the two islands may have some effect on resistance to use of contraceptives, it does not have a great effect on sex outside of marriage. Therefore, the reader could speculate that the girls of St. Lucia and Grenada are equally exposed

141

to conditions that can lead to pregnancy outside of wedlock. However, the greater moral resistance of the St. Lucians to contraceptive techniques makes them more vulnerable to pregnancy.

From the standpoint of introducing family planning programs in these two islands, one must recognize that such efforts will not be welcomed with equal enthusiasm by the two populations. The Grenadian girls would seem to be experiencing significantly less internal conflict between their overt religious practices and sentiments, on the one hand, and their sexual licenses on the other. The data suggest, then, that family planning policies should take into account these differences. What might be effective family planning in the more liberal atmosphere of Grenada might be less effective in the more conservative atmosphere of St. Lucia. However, before a fertility control policy is designed, it is necessary to take into account other important social characteristics, e.g., rural and urban social settings with their respective attitudes toward intercourse outside of marriage, not to overlook the willingness of young people of both sexes to employ various means to prevent conception.

Rural-Urban Differences. The next ten tables analyze responses to the schedule in terms of the rural and urban residences of the respondents. The urban residents are defined as those living in the cities of St. George's Grenada, and Castries, St. Lucia. All other respondents are classified as rural. Out of the 100 respondents interviewed, 52 claimed residence in the two cities; 48 lived in the rural areas. I begin the analysis of the rural-urban portion of the schedule with the hypothesis that it is by no means clear that the likely effect of further urbanization or industrialization on West Indian fertility will be a significantly reduced birth rate. This hypothesis is not in accord with "standard" theory,[9] but the analysis would seem to confirm it. Warren C. Robinson and Elizabeth H. Robinson give support to this hypothesis in discovering a narrowing rural urban fertility differential in Mexico.[10] They described a rising urban birth rate and a fairly stable rural fertility, stating: "The notion that rural-urban fertility differentials in Mexico are attributable to the effects of industrialization is open to question. Surely, Mexico was less industrialized in 1930, than in 1950, yet urban fer-

[9] Cf Wilber E. Moore, *Industrialization and Labor* (Ithaca: Cornell University Press, 1951), p. 221; Nathan L. Whetten, *Rural Mexico* (Chicago: Chicago University Press, 1948), pp. 389-393; Kingsley Davis, "Population Trends and Policies in Latin America", *Some Economic Aspects of Post-war Inter-American Relations,* Latin American Studies II (Austin: University of Texas, 1946), pp. 35-39; Kingsley Davis and Anna Cass, "Urbanization in Latin America", *Milbank Memorial Fund Quarterly,* (April, 1946), pp. 186-207, and (June, 1946), pp. 292-314.

[10] Warren C. Robinson and Elizabeth H. Robinson, "Rural-Urban Fertility Differentials in Mexico", *American Sociological Review,* (February, 1960), pp. 77-81.

tility appears to have been higher in 1950 than in 1930."[11] They admit that their fertility-ratio analysis is subject to error. Perhaps a fertility expectation analysis might add additional evidence to their tentative conclusions. From my research, West Indian rural adolescents are more anxious to reduce their offspring, or at least hold the rates stable, than urban adolescents. Supporting evidence is developed in the following set of tables.

Urban-rural differences often reflect religious practices and commitment. The effects of the urban setting on fertility might be due to the more liberal religious belief often found in the urban community. Therefore, the task becomes one of examining possible differences in the rural and urban samples with respect to church attendance and belief. Responses to the question: "How often do you attend church?" were classified by rural and urban residence. The data are presented below.

Q. 19. How often do you attend church?

	Urban	Rural
Once or more a week	19 (18)	15 (16)
About once a week	27 (24)	20 (23)
Almost never	6 (10)	13 (9)

$$\chi^2 = 3.935 \quad df = 2 \quad p < .20$$

From these data, we conclude that there are no significant differences between the urban and rural groups with respect to church attendance. A preponderance of the girls stated that they attended church "about once a week." One fifth of the sample indicated that they "almost never" attended church. However, there was no significantly greater tendency for the urban group not to attend church than for the rural group. Therefore, any differences in the sexual practices and attitudes toward contraceptives that appeared in the rural-urban samples are not a function of differences in religious practices.

Although no differences were found between the rural and urban groups in church attendance there were significant differences in degree of religious commitment. In response to the question: "Are you very religious, just average, or not very religious?" the urban girls revealed a greater tendency to define their religious sentiments as "average."

Q. 24. Are you very religious, just average, or not very religious?

	Urban	Rural
Very religious	6 (10)	14 (10)
Just average	39 (29)	16 (26)
Not very religious	7 (13)	18 (12)

$$\chi^2 = 17.52 \quad df = 2 \quad p < .001$$

---

[11] *Ibid.*, p. 81.

A very interesting feature of the data in the above table is that the rural girls are either very committed or are highly uncommitted to religion. So, even though there is a very significant difference in the nature of the urban and rural religious sentiment, we cannot say that the urban group is less religious, on the average than the rural group. Therefore, any attempt to account for rural-urban differences in sex conduct and attitude toward contraception is not a simple reflection of rural-urban differences in religious practice and sentiment. This leaves a provocative problem, one which, unfortunately, cannot be resolved with the data available in this study. I refer to the problem of ascertaining which is more important in bringing about acceptance of family planning, decline in religious commitment or residence in an urban setting.

The next table pertains to the educational attainments of the urban and rural groups. The data show quite conclusively, and as the reader might expect, that the urban group has a significantly larger number of persons with secondary school education. Among the rural girls, 40 out of 48 interviewees did not have secondary schooling.

Q. 20. How long did you go to school?

	Urban	Rural
Primary	16 (29)	40 (27)
Secondary	36 (23)	8 (21)

$$\chi^2 = 27.987 \quad df = 1 \quad p < .001$$

The above table suggests that the differences between rural and urban populations with respect to the use of contraceptives may be a reflection of more advanced level of education. This is suggested only as a hypothesis accounting for the differences observed in the tables that follow.

Now, turning to a question that deals with attitudes toward fertility and contraception, we find significant differences between the rural and urban samples. The question was asked: "Doctors are making a pill which will keep you from having babies for a short time. These pills will not make you sick or permanently sterile. If doctors gave you these pills without their costing you anything, would you want to take them once in a while?" In response to this item, the rural girls were much more willing to make use of such a pill than one might expect on the basis of chance.

Q. 28. Doctors are making a pill which will keep you from having babies for a short time. These pills will not make you sick or permanently sterile. If doctors gave you these pills without their costing you anything, would you want to take them once in a while?

144

	Urban	Rural
Yes	21 (32)	40 (29)
No	19 (12)	4 (11)
Uncertain	12 (8)	4 (8)

$$\chi^2 = 19.568 \quad df = 2 \quad p < .001$$

More urban girls indicated unwillingness to use such a pill than one might expect on the basis of no difference between the urban and rural groups. Out of the total sample of 100 girls, 61 were willing to use the pill and 23 were unwilling to use it. Only 4 out of the 48 rural girls were unwilling to use the pill whereas 19 out of 52 of the urban girls expressed unwillingness to use it. The urban girls also indicated a slightly greater tendency to be more uncertain about the use of such a pill than were the rural girls. This finding is surprising in that the general impression to be gained from the study thus far is that better educated urban girls are more inclined toward experimentations, not being "uncertain." In other words, one is now led to conclude that resistance to family planning programs would be lower in the rural areas than in the urban areas. And I propose that in further research, investigators consider factors that might account for this observation. Tentative possibilities are: first, it is possible that a more extensive survey may show that urban groups are not as resistant as this study indicates; second, it is possible that if this difference is real, it is because the urban girls are more inclined to accept conventional techniques, and are resistant to something new; third, that the urban girls, by being better educated, may fear both physiological damage and greater expense. But these are offered only as tentative suggestions for further research.

The sample was also asked: "If you knew of a very easy way to keep from having babies, which did not stop you from having a good time (sport), do you think you might use it?" Once again, the data revealed significant differences between the rural and urban samples in response to this question. While 71 out of 97 respondents said "yes" they would use it, the tendency was for rural girls to be more inclined to use it than urban girls.

Q. 27. If you knew of a very easy way to keep from having babies, which did not stop you from having a good time (sport), do you think you might use it?

	Urban	Rural
Yes	30 (36)	41 (35)
No	19 (13)	7 (13)

$$\chi^2 = 7.241 \quad df = 1 \quad p < .01$$

Had there been no difference between the urban and rural groups, 35 rural girls should have said "yes." Actually, 41 said that they would use it. Conversely, one would have expected, statistically speaking, 36 of the urban girls

145

replying in the affirmative. Actually, only 30 indicated a willingness to employ an easy way of avoiding childbirth. These differences are significant and could not have happened by chance more than once out of 100 times. Once again, the data indicate a greater resistance to the use of easy contraceptives on the part of the urban girls. Thus family planning programs should encounter less resistance in rural areas than in urban districts. Please be mindful, however, that the majority of girls in both the urban and rural settings were favorably inclined to the idea of using easy ways of controlling fertility.

In responding to the question: "Do you think it is all right for a girl to have experience (sport) before she is married?" no significant difference was found between the urban and rural girls.

Q. 26. Do you think it is all right for a girl to have experience (sport) before she is married?

	Urban	Rural
All right	31 (35)	35 (31)
Not all right	21 (17)	11 (15)

$$\chi^2=3.008 \quad df=1 \quad p<.10$$

Both groups had a greater number of girls indicating the belief that such a practice is all right. Out of the urban group, 31 girls felt that it is permissible, while 21 believed that it is not. A somewhat similar distribution was found for the rural group: 35 girls believed that it is all right and 11 believed that it is not. In conclusion, then, the sexual mores binding on girls in the urban and rural sectors of these islands are no less permissive in the one instance than they are in the other. In both the rural and urban settings sexual morality appears to be relatively permissive. This is a relevant finding to the extent that these expressions reveal high exposure to fertility among unmarried women.

The responses to the next item suggest, as I have already speculated, that the urban girls are as familiar with the problem of coping with pregnancy as are the rural girls. When asked the question: "When having sport with your lover, have you ever tried to keep from getting pregnant?" 25 out of 35 of the urban girls stated that they made use of some means of preventing conception. Thirty-three out of the 46 rural girls responded in a like manner.

Q. 25. When having sport with your lover, have you ever tried to keep from getting pregnant?

	Urban	Rural
Yes	25 (25)	33 (33)
No	10 (10)	13 (13)

$$\chi^2=0.000 \quad df=1 \quad p<.98$$

146

The pattern of responses for the rural and urban samples was practically identical—there were no significant differences between the two groups in their response to this question. Out of 100 girls interviewed, 19 indicated that the question did not apply to them. These girls were omitted from the table. It is interesting to note, however, that a smaller proportion of the rural girls felt that this question did not apply than was the case for the urban girls. On the basis of these data, one is led to the conclusion that a preponderance of girls is engaged in premarital sexual experiences and that of this group a majority is concerned with avoiding pregnancy and using, therefore, some appropriate technique to achieve this end. The most common method of avoiding conception throughout the world is the simplest, coitus interruptus, or withdrawal just before emission. This is probably nearly as old a method as the group life of man.[12] It requires no preparations or appliances, and costs nothing. However, it does have two disadvantages: usually it ultimately fails to prevent impregnation, and it requires that the male be motivated strongly enough to frustrate his desire at the moment of highest excitation. My informants in the West Indies have indicated that the woman often takes the initiative in the thrusting of the male away from her prior to climax. A replication of this study requires that some questions elicit responses concerning specific techniques, i.e., mechanical versus "natural" procedures.

Traditional conceptions of rural-urban fertility patterns view the urban girl as less desirous of having children as soon as possible. The question was asked: "Do you think a girl should have a baby as early in life as possible, or do you think she should wait a while?" Responses to this question reveal that out of 98 persons responding, 83 felt that a girl should wait a while.

Q. 22. Do you think a girl should have a baby as early in life as possible, or do you think she should wait a while?

	Urban	Rural
Soon as possible	10 (8)	5 (7)
Wait a while	41 (43)	42 (40)

$$\chi^2 = 1.512 \quad df = 1 \quad p < .30$$

Fifteen out of the 98 respondents thought that a girl should have a baby as soon as possible. There was a slight tendency for more urban girls to believe that a baby should be had as soon as possible. However, this tendency was not significant and requires the conclusion that there is no greater desire on the part of rural girls to have babies early than is true of urban

---

[12] Norman E. Himes, *Medical History of Contraception* (Baltimore: Williams & Wilkins, 1936), pp. 183-184.

girls. Once again, the responses of these West Indians leads us to believe that the climate of opinion is one which would be receptive to family planning training. The problem is not one of overcoming resistance to the idea of not having children, but rather one of designing programs that generate an ability on the part of the girls to view the problems of family planning more broadly than they do now.

In earlier chapters, I indicated a relatively high incidence of pregnancies outside of wedlock. I was interested in determining whether or not such pregnancies were viewed more favorably by women in the rural sample than by women in the urban sample. In response to the question: "Do you think it is all right for a girl to have a baby before she is married?" 78 out of 98 girls expressed the opinion that this is not all right. About one-fifth of the girls thought that this is permissible, hence the conclusion that the climate of opinion is not particularly permissive with respect to having children out of wedlock, although it is permissive with respect to having sexual experience out of wedlock. A comparison between the rural and urban girls revealed a significant tendency for the rural girls to believe that such pregnancies were all right.

Q. 21. Do you think it is all right for a girl to have a baby before she is married?

	Urban	Rural
All right	6 (10)	14 (10)
Not all right	44 (40)	34 (38)

$$\chi^2 = 4.433 \quad df = 1 \quad p < .05$$

Had there been no difference between the urban and rural groups one would have expected 10 of the rural girls to say that this is "all right." Actually, fourteen indicated that they thought such pregnancies were "all right." The difference, though not great, is significant at the .05 level.

One technique of fertility control is infanticide. I was interested in the extent to which urban and rural girls recognized the existence of infanticide as a means of dealing with unwanted births. On the basis of considerations developed in other chapters, I hypothesized that in the rural areas, infanticide was more generally recognized though not necessarily more acceptable than in urban areas. The girls were asked: "Do some girls let their babies die because they don't want them?" The results, shown in the table below, indicate that the speculation was correct.

Q. 7. Do some girls let their babies die because they don't want them?

	Urban	Rural
Yes	21 (26)	30 (25)
No	28 (23)	17 (22)

$$\chi^2 = 4.233 \quad df = 1 \quad p < .05$$

The rural girls to a significant extent are more aware of infanticide as a means of fertility control than are the urban respondents. Thirty out of the 47 rural respondents said that some girls let their babies die; only 21 out of the 49 urban respondents revealed similar knowledge. The difference between the two groups, though not very great, is statistically significant and in the direction hypothesized earlier. Several ideas are suggested by these data. One is that possibly the rural sample is more eager to find easy means of controlling pregnancy in order to avoid the harshness of infanticide, something of which they are more fully aware than their urban counterparts. Another idea is one aimed at those who are opposed to contraception, namely: the morality of family planning involves more than simply Victorian codes of sexual purity and physical pleasure. Family planning in underdeveloped areas involves human beings in the broader morality that has to do with the sanctity of life itself. Could it be that some West Indian leaders, because of their moral resistance to contraceptives, are tacitly condoning infanticide?

Catholic versus non-Catholic responses. From the foregoing analysis, significant dissimilarities in response by place were noted. The next task is to measure the responses of these 100 adolescent women in terms of Catholic and non-Catholic membership. An earlier study in Jamaica, by J. Mayone Stycos and Kurt Back, found that membership in either Catholic or non-Catholic churches is of little importance insofar as attitudes toward and practice of birth control are concerned.[13] The data for Grenada and St. Lucia, support a similar conclusion. Catholic and non-Catholic girls differ but little on the respectability of birth control. The one difference that is significant shows the Catholic girls somewhat more permissive with respect to the right to "live in sin."

The next eight tables present evidence having to do with attitudes toward fertility among Catholics and non-Catholics. When asked the question: "Do you feel like you had too few brothers and sisters, about right, or too many?" significant differences were observed between the two groups.

Q. 5. Do you feel like you had too few brothers and sisters, about right, or too many?

	Catholic	Non-Catholic
Too few	16 (13)	4 (7)
About right	40 (38)	18 (20)
Too many	9 (14)	13 (8)

$$x^2=7.989 \quad df=2 \quad p<.02$$

[13] J. Mayone Stycos and Kurt Back, "Contraception and Catholicism in Jamaica", *Eugenics Quarterly*, (December, 1958), pp. 216-220.

Of the 65 Catholic respondents, only 9 felt they had "too many." If Catholic membership had had no effect one would have expected 14 to respond by saying that they had had "too many" in their families. Non-Catholics were more inclined to feel that their family size had been too large. The relationship as it appears in the above table is not marked but is nevertheless statistically significant. It could not have happened by chance more than twice out of 100 times. The table suggests that Catholic ideology has a slight tendency to provide the girls in this sample with the feeling that their families of orientation were the "right" size or even too small. I speculate, then, that the Catholics found their families of orientation ideal in size. If one may assume that both groups came from similar sized families then it is possible that Catholics, by virtue of their religious background, tend to find larger families of orientation emotionally satisfying. Part of the effectiveness of Catholic ideology in the West Indies in sustaining attitudes favorable to high fertility stems, it seems, not merely from the content of the ideology but from the ability of that ideology to produce primary emotional satisfactions within the social context of the large family. Though this is set forth only as a hypothesis, I would suggest that the resistance to fertility control on the part of a small number of Catholics derives not simply from an ideological or moral commitment but derives as well from the belief on the part of the respondent that her personal, factual experiences support the conclusion that the large family is a good thing.

When the matter of church attendance is examined, I found no significant difference between Catholics and non-Catholics. In response to the question: "How often do you attend church?" I found a slight tendency for Catholics to attend more regularly than non-Catholics.

Q. 19. How often do you attend church, once or more each week, about twice a week, almost never?

	Catholic	Non-Catholic
Once or more	27 (22)	7 (12)
About twice	26 (31)	21 (16)
Almost never	12 (12)	7 (7)

$$\chi^2 = 5.065 \quad df = 2 \quad p < .10$$

The difference between the two groups in regularity of attendance was not statistically significant, hence the conclusion that any difference that might exist between the two groups is not a result of greater degree of religious practice on the part of the Catholics as opposed to the non-Catholics. Instead, such differences will have to be attributed to some other aspect of religious membership in the two categories.

The study reveals that the intensity of religious commitment does not differ significantly between the two groups. In response to the question: "Are you very religious, just average, or not very religious?" the Catholics were slightly more inclined to express the view that they are "very religious." The degree of difference, however, is not significant.

Q. 24. Are you very religious, just average, or not very religious?

	Catholic	Non-Catholic
Very religious	16 (13)	4 (7)
Just average	33 (36)	22 (19)
Not very	16 (16)	9 (9)

$$\chi^2 = 2.590 \quad df = 2 \quad p < .30$$

Again, one is led to the conclusion that any differences between these two groups in their attitudes toward patterns of sexual conduct are not a product of degree of religious sentiment. More likely, any difference found is a product of differences in the substantive content of the religious beliefs adhered to by the Catholic and non-Catholic groups.

With respect to schooling, Catholic and non-Catholic girls did not show any significant differences. The data below reveal the responses of the two groups to the question: "How long did you go to school?" While there was a slight tendency for the Catholic girls to have less secondary school education, the degree of relationship was statistically non-significant.

Q. 20. How long did you go to school?

	Catholic	Non-Catholic
Primary	41 (36)	15 (20)
Secondary	24 (29)	20 (15)

$$\chi^2 = 3.773 \quad df = 1 \quad p < .10$$

Now, the data in the following table support the Stycos-Back findings in Jamaica to the effect that affiliation with the Catholic Church has no significant effect on attitudes toward the use of simple contraceptives. In reply to the question: "If you knew of a very easy way to keep from having babies, which did not stop you from having a good time (sport), do you think you might use it?" the Catholic girls were just as inclined to say "yes" as the non-Catholic girls. As found earlier, a preponderance of respondents stated they would use such a device. In this instance, 44 out of 63 Catholic girls said they would use it.

Q. 27. If you knew of a very easy way to keep from having babies, which did not stop you from having a good time (sport), do you think you would use it?

151

	Catholic	Non-Catholic
Yes	44 (46)	27 (25)
No	19 (17)	7 (9)

$$\chi^2=1.025 \quad df=1 \quad p<.50$$

Twenty-seven out of 34 non-Catholic girls said they would use it. The conclusion is drawn, then, that membership in the Catholic Church should not act as a strong bar to the development of effective family planning programming in these two islands.

The assertion above is given further support by the responses of the girls to the question: "Doctors are making a pill which will keep you from having babies for a short time. These pills will not make you sick or permanently sterile. If doctors gave you these pills without their costing you anything, would you want to take them once in a while?" Again, the data indicate that the Catholic girls are as willing to employ such a contraceptive technique as are the non-Catholic girls. In other words, there are no significant differences between the Catholic and non-Catholic categories of respondents.

Q. 28. Doctors are making a pill which will keep you from having babies for a short time. These pills will not make you sick or permanently sterile. If doctors gave you these pills without their costing you anything, would you want to take them once in a while?

	Catholic	Non-Catholic
Yes	36 (39)	25 (22)
No	18 (15)	5 (8)

$$\chi^2=2.685 \quad df=1 \quad p<.20$$

Generalizing from these data, membership in the Catholic Church has no great effect on the attitude of respondents toward any type of contraceptive technique. What these people are probably interested in is not the moral issue of contraception but the economic, physiological and sensual aspects of contraception.

In response to the question: "When having sport with your lover, have you ever tried to keep from getting pregnant?" again we find the Catholic respondents not differing significantly from the non-Catholic respondents. A majority of both groups stated that they did employ means of preventing conception.

Q. 25. When having sport with your lover, have you ever tried to keep from getting pregnant?

	Catholic	Non-Catholic
Yes	34 (37)	24 (21)
No	18 (15)	5 (8)

$$\chi^2=2.755 \quad df=1 \quad p<.10$$

Unfortunately, this question does not distinguish between the use of so-called natural contraceptive techniques and mechanical ones. It is possible that the Catholic and non-Catholic groups differ in the extent to which mechanical techniques are employed to prevent pregnancy resulting from pre-marital sexual experience. Further research is suggested.

The one significant difference found between the Catholic and non-Catholic girls was in response to the question: "Do you think it is all right for a girl to have experience (sport) before she is married?" Responses to this question appear in the table below.

Q. 26. Do you think it is all right for a girl to have experience (sport) before she is married?

	Catholic	Non-Catholic
All right	47 (42)	19 (24)
Not all right	16 (21)	16 (11)

$$\chi^2 = 4.220 \quad df = 1 \quad p < .05$$

From this table, the Catholic girls were more inclined to believe that it is permissible for a girl to engage in premarital sexual relationships. The relationship is significant at the .05 level. Interestingly, for every non-Catholic girl who did not consider this permissible there was one among her group who thought it was all right; for every Catholic girl who thought this was not permissible there were three within her group who thought it was.

Summarizing, the Catholic girls are not significantly different from the non-Catholic girls in their attitudes toward birth control. The one exception was the degree of permissiveness toward premarital sex experience. One cannot attribute this permissiveness on the part of the Catholic girls either to their educational background, their intensity of religious commitment or their regularity of church attendance. In all of these respects, the Catholic girls are not significantly different from the non-Catholic girls.

Island differences among Catholics. Of the 100 adolescent girls in the sample, 65 were Roman Catholics. Are these Catholics of "one mind" concerning sex and conjugal matters? To answer this question the responses were divided into two groups: St. Lucia Catholics and Grenada Catholics. As will be seen in the following analysis, the two groups tended to react differently. Spatial isolation apparently disrupts any potential consensus, particularly on birth control matters.

St. Lucian and Grenada Catholics studied in this survey showed significant differences with respect both to church attendance and degree of religious sentiment. From the data below, it is seen how the St. Lucian Catholics were more inclined to be regular attenders at church than the Catholics of Grenada, the difference being significant at the .01 level.

153

Q. 19. How often do you attend church, once or more a week, about twice a week, almost never?

	St. Lucia Catholics	Grenada Catholics
Once or more a week	18 (12)	9 (15)
About twice a week	9 (12)	17 (14)
Almost never	2 (5)	10 (7)

$\chi^2=10.140$ df$=2$ p$<.01$

Data with respect to degree of religious sentiment also reveal the St. Lucian Catholics as girls significantly more inclined to consider themselves very religious in nature, the difference being significant at the .01 level.

Q. 24. Are you very religious, just average, or not very religious?

	St. Lucia Catholics	Grenada Catholics
Very	10 (7)	6 (9)
Just average	17 (15)	16 (18)
Not very	2 (7)	14 (9)

$\chi^2=9.386$ df$=2$ p$<.01$

In referring to responses dealing with contraception and sexual activity, the remaining task is to determine the degree to which St. Lucian Catholics reflect more closely the moral sentiments of their Church.

When asked the question, "If you knew of a very easy way to keep from having babies, which did not stop you from having a good time (sport), do you think you might use it?" of the 63 Catholic girls who answered either "yes" or no," twice as many answered in the affirmative as in the negative. Significant differences appeared in the responses of the St. Lucian Catholics and the Grenadian Catholics. The St. Lucian Catholics were less inclined to

Q. 27. If you knew of a very easy way to keep from having babies, which did not stop you from having a good time (sport), do you think you might use it?

	St. Lucia Catholics	Grenada Catholics
Yes	15 (20)	29 (24)
No	13 (8)	6 (11)

$\chi^2=6.345$ df$=1$ p$<.02$

make use of an easy way of preventing pregnancy. Among the Grenadian Catholics nearly five times as many girls said they would use it as said they would not. Among the St. Lucian Catholics, the number who said they would use it was about the same as the number who said they would not. Earlier, the point was made that the St. Lucian Catholics both attend church more regularly and consider themselves more religious. Their responses to this question are about in keeping with what we might expect to result from a commitment to Catholic moral precepts.

While the above data are fairly consistent, other data reveal that the difference between St. Lucian and Grenadian Catholics is not always in the direction of more conservative attitudes as shown by the St. Lucian women. For example, in reply to the question: "Doctors are making a pill which will keep you from having babies for a short time. These pills will not make you sick or permanently sterile. If doctors gave you these pills without their costing you anything, would you want to take them once in a while?" the St. Lucians were no more inclined than the Grenadians to accept or reject the use of such a device.

Q. 28. Doctors are making a pill which will keep you from having babies for a short time.. These pills will not make you sick or permanently sterile.. If doctors gave you these pills without their costing you anything, would you want to take them once in a while?

	St. Lucia Catholics	Grenada Catholics
Yes	10 (8)	8 (10)
No	10 (12)	18 (16)
Uncertain	9 (8)	10 (11)

$$\chi^2=1.823 \quad df=2 \quad p<.50$$

Furthermore, there was no significant difference between the two groups of Catholics with respect to their degree of uncertainty about the use of such a device.

In reply to the question: "When having sport with your lover, have you ever tried to keep from getting pregnant?" the Grenada Catholics were more inclined to indicate that they had attempted to avoid pregnancy than was the case for the St. Lucian Catholic. Out of 52 Catholics responding either "yes" or "no" to this item, 34 indicated utilizing some means of avoiding conception.

Q. 25. When having sport with your lover, have you ever tried to keep from getting pregnant?

	St. Lucia Catholics	Grenada Catholics
Yes	10 (15)	24 (19)
No	13 (8)	5 (10)

$$\chi^2=8.748 \quad df=1 \quad p<.01$$

Among the Grenadian Catholics, nearly five times as many said "yes" they tried to avoid pregnancy as said "no." Among the St. Lucian Catholics, the ratio of "yes" respondents to "no" respondents was slightly less than one-to-one. The difference between St. Lucian and Grenada Catholics to this item was statistically significant at the .01 level. The direction of the relationship is consistent with the presumed greater religious conservatism of the St. Lucian Catholics.

Having noted how the St. Lucian Catholics were more resistant to the idea of birth control, how did they respond to the question: "Do you think it is all right for a girl to have a baby before she is married?"

Q. 21. Do you think it is all right for a girl to have a baby before she is married?

	St. Lucia Catholics	Grenada Catholics
Yes	9 (6)	4 (7)
No	19 (22)	31 (28)

$$\chi^2 = 4.068 \quad df = 1 \quad p < .05$$

From the above table, the St. Lucian Catholic girls gave responses consistent with their attitudes toward birth control. Although 50 out of the 63 Catholics responding to this question said "no" it is not all right, the St. Lucian Catholics were significantly less inclined to answer in the negative. Only twice as many St. Lucians said "no" to this question. This difference was tested statistically and found to be significant at the .05 level, hence the conclusion: negative attitudes toward birth control have a tendency to support acceptance of childbirth outside of wedlock within a Catholic population.

Although a significant difference was found between the St. Lucian and Grenadian Catholics on issues of birth control and the propriety of having children out of wedlock, I could find no significant differences between these two groups with respect to having sexual relationships prior to marriage. Out of the 63 Catholic girls responding to the question: "Do you think it is all right for a girl to have experience (sport) before she is married?" 47 said

Q. 26. Do you think it is all right for a girl to have experience (sport) before she is married?

	St. Lucia Catholics	Grenada Catholics
All right	21 (20)	26 (27)
Not all right	6 (7)	10 (9)

$$\chi^2 = 0.250 \quad df = 1 \quad p < .70$$

they thought it was "all right." Slightly over three times as many St. Lucians thought this was "all right" as thought it was "not all right." The difference between the two groups replying to this question is not statistically significant, hence the conclusion: the differences that exist between these groups fall in the province of birth control and the having of children outside of wedlock; not to sexual activity itself.

Conclusions

From the foregoing analysis, in combination with material appearing elsewhere in this book, the following conclusions seem in order:

First, in spite of the limitations of the sample, the responses were consistent with conclusions derived from case materials, cultural soliloquies, and open-ended interviews gathered in the two islands.

Second, my insistence that the Islands are composed of internally diverse island peoples and that we are in the presence of cultural pluralism is documented here.

Third, the rural-urban dichotomy is fundamental in the ordering-up of self-images, including religious values, educational aspirations, and conjugal and reproductive expectations. Urban girls are not ready to succumb to the purported influences of industrialization or city life upon fertility practices, i.e., they are not going to lower their birth rates at a greater pace than rural girls.

Fourth, the assertion that the "West Indians do not take their institutions seriously," is more true than false. Catholic churches and schools in particular appear to have failed in exercising sweeping controls over extra-marital sex relations and the use of contraceptives. The degree of effectiveness of these controls is relative to place, however.

Fifth, West Indian adolescent girls revere the institution of marriage. But by reason of the barriers placed in front of these aspirations, particularly the low marriage aspirations of men, they justify extra-marital sex relations on these grounds. Consensual unions are felt by many to be prerequisites to legal marriage. But they prefer to postpone having their families until legally wed. Virginity is not essential for marriage; in fact it can act as a deterrent.

Sixth, the mothers of tomorrow will prefer fewer children than the mothers of today. Contrary to findings in the United States,[14] those who are emotionally and rationally identified with large families are not expecting a relatively large number of offspring of their own.

Seventh, most adolescent girls in the sample practice some kind of contraception.

---

[14] Kiser, E. and Whelpton, P., *The Indianapolis Study of Social and Psychological Factors Affecting Fertility*. A Study conducted in 1941 under the sponsorship of the Milbank Memorial Fund; George K. Tokuhata, "Behavioral Factors Affecting Fertility Expectations: Introduction to Behavioral Demography", Doctoral dissertation, 1956, *State University of Iowa*.

Eighth, family planners concerned with finding the most responsive locus for fertility control, should concentrate their efforts on those communities and social groups that cultivate the following type of adolescent girl:

a. A girl of Grenadian residence. She will be more cooperative but may have found satisfactory control techniques, thus have less need for advice. A St. Lucian girl could best use the help but will be less cooperative.
b. A girl who is average-to-not-very religious, the faith itself not being too important, particularly in Grenada.
c. A girl who feels that she had "about right" number or "too many" siblings. Size of family or orientation is not important.
d. A girl of rural residence.

Chapter VIII

What It All Means:
Countervailance and Social Action

We turn now to the more positive task of integrating the several dimensions of the West Indies population problem. I should like to approach this objective by raising the level of inquiry to a different plane: designing for planning. With theoretical research oriented to *cause*, and practical research to *purpose*, my task becomes one of moving from the former into the latter. And my position is: given the conclusion that the present way of life in the Islands is leading the people to their own self-destruction, the scientist faces responsibility of showing the populace how they might best modify their norms and values in such a way that internal strife or outright social disintegration may be avoided.

PLANNING FOR COUNTERVAILANCE

The West Indian population problem is neither a single problem, an isolated problem, nor a static problem. It carries complex and intertwining characteristics. The variations in material conditions of existence, in ideas, attitudes, and values are all involved. In addition, the "population problem" is a general over-all term intended to include phases of a large number of specific problems—privacy, poverty, leisure time, illegitimacy, education, housing, and diet. The list is endless. With these various components of the population problem so interdependent, the solution of one is conditional on the solution of others. In addition, these solutions are likely dependent on the solution of problems which may seem to be rather remote in both physical and social space from the population problem itself. For this reason, one encounters specialists from many fields trying to cope with the increased numbers of people. Yet the mere giving away of contraceptives, the building of more and better houses and schools, the enticing of more industry into the Islands will not solve the population predicament. It would still be necessary to grapple with the concept of good living of which population growth is only one part. This involves attention to public services such as recreation, cultural opportunities, aesthetic values, and other needs and desirable ends with which population planning must be coordinated.

Now I do not propose that the theory of countervailing power is complete in the sense of supplying full theoretical explanation or constituting a final plan of action to the problem enumerated above. The light that an incomplete theory can shed always depends on the extent to which it contains

159

or leads to important propositions that have empirical practical value. To ascertain whether the proposal about to be presented here from the theory requires further efforts of both theoretical and empirical nature must be left to my colleagues. But I have seen how the rise of the scientific method and of technology have resulted in complex changes in the West Indies, not only in lowering the death rate but in supplying somewhat better health, better transportation and more efficient ways of working the soil. Yet this is not to imply that counter forces have not been at work to arrest, rearrange, deflect, and corrupt their operation. There is particular conflict between current group practices and habits originating in the pre-scientific and pre-technological age, and new forces generated by science and technology. I would draw attention to the fact that within the hum-drum routines of life do we find the very locus for the liberation of intellectual, aesthetic and companionship values. That is, the transfer of the burden of material production from human muscles and brain to steam, electricity and chemical processes now makes possible the effective actualization of this potential. Needs, wants and desires are always the moving forces in generating creative action. And new mechanical forces of production become the means of emancipation from the apathy which attends West Indian socio-economic organization. But up to the present time, new technology has intensified a reversal of the true relation between means and ends, compounding apathy and strife. Yet its termination cannot be effected by preaching to people that they should place incorporeal ends above material means and satisfactions. To bring births, deaths and wealth into a satisfying relationship requires that ideas be organized, and this organization implies a group of individuals who hold these ideas and whose faith is ready to translate itself into action. And translation into action signifies that a general creed of liberalism be formulated as a concrete program of action. *Thus to alter a demographic situation means to educate in the broader sense of the term—a task not to be accomplished merely by working upon men's minds.* An action program must embrace actual change in institutions, associations and conventions. The idea that dispositions and attitudes can be altered by merely "moral" means conceived of as something that goes on wholly inside the person is itself one of the old patterns that has to be changed. *Thought, desire and purpose exist in a constant give and take of interaction with environing conditions.* Resolute thought, however, is the first step in that change of action that will itself breed the needed change in patterns of mind and character.

Succinctly put, the seeds of liberalism must germinate into radicalism, meaning by "radical" a perception of the necessity of thorough-going changes in the structure of communities, institutions and life organizations to bring quick changes to pass. For the gulf between what the actual situation makes possible and the actual state itself, is so great in the Islands that it cannot be bridged by piecemeal policies undertaken *ad hoc*. "Reforms" that deal now with this abuse and now with that, without having a social goal based upon an inclusive plan, differ entirely from effort at re-forming, in its literal sense, the associational scheme of things. While I recognize that the process of producing changes in the social ethos will be, in any case, a gradual one, the tempo can be heightened with skilled effort, and is superior to improvization. The job is to make new routines a vital part of life perspectives as soon as possible.

Because the West Indian masses make no distinction between freedom and *laissez-faire*, the planner must formulate his program on this knowledge. His problem consists in the creation of free zones within the planned structure: freedom of movement, of expression, of opinion, of association. These are special obligations which must be met in a planful society. Throughout a planned society is the necessity of guaranteeing the maintenance of the individual capacity for adjustment, this serving to preserve vitality and strengthen initiative. Socialized procreation dictated from above will obviously not work. So long as West Indians retain the private system of human procreation and economic effort, any family planning program must be designed so as not to interfere unduly with that system.

This society need not be anarchically one in which a great minority is breeding itself into ever poorer health; nor need it become a nation bursting with health but at the same time bursting with revolutionary resentment against a body of state doctors and functionaries manhandling everybody with remedial medicines, contraceptives and housing assignments. I am only saying that in every field of individual and social life one encounters regulations on morals, marriage, divorce, duty to family, religion, property, theft, libel, slander, contract, business—the list is long. These controls do not come out of the blue, produced without careful reflection and weighing of choices. Human societies gradually develop general principles of action to which they subordinate certain values in order that they might better organize their lives. West Indians have had, by and large, comparatively little interest in population policies because population growth and change, like other social changes, were supposed to work out to the greatest welfare of the community if no effort were made at public control, i.e., if a *laissez-faire* policy were followed. As a result, the growth of population has been almost incidental, a by-product, of the social, economic and scientific development of this era in this region. And because it has continued for so long and has been accompanied by increasing welfare measures, population growth has come

161

to be regarded as natural, and talk of population policy is looked upon as something new and perhaps dangerous. With the emerging knowledge that the pursuit of individual interests is not promoting automatically the general welfare, this is the opportune moment to press for a population policy geared to the distant horizon of non-economic, non-material needs and their satisfactions. Recognizing that a depressed country must first survive before it can seek higher values, nevertheless the course of social organization in the Islands during the next two generations requires a change in prevailing moral philosophy. The burden rests, at the outset, on individuals in position of power and decision-making.

A Sound Public Policy

In emergency or "crash" fertility planning, the West Indies is faced, unfortunately, with making action designs without a model. We know how old formulas, such as out-migration, increased schooling, more contraceptive-dispensing clinics, more tourism, have proved ineffective. To compound this failure, the people have no important ancient skills inherited from earlier times and they have acquired very few new skills since slavery. Only the more privileged brown people are attempting to acquire the tastes and standards necessary for a high standard of living. Thanks to recent years of social reform, gratuitous education, improvement in communication within and between islands (including exposure to Hollywood motion pictures), the colored (brown) population is showing increasing restlessness to improve the lot of the Islands. Some might say that "given the time," the values for self-improvement found among these people will soon trickle downward and permeate the values of the less advantaged black people. But the "take-it-slow" formula will not meet the crisis of high fertility and low mortality. The task is clear: to bring the Islands, within a generation, closer to the standard of living of the industrial states of the West. "Priming the pump" through economic tinkering is not enough. Population control comes first. And it must be tied to informal education, by reason of its diffusing qualities insofar as other life activities are concerned. Indeed, the area needs many things: more industry and capital, more exports, more everything except babies.

Hungry, poor and illiterate West Indians need to be approached with a clear statement of a "creed of democracy"—a creed reflected in a fertility-control movement that they can understand and through which they can see hope for the satisfaction of basic needs and the fulfillment of fresh aspirations. To accomplish such an objective requires a back-door approach—

moving with the social tide and not through imposing a creed from the top-down. At base, it must be a grass-roots approach, the masses making their own compromises, resolving their own conflicts. The planning effort should be aimed at those communities expressing interest in reducing family size. To appeal to these people in terms of the "national interest" is all too remote and vague to arouse cooperative response. The male's sexual authority will prove to be the most important barrier to the program. For a concubine or wife is first and last sexual property. And a girl's fear of spinsterhood and childlessness, in the presence of a possessive male, is a formidable block to any secret use of contraceptives. For this reason latent competing interests with those of sex and fertility must be brought forward with ingenuity by the decision-makers.

A crash fertility control program is proposed in which spokesmen for public rights will plant the initiative. The primary reason for state involvement in fertility control is that the individual West Indian will never carry it out of his or her own initiative. While the man of the street is unschooled on the obligations of the socialized self, he does have dignity and is unwilling to sacrifice it. He wants recognition among his peers. He wants to be a local somebody; to be a non-entity is to be non-human. In the past, the opportunity for recognition was confined by the limits of the plantation and local community to which the individual belonged. The crude artisan gained recognition by his humble skill, the servant by his value to his master. But beyond that of being a faithful servant and an artisan he was nothing. The barriers were political and racial. Honoring this dignity, the task of governmental leaders is to identify the objectives, spell out the logic, and strategically encourage the populace to fill in the details of means-to-ends. The woman concerned about unwanted children, should have complete control of whatever technique she would employ. So long as sex and fertility remain such master ego-reinforcing agents they will most assuredly destroy any family planning program that is interpreted by the public as a transparent trick aimed at belittling its reproduction values.

Birth Control Compensation—The Catalytic Agent

The West Indies needs persistent experimentation, enthusiasm, imagination, and ability to face population facts bravely. The fertility problem must be corrected by drastic means because the several millions who are in want, by viewing the prosperity in other nations, will not forever stand by indifferently while the things to satisfy their felt-needs are within reach. The development of special measures conducive to fertility reduction at a high qualitative level is needed. Because reproduction is definitely a private matter, it is important that conditions affecting attitudes toward childbearing be such that the most capable and well-adjusted persons will tend to prefer families that are, on the average, smaller than those of their parents. The special measures must contribute to the release of opportunity for better health, education and the development of prized institutions. But the inducement must not be discriminatory, being available to groups with superior opportunities for physical, material and intellectual development, yet equally available to less privileged groups.

The procedure is to reverse completely the European experiment of a generation ago wherein endowments for high fertility met with some success. I say "some" because once the idea of birth control had been seized by Europeans, the birth rates continued downward in many districts despite inducements to thwart it. Ungern-Sternberg[1] in 1931 commented that the example of Vienna proved how little could be done to check the falling birth rate, for there, in spite of an ample supply of cheap lodging and an extensive public child-welfare program, the birth control movement was too well entrenched, the consequence of prior indirect and pervasive efforts to redefine life goals.

Given endowments, preferably in the form of cash subsidies to productive-age women, varying in inverse proportion to number of children born to them, West Indian females can employ their own techniques of control and use their annual payments to pursue previously unrealizable goals. Obviously, payments proportional to income would accomplish nothing, and might even increase the fertility rate. Upon seeing how monetary inducements further their personal interests (other than prolific reproduction) these women may become the charter member educators for family planning in the succeeding generation. The monetary plan can thus be stopped when the norms for fertility control become self-generating. The mores on reproduction will be placed in competition with other values such as learning trades, personal adornment, travel, and housing, all this without officious encouragement from the state, but largely as a matter of unconscious drift toward a new standard. New mores can arise, and with them new practices, without the exercise of undemocratic state policies. The power of birth control compensation rests in the fact that it does not defy private interest in the determination of family size because it is voluntary and yet meets the ends of public policy. Furthermore, it does not insult the

---

[1] Roderich von Ungern-Sternberg, *The Causes of the Decline in Birth Rate Within the European Sphere of Civilization,* translated by Hilda H. Wullen, (Cold Spring Harbor, New York: Eugenics Research Association, 1931), p. 103.

views of Roman Catholicism because there is no coercion for the use of artificial contraception. It cannot be dubbed a "moral evil" or an effort to promote any particular technique of fertility control.[2]

No outside nation should alone underwrite the program (supply the grants). It should be sponsored by an international body such as the Organization of American States, the United Nations, or failing those, by international financing agencies. Support might be had from philanthropic agencies, private gifts or a combination of all of these.

Many demographers believe that the differential birth rate will correct itself in large part through the gradual diffusion of upper or middle class family limitation practices to the lower classes. But the urgency of the problem does not permit this chance possibility. And if the decision-makers yielded to this formula, a catalyst such as birth control compensation would still be necessary to generate the "trickle-down" process for quick success.

For some female cohorts, an economic inducement will prove insufficient for the voluntary reduction of their reproductive rates. And others will already have accepted the family planning ideal, leaping at the compensation program because it is "free." However, these folk unwittingly become the agitators for the plan—self-appointed spokesmen for "easy income." Still other females will respond in secret by reason of fear of sanctions from their men. While soon exposed, they can draw their men into some cooperation by the strategy of sharing the subsidies. Thus birth control compensation can serve as the accelerator of both money and fertility control incentives.[3] And, as stated, it has a point of termination: when individual control incentives become group incentives thus a respected mos. It is offered, therefore, as a short-run experiment. If it fails, admit it and seek another plan. But I doubt that it will fail because it is compatible with so many incentives of West Indians: (a) the love of money gained with modest effort, (b) the desire for public attention through display of material things, such as bicycles, costume jewelry, and new clothes, (c) the desire to raise healthy children.

Please be mindful that birth control compensation serves only as the detonator for the reorganization of fertility values. After all, birth rates have many causes, causes inherent in socio-economic group patterns in which the family functions. While a change in fertility mores is essential to a surviving

---

[2] Assuming for the moment, that the Catholic Church found reason to reject birth control compensation, the islands of St. Vincent (Methodist) and Barbados (Anglican) would be the recommended territories to launch the plan.

[3] See the proposal by Stephen Enke, "The Gains to India from Population Control: Some Money Measures and Incentive Schemes", *The Review of Economics and Statistics*, (May, 1960) 175-181.

democratic West Indies, it cannot be altered by fiat but by a more indirect and powerful ferment of hidden or secondary values.

The plan can strengthen the marriage institution, making inroads into illegitimacy and desertion through supplying otherwise promiscuous girls with the material means for the acquisition of attention-getting symbols necessary for marriage. A young lady with a compensation check would be a preferred spouse. And upon entering motherhood she could better meet the problems of housing space, expense of obstetrical care and a sustaining standard of living. She would discover that family planning permitted the continuation of those contacts and privileges enjoyed prior to having children, e.g., greater freedom of mobility, greater freedom of participation in many kinds of social and play activities.

A sound public policy would encourage all groups, religious as well as civic and professional, to proffer their own prescribed techniques for family limitation. While some techniques will not be as effective as others, the state must not interfere, leaving the matter entirely in the hands of private sources. For only in this way can the over-all program invite support from those who guard the prevailing fertility values. The state, through its maternity clinics and hospitals can make birth control information and contraceptives available, but the response must be voluntary. Anxieties and tensions must be kept to the minimum within persons, small groups and institutions.

Subsidies in cash at fixed rates will provide greatest inducement, relatively, where levels of living are lowest. These allowances will raise income available for personal expenditures of women (and husbands, if present) with the fewest children at the lowest wage levels above that of women with many children. The temptation will be great to subsidize the large families, thereby making the entire plan abort. A fixed-rate system has the advantage of providing economic aid and raising consumption levels for those women and children who are in considerable need thus improving the quality-potential (through increased health and educational opportunities) of the offspring. Naturally the fixed-rate plan does little to relieve the economic strain experienced by parents of larger families among the higher-earning clerical, business and professional groups, whose standards are set up by their own experience and the expenditure patterns of their associates. Nevertheless the formula must not be sabotaged by those who would turn it into an aid-the-needy program.

The principle of subsidy in cash to women does not make direct provision for the basic needs of dependent children at a standard which is generally acceptable to the community. To the contrary, it is aimed at those persons who would nurture those prestigeful symbols other than those which spring from childbirth. The intent of birth control compensation is not to improve child welfare directly, although it represents an indirect expression of public interest in parenthood and child life. I fully believe that the program should be an expression of public policy for responsible parenthood. And participants in the subsidy plan can be reminded constantly of opportunities to invest their payments in improved housing, in better child care through seeking medical aid and providing nutritious lunches for school-age children. In this way education is made to tie-in with experience. After all, the means for a democratic population policy must include both educational influences and socio-economic reforms. I have said how sheer moralization and exhortations of duty to nation and family are futile. Psychological attitudes may be changed somewhat by formal education on matters parental and familial. But without informal education no reforms will be supported; without socio-economic reforms educational sermons on the value of small families are a waste of breath.

The English social philosopher, John Stuart Mill, a hundred years ago, in his classic plea for individual freedom, *On Liberty*, outlined the West Indian challenge when he wrote:

". . . And in a country either overpeopled, or threatened with being so, to produce children, beyond a very small number, with the effect of reducing the reward of labor by their competition, is a serious offense against all who live by the remuneration of their labor. . ."

Appendix

TABLE A1
WEST INDIES FEDERATION

Year	Population	Births	Deaths	Excess of Births	Population Change from Previous Year	Inflow	Outflow	Natural Growth
1932	1,967,845	61,928	33,288	28,640	....	....	....	....
1933	2,001,840	64,352	37,411	26,941	33,995	7,054	....	1,996,485
1934	2,032,540	62,929	35,534	27,395	30,700	3,305	....	2,023,426
1935	2,064,411	67,519	35,945	31,574	31,871	297	....	2,050,821
1936	2,097,152	68,926	36,029	23,897	32,741	....	156	2,082,395
1937	2,125,176	67,220	34,530	32,690	28,024	....	4,666	2,115,292
1938	2,159,694	70,065	35,926	34,139	34,518	379	....	2,147,982
1939	2,195,520	69,405	34,576	34,829	35,826	947	....	2,182,121
1940	2,235,983	70,511	34,866	35,645	40,463	4,818	....	2,216,950
1941	2,283,070	72,252	35,325	36,927	47,087	10,160	....	2,252,595
1942	2,356,074	74,992	36,327	38,665	73,004	34,339	....	2,289,522
1943	2,363,333	77,399	35,364	42,035	7,259	....	34,876	2,328,587
1944	2,397,592	80,813	36,490	44,323	34,259	....	10,064	2,370,222
1945	2,429,654	78,391	35,656	43,735	32,062	....	11,673	2,414,545
1946	2,462,971	80,772	34,469	46,303	−(2,683)	....	48,986	2,458,280
1947	2,483,411	85,509	35,828	49,683	56,440	6,757	....	2,504,583
1948	2,531,087	85,105	34,208	50,897	47,676	....	3,221	2,554,266
1949	2,574,000	87,567	32,558	55,009	42,913	....	12,096	2,605,163
1950	2,632,000	90,903	32,706	58,197	58,000	....	197	2,660,172
1951	2,691,000	94,117	34,153	59,964	59,000	....	964	2,718,369
1952	2,747,000	94,316	34,019	60,297	56,000	....	4,297	2,778,333
1953	2,803,000	99,894	30,416	69,478	56,000	....	13,478	2,838,530
1954	2,870,000	107,138	30,750	76,388	67,000	....	9,388	2,908,108
1955	2,934,000	112,402	31,262	81,140	64,000	....	17,140	2,984,496
1956								3,065,636

TABLE A2

MALES PER 1000 FEMALES, JAMAICA, BARBADOS, LEEWARD ISLANDS, TRINIDAD-TOBAGO, WINDWARD ISLANDS, AND U.S.A.

Area		Under 5	5-9	10-14	15-19	20-24	25-29	30-34	35-39
Jamaica[a]	Males	78,300	78,225	70,340	55,060	53,386	49,925	46,017	39,357
	Females	78,065	77,854	69,502	60,968	62,150	57,103	47,875	40,963
	Sex Ratio	1005	1005	1012	903	859	872	962	961
Barbados[b]	Males	11,297	10,695	9,578	8,751	7,079	6,494	6,416	6,562
	Females	11,580	10,943	9,926	9,551	8,227	7,863	7,902	7,954
	Sex Ratio	976	977	965	916	860	826	812	825
Leeward Islands[b]	Males	7,549	6,557	6,212	4,990	4,483	3,794	3,508	3,244
	Females	7,794	6,692	6,121	5,381	4,890	4,496	4,215	4,058
	Sex Ratio	969	980	1015	927	917	844	832	799
Trinidad-Tobago[b]	Males	41,715	34,202	27,321	23,407	25,096	23,356	21,120	19,148
	Females	41,177	33,913	26,687	25,752	26,150	23,119	20,409	18,528
	Sex Ratio	1013	1008	1024	909	960	1010	1035	1033
Windward Islands[b]	Males	17,979	18,121	16,557	12,541	9,475	7,500	6,118	5,684
	Females	18,032	17,563	16,004	13,445	11,775	10,005	8,069	7,818
	Sex Ratio	997	1032	1034	933	805	750	758	727
U.S.A.[c]	Males	8,236,164	6,714,555	5,660,399	5,311,342	5,606,293	5,972,078	5,624,723	5,517,544
	Females	7,927,407	6,485,130	5,458,869	5,305,256	5,875,535	6,270,182	5,892,284	5,728,842
	Sex Ratio	1039	1035	1037	1001	954	952	955	963

Area		40-44	45-49	50-54	55-59	60-64	65-74	75-84	85-and over
Jamaica[a]	Males	34,671	24,697	19,588	13,534	13,451	14,408	5,819	1,233
	Females	34,623	25,296	22,456	15,732	15,893	18,229	9,004	2,403
	Sex Ratio	1001	976	872	860	846	790	646	513
Barbados[b]	Males	5,438	3,959	2,723	1,689	1,493	2,474	937	136
	Females	6,716	5,994	4,639	3,866	3,369	5,610	2,447	485
	Sex Ratio	810	660	587	437	443	441	383	280
Leeward Islands[b]	Males	2,364	1,675	1,241	984	908	1,187	547	101
	Females	3,246	2,687	2,199	1,833	1,823	2,491	1,218	292
	Sex Ratio	728	623	564	537	498	477	449	346
Trinidad-Tobago[b]	Males	16,031	13,381	9,383	7,542	6,427	8,339	2,187	470
	Females	14,714	12,195	8,848	6,873	5,921	9,835	2,920	803
	Sex Ratio	1089	1097	1060	1097	1085	848	749	585
Windward Islands[b]	Males	4,788	4,209	3,188	2,463	2,231	2,747	1,222	326
	Females	6,676	6,253	4,999	4,093	3,726	4,781	2,386	763
	Sex Ratio	717	673	638	602	598	575	512	427
U.S.A.[c]	Males	5,070,269	4,526,366	4,128,648	3,630,046	3,037,838	4,053,390	1,506,756	236,828
	Females	5,133,704	4,544,099	4,143,540	3,605,074	3,021,637	4,361,495	1,770,995	340,073
	Sex Ratio	988	996	996	1007	1005	929	851	696

[a] Census of Jamaica, 1943, pp. 28-30.
[b] West Indian Census, 1946, Part A, Table 3, p. 93.
[c] United States Census of Population, 1950, Vol. II, Part 1, Table 38, p. 190.

TABLE A3

FERTILITY EXPECTATIONS, GRENADA AND ST. LUCIA, 1959

Schedule	How many children have you given birth to?	If you could have as many children as you wanted, how many children would you have?	How old are you?	Are you expecting a baby?			Do you feel like you had too few brothers and sisters, about right, or too many?			Have you ever been married?		Do some girls let their babies die because they don't want them?		
	1	2	3	4			5			6		7		
	(Totals)	(Mean Number)	(Mean Age)	Yes	No	Other	Too few	About Right	Too Many	Yes	No	Yes	No	Don't Know
Responses														
Grand Total (100)	23	3.20	17.85	5	93	2	20	58	22	5	95	51	45	4
Grenada (71)	21			2	67	2	10	41	20	4	67	36	33	2
St. Georges (35)	6	3.81	18.83	1	34	1	8	24	3	2	33	11	22	2
Perdmontemps (26)	10	2.46	17.77	1	24	1	1	11	14	2	24	19	7	0
Wobourn (10)	5	3.00	17.50	0	10	0	1	6	3	0	10	6	4	0
St. Lucia (all Catholics) (29)	2			3	26	0	10	17	2	1	28	15	12	2
Castries (17)	0	3.35	18.47	1	16	0	6	9	2	0	17	10	6	1
Ciceron (6)	1	3.33	15.67	1	5	0	3	3	0	0	6	3	2	1
Labayee (6)	1	2.83	16.83	1	5	0	1	5	0	1	5	2	4	0
Urban (52)	6			2	49	1	14	33	5	2	50	21	28	3
Rural (48)	17			3	44	1	6	25	17	3	45	30	17	1
Roman Catholic (65)	15			3	61	1	16	40	9	3	62	34	29	2
Catholic (Grenada) (36)	13			0	35	1	6	23	7	2	24	19	17	0
Non-Catholic (35)	8			2	32	1	4	18	13	2	33	17	16	2
Methodist and Presbyterian (16)	5			0	16	0	3	10	3	2	14	7	9	0
Anglican (9)	0			1	8	0	1	4	4	0	9	2	6	1
Plymouth Brethern and Gospel Hall (7)	2			0	7	0	0	2	5	0	7	5	1	1

Fertility Expectations, Grenada and St. Lucia, 1959 (Continued)

Schedule	Would you like to get married right away, or would you prefer to wait until you are a little older?		What is the best age for a girl to get married?	What is the best age for a boy to get married?	How do you think most men feel about getting married?					What do you think is the right age for a girl to have her first baby?	Are you making money now?		Do you think that most girls want to be married?	
	8		9	10	11					12	13		14	
	Marry Now	Wait	Mean Age	Mean Age	Very Anxious	Somewhat Anxious	Not very Anxious	Avoid It	Other	Mean Age	Yes	No	Yes	No
Responses														
Grand Total (100)	21	79	21.8	24.7	1	7	64	24	4	21.2	54	46	92	8
Grenada (71)	16	55			0	4	49	17	1		43	28	69	2
St. Georges (35)	7	28	22.3	25.1	0	4	18	12	1	21.8	31	4	33	2
Perdmontemps (26)	5	21	21.9	24.5	0	0	21	5	0	21.7	9	17	26	0
Wobourn (10)	4	6	22.8	25.0	0	0	10	0		23.5	3	7	10	0
St. Lucia (all Catholics) (29)	5	24			1	3	16	7	3		11	8	23	6
Castries (17)	3	14	20.6	24.1	1	2	7	6	1	20.6	8	9	14	3
Ciceron (6)	1	5	15.3	21.0	0	0	5	0	1	16.2	1	5	4	2
Labayee (6)	1	5	19.7	23.2	0	1	3	1	1	19.3	2	4	5	1
Urban (52)	10	42			1	6	25	18	2		39	13	47	5
Rural (48)	11	37			0	1	39	6	2		15	33	45	3
Roman Catholic (65)	12	53			1	5	39	16	4		32	33	58	7
Catholic (Grenada) (36)	7	29			0	2	24	9	1		21	15	35	1
Non-Catholic (35)	9	26			0	2	25	8			22	13	34	1
Methodist and Presbyterian (16)	6	10			1	12	3				10	6	16	0
Anglican (9)	1	8			1	5	3				7	2	8	1
Plymouth Brethren and Gospel Hall (7)	1	6			6	1					6	1	7	0

FERTILITY EXPECTATIONS, GRENADA AND ST. LUCIA, 1959 (Continued)

Schedule	Tell me where your babies were born.			Do you think that it is better for babies to be born in the hospital or the mother's home?		Do you think that it is all right for unmarried women to have more children than married women?			Do you think unmarried mothers take better care of their babies than married mothers?			How often do you attend church?		
	15			16		17			18			19		
	Hospital	Home	No Children	Hospital	Home	All right	Not All right	Doesn't Know	Yes	No	Uncertain	Once or More a Week	Almost Once a Week	Almost Never
Responses														
Grand Total (100)	16	5	78	90	10	0	96	4	13	83	3	34	47	19
Grenada (71)	13	5	52	62	9	0	70	1	6	64	1	16	38	17
St. Georges (35)	3	1	31	26	9	0	35	0	5	29	1	10	20	5
Perdmontemps (26)	8	2	16	26	0	0	26	0	1	25	0	2	14	10
Wobourn (10)	2	3	5	10	0	0	9	1	0	10	0	4	4	2
St. Lucia (all Catholics) (29)	2	0	27	28	1	0	26	3	7	20	2	18	9	2
Castries (17)	0	0	17	16	1	0	15	2	4	12	1	9	7	1
Ciceron (6)	1	0	5	6	0	0	5	1	2	3	1	4	1	1
Labayee (6)	1	0	5	6	0	0	6	0	1	5	0	5	1	0
Urban (52)	3	1	48	42	10	0	50	2	9	41	2	19	27	6
Rural (48)	13	4	30	48	0	0	46	2	4	43	1	15	20	13
Roman Catholic (65)	12	2	50	61	4	0	62	3	10	52	3	27	26	12
Catholic (Grenada) (36)	10	2	24	33	3	0	36	0	3	32	1	9	17	10
Non-Catholic (35)	3	3	28	29	6	0	34	1	3	32	0	7	21	7
Methodist and Presbyterian (16)	2	3	11	12	4	0	15	1	1	15	0	5	9	3
Anglican (9)	0	0	9	7	2	0	9	0	0	9	0	1	8	0
Plymouth Brethren and Gospel Hall (7)	1	1	5	7	0	0	7	0	1	6	0	0	3	4

FERTILITY EXPECTATIONS, GRENADA AND ST. LUCIA, 1959 (Continued)

Schedule	How long did you go to school? 20		Do you think that it is all right for a girl to have a baby before she is married? 21			Do you think a girl should have a baby as early in life as possible, or do you think she should wait awhile? 22			If you could, would you like to live in the city? 23		Are you very religious, just average, or not very religious? 24		
	Primary	Secondary	All right	Not All right	Uncertain	Soon as Possible	Wait	Don't Know	Yes	No	Very Religious	Average	Not Very
Responses													
Grand Total (100)	56	44	20	78	2	15	83	2	54	46	20	55	25
Grenada (71)	42	29	11	59	1	8	62	1	39	32	10	38	23
St. Georges (35)	10	25	2	32	1	6	28	1	23	12	4	26	5
Perdmontemps (26)	25	1	4	22	0	1	25	0	12	14	2	8	16
Wobourn (10)	7	3	5	5	0	1	9	0	4	6	4	4	2
St. Lucia (all Catholics) (29)	15	15	9	19	1	7	21	1	15	14	10	17	2
Castries (17)	6	11	4	12	1	4	13	0	8	9	2	13	2
Ciceron (6)	4	2	4	2	0	1	5	0	3	3	3	3	0
Labayee (6)	4	2	1	5	0	2	3	1	4	2	5	1	0
Urban (52)	16	36	6	44	2	10	41	1	31	21	6	39	7
Rural (48)	40	8	14	34	0	5	42	1	23	25	14	16	18
Roman Catholic (65)	41	24	13	50	2	10	53	2	36	29	16	33	16
Catholic (Grenada) (36)	27	9	4	31	1	3	32	1	21	15	6	16	14
Non-Catholic (35)	15	20	7	28	0	5	30	0	18	17	4	22	9
Methodist and Presbyterian (16)	5	11	4	12	0	3	13	0	6	10	3	10	3
Anglican (9)	3	6	1	8	0	1	8	0	5	4	0	9	0
Plymouth Brethren and Gospel Hall (7)	5	2	1	6	0	0	7	0	5	2	0	2	5

FERTILITY EXPECTATIONS, GRENADA AND ST. LUCIA, 1959 (Concluded)

Schedule	When having sport with your lover, have you ever taken steps to keep from getting pregnant?			Do you think it is all right for a girl to have experience (sport) before she is married?			If you knew of a very easy way to keep from having babies which did not stop you from having a good time (sport), do you think you might use it?			Doctors are making a pill which will keep you from having babies for a short time. Would you want to take them once in a while?		
	25			26			27			28		
Responses	Yes	No	Doesn't Apply	All right	Not All right	Uncertain	Yes	No	Uncertain	Yes	No	Uncertain
Grand Total (100)	58	23	19	66	32	2	71	26	3	61	23	16
Grenada (71)	48	10	13	45	26	0	56	13	2	51	13	7
St. Georges (35)	18	6	11	18	17	0	20	13	2	17	13	5
Perdmontemps (26)	25	1	0	22	4	0	26	0	0	26	0	0
Wobourn (10)	5	3	2	5	5	0	10	0	0	8	0	2
St. Lucia (all Catholics) (29)	10	13	6	21	6	2	15	13	1	10	10	9
Castries (17)	7	4	6	13	4	0	10	6	1	4	6	7
Ciceron (6)	1	5	0	5	1	0	3	3	0	3	2	1
Labayee (6)	2	4	0	3	1	2	2	4	0	3	2	1
Urban (52)	25	10	17	31	21	0	30	19	3	21	19	12
Rural (48)	33	13	2	35	11	2	41	7	0	40	4	4
Roman Catholic (65)	34	18	13	47	16	2	44	19	2	36	18	11
Catholic (Grenada) (36)	24	5	7	26	10	0	29	6	1	8	18	10
Non-Catholic (35)	24	5	6	19	16	0	27	7	1	25	5	5
Methodist and Presbyterian (16)	8	4	4	6	10	0	12	4	0	12	3	1
Anglican (9)	8	1	0	5	4	0	7	2	0	5	1	3
Plymouth Brethern and Gospel Hall (7)	6	0	1	6	1	0	5	1	1	6	1	0

Selected Bibliography

BOOKS

ALFORD, C. E. R., *The Island of Tobago, B.W.I.*, Dorchester, England: Longmans, 1949.

ARROW, KENNETH, J., *Social Choice and Individual Values*, New York: John Wiley & Sons, Inc., 1951.

BANFIELD, EDWARD C., *The Moral Basis of a Backward Society*, Glencoe, Illinois: The Free Press, 1958.

BEARD, J. S., *The Natural Vegetation of the Windward and Leeward Islands*, Oxford: Clarendon Press, 1949.

BEASLEY, C. G., *Fiscal Survey of Barbados*, Bridgetown, Barbados: Barbados Advocate Printery, 1952.

BECKWITH, MARTHA W., *Black Roadways: A Study of Folk Life in Jamaica*, Chapel Hill: University of North Carolina Press, 1929.

BENNS, F. L., *The American Struggle for the British West Indian Carrying Trade, 1815-30*. Bloomington: University of Indiana Press, 1923.

BERGER, MORROE, THEODORE ABEL AND CHARLES PAGE (eds.), *Freedom and Control in Modern Society*, New York: D. Van Nostrand Co., 1954.

BIERSTEDT, ROBERT, *The Social Order*, New York: McGraw-Hill Book Co., Inc., 1957.

BLAKE, JUDITH, *Family Instability and Reproductive Behavior in Jamaica*, New York: Milbank Memorial Fund, 1955.

BLANSHARD, PAUL, *Democracy and Empire in the Caribbean: A Contemporary View*, New York: Macmillan Co., 1947.

BROWN, W. J. *Jamaican Journey*, London: George Allen & Unwin Ltd., 1948.

BRYCE, WYATT (ed.), *Reference Book of Jamaica*, Kingston: Gleanor Co., 1946.

BURN, WILLIAM LAURENCE, *The British West Indies*, New York: Hutchinson House: Hutchinson's University Library, 1951.

BURNS, SIR ALAN CUTHHURT, *History of the British West Indies*, London: George Allen & Unwin, Ltd., 1954.

CARLSON, A. J. AND HEOLZEL F., *Overnutrition: Its Causes and Consequences*, Springfield, Illinois: Charles C. Thomas, 1950.

CARLSON, FRED A., *Geography of Latin America*, New York: Prentice Hall Inc., 1936.

CHANDRASEKHAR, S., *Population and Planned Parenthood in India*, George Allen & Unwin, Ltd., 1955.

CHAPMAN, ESTHER, *Pleasure Island, a Book of Jamaica*, Kingston: Arawak Press, 1952.

COALE, ANSLEY, *Population Growth and Economic Development in Low Income Countries*, Princeton: Princeton University Press, 1959.

CUNDALL, FRANK, *Bibliography of West Indies*, Kingston: Institute of Jamaica, 1909.

———. *Political and Social Disturbance in the West Indies*, Kingston: Institute of Jamaica, 1906.

CURTIN, PHILIP D., *Two Jamaicas—The Role of Ideas in a Tropical Colony, 1830-1865*, Cambridge: Harvard University Press, 1955.

DAVENPORT, C. B. and others, *Race Crossing in Jamaica*, Washington: Carnegie Institution of Washington, 1929.

DAVIS, KINGSLEY, *The Population of India and Pakistan*, Princeton: Princeton University Press, 1951.

DAVIS, WILLIAM MORRIS, *The Lesser Antilles*, New York: American Geographical Society of New York, 1926.

DEANE, PHYLLIS, *The Measurement of Colonial National Incomes*, Cambridge: Harvard University Press, 1948.

DE CASTRO, JOSUE, *The Geography of Hunger*, Boston: Little, Brown and Co., 1952.

DETOQUEVILLE, ALEXIS, *Democracy in America*, New York, 1897.

EATON, JOSEPH AND MAYER, A. J., *Man's Capacity to Reproduce: The Demography of a Unique Population*, Illinois: Glencoe Free Press, 1954.

FOX, ANNETTE B., *Freedom and Welfare in the Caribbean—A Colonial Dilemma*, New York: Harcourt, Brace, 1949.

FRANCIS, ROY G., *The Population Ahead*, Minneapolis: University of Minnesota Press, 1958.

FREEDMAN, RONALD, WHELPTON, P. K., AND CAMPBELL, A. A., *Family Planning, Sterility and Population Growth*, New York: McGraw-Hill Book Company, 1959.

GITTENS, G. L., *Why Birth Control? The Need for Planned Parenthood by the Family and the Island*, Barbados, Bridgetown: Advocate Co., 1954.

HAGOOD, MARGARET, *Mothers of the South*, Chapel Hill: University of North Carolina Press, 1939.

HALL, G. STANLEY, *Adolescence*, New York, 1904.

HARLOW, VINCENT T., *A History of Barbados, 1624-1685*, Oxford: Oxford University Press, 1926.

HATT, PAUL K. (ed.), *World Population and Future Resources*, New York: American Book Company, 1952.

HENRIQUES, FERNANDO, *Family and Colour in Jamaica*, London: Eyre and Spottiswoode, 1953.

———. *Jamaica, Land of Wood and Water*, London: Mac-Gilihon and Kee, 1957.

HENSHAW, PAUL S., *Adaptive Human Fertility*, New York: McGraw-Hill Book Company, Inc., 1955.

HERSKOVITZ, MELVILLE J., AND FRANCES, S., *Trinidad Village*, New York: Alfred Knopf, 1947.

HERTZLER, J. O., *The Crises in World Population*, Lincoln: University of Nebraska Press, 1956.

HOFSTRA, S., *Developments Toward Self-Government in the Caribbean*, Chicago: Quadrangle Books, Inc., 1956.

HOLTON, JOHN CAMDEN, *Biography of Barbados*, New York: G. A. Baker & Co., Inc., 1931.

HOMANS, GEORGE C., *The Human Group*, New York: Harcourt Brace & Co., 1950.

HOSELITZ, BERT F. (ed.)., *Economic Development and Cultural Change*, Chicago: University of Chicago Press, 1955.

ISAAC, JULIUS, *Economics of Migration*, London: K. Paul, Trench, Trubner & Company, 1947.

BIBLIOGRAPHY

JACOB, OSER, *Must Men Starve? The Malthusian Controversy,* New York: Abelard, Schuman, Ltd., 1957.

KEYS, A., *et al., Human Starvation,* Minneapolis, University of Minnesota Press, 1950.

KUCZYNSKI, ROBERT R., *Demographic Survey of the British Colonial Empire,* Vol. III, London: Oxford University Press, 1953.

LEIBENSTEIN, HARVEY, *A Theory of Economic-Demographic Development,* Princeton: Princeton University Press, 1954.

LORIMER, FRANK, *Culture and Human Fertility,* UNESCO publication, Zurich: Berichthaus, 1954.

———, WINSTON, E., AND KISER, L. K., and others, *Foundations of American Population Policy,* New York: Harper and Brothers Publishers, 1940.

LUCAS, C. P., *Historical Geography of the British Colonies* (Vol. II), Oxford: West Indies Clarendon Press, 1905.

MacIVER, R. M., *The More Perfect Union,* New York: The Macmillan Co., 1948.

MADDOX, JAMES G., *Technical Assistance by Religious Agencies in Latin America,* Chicago: University of Chicago Press, 1956.

MALINOWSKI, BRONISLAW, *The Sexual Life of Savages in Northwestern Melanesia,* London: Routledge, 1929.

———. *Argonauts of the Western Pacific,* London: Routledge, 1922.

MATTHEWS, DOM BASIL, *Crises of the West Indian Family,* Kingston, Jamaica: U.C.W.I., Extra-Mural Department of Caribbean Affairs Publication, 1954.

MERTON, ROBERT K., *Social Theory and Social Structure,* Glencoe, Illinois: Free Press, 1949.

MILL, JOHN STUART, *On Liberty,* London, 1859.

MOORE, WILBER E., *Industrialization and Labor,* Ithaca: Cornell University Press, 1951.

MOSHER, ARTHUR T., *Technical Cooperation in Latin American Agriculture,* Chicago: University of Chicago Press, 1957.

MYRDAL, GUNNAR, *An American Dilemma,* New York: Harper & Brothers, 1944.

OGBURN, WILLIAM F., ADAMS, J. L., AND S. C. GILFILLAN, *The Social Effects of Aviation,* New York: Houghton Mifflin Co., 1946.

OLDMIXON, JOHN, *The British Empire in America,* (Vol. II), London, 1741.

PARES, RICHARD, *War and Trade in West Indies,* Oxford: Clarendon Press, 1936.

PEARL, RAYMOND S., *The Biology of Population Growth,* New York: Alfred A. Knopf, 1925.

PERKINS, DEXTER, *The United States and the Caribbean,* Cambridge: Harvard University Press, 1947.

PITMAN, FRANK WESLEY, *Development of the B.W.I., 1700-1763,* New Haven: Yale University Press, 1917.

POYER, JOHN, *The History of Barbados,* London, 1808.

PROUDFOOT, MARY, *Britain and the U.S. in the Caribbean,* London: Faber and Faber, 1954.

RAGATZ, L. J., *A Guide for the Study of British Caribbean History, 1763-1834,* Washington: United States Government Printing Office, 1932.

REID, I. D., *The Negro Immigrant,* New York: Columbia University Press, 1939.

ROBERTS, GEORGE W., *The Population of Jamaica,* New York: Cambridge University Press, 1957.

Roberts, W. Adolphe, *Jamaica: The Portrait of an Island*, New York: Coward-McCann, 1955.

Sewell, W. G., *The Ordeal of Free Labour in B.W.I.*, New York: 1861.

Siegal, Sidney, *Nonparametric Statistics for the Behavioral Sciences*, New York: McGraw-Hill, 1956.

Shannon, Lyle W., *Underdeveloped Areas*, New York: Harper and Brothers Publishers, 1957.

Simpson, George and Yinger, J. Milton, *Racial and Cultural Minorities*, New York: Harper and Brothers, 1953.

Simon, Lord (of Wythenshawe), *Population and Resources of Barbados*, Didsbury, England: Bloomcraft, 1954.

Sims, N. L., *The Problem of Social Change*, New York: Crowell Publishing Co., 1939.

Smith, M. G., *A Framework for Caribbean Studies*, Jamaica: University College of the West Indies, 1955.

Spengler, Joseph J., and Duncan, Otis D., *Demographic Analysis*, Glencoe, Illinois: The Free Press, 1956.

———. *Population Theory and Policy*, Glencoe, Illinois: The Free Press, 1956.

Starkey, Otis P., *The Economic Geography of Barbados*, New York: Columbia University Press, 1939.

Steel, Robert Walter, *Geographical Essays of British Tropical Lands*, London: G. Philip & Son, 1956.

Steward, Julian H. (ed.), *Handbook of South American Indians*, Vol. 4, Washington: United States Government Printing Office, 1948.

Stonequist, Everett V., *The Marginal Man: A Study in Personality and Culture Conflict*, New York: Scribner's Sons, 1937.

Thome, James A., and Kimball, J. H., *Emancipation in the West Indies*, New York, 1838.

Ungern-Sternberg, Roderick von, *The Causes of the Decline in Birth Rates Within the European Sphere of Civilization* (trans. by Hilda H. Wullen), Cold Spring Harbor, New York: Eugenics Research Association, 1931.

Weber, Max, *From Max Weber: Essays in Sociology* (trans. by H. H. Gerth & C. W. Mills), New York: Oxford University Press, 1946.

Wesley, Charles, H., *The Negro in the Americas*, Washington: Howard University, 1940.

Whetton, Nathan L., *Rural Mexico*, Chicago: University of Chicago Press, 1951.

White, Leslie A., *The Science of Culture*, New York: Grove Press Inc., 1949.

Wilgus, A. Curtis (ed.), *The Caribbean: Peoples, Problems and Prospects*, Gainesville: University of Florida Press, 1952.

———. *The Caribbean, Its Economy*, Gainesville: University of Florida Press, 1954.

Williams, Eric, *Economic Development of Caribbean up to Present in The Economic Future of the Caribbean*, Washington: Howard University, 1944.

———. *The Negro in the Caribbean*, New York: The Williams Press, Inc.

Winshold, Karl, *Deutsche Frauen in Mittelalter*, Wien, 1882.

Wolf, Charles, Jr., and Sufrin, Sidney C., *Capital Formation and Foreign Investment in Underdeveloped Areas*, Syracuse: Syracuse University Press, 1955.

BIBLIOGRAPHY

ARTICLES

AUGELLI, JOHN P., "Patterns and Problems of Land Tenure in Lesser Antilles: Antigua, B.W.I.", *Economic Geography*, Vol. 29 (October, 1953), 362-367.

AYRES, CLARENCE E., "The Role of Technology in Economic Theory", *American Economic Review*, Vol. 43 (May, 1953) 279-287.

BALL, Z. B., BARNES, R. H., AND VISSCHER, M. B., "The Effects of Caloric Restriction on Maturity, Senescence, with Particular Reference to Fertility and Longevity", *American Journal of Physiology*, Vol. 150 (1947), 511.

BANKS, E. P., "A Caribbean Village in Dominica", *Social and Economic Studies*, Vol. V (March, 1956), 74-86.

BARNES, ARTHUR C., "Sugar: Mainstay of British West Indies", *World Crops*, (August, 1950), 325-327; (September, 1950), 365-369.

BEARD, J. S., "The Classification of Tropical Vegetation Types", *Ecology*, Vol 36 (January, 1955), 89-100.

BENNETT, H., "Exposure of Infants in Ancient Rome", *Classical Journal*, Vol. 18 (March, 1923), 341-51.

BILLMEYER, JAMES H. S., "The Cayman Islands", *Geographical Review*, Vol. 36 (January, 1946), 29-43.

BLUMER, HERBERT, "Sociological Analysis and the 'Variable' ", *American Sociological Review*, Vol. XXI (December, 1956), 686.

BRAITHWATE, LLOYD, "Sociology and Demographic Research in the British Caribbean", *Social and Economic Studies*, Vol. VI (No. 4), 523.

———. "The Problem of Cultural Integration in Trinidad", *Social and Economic Studies*, June, 1954, 32-96.

———. "The Development of Higher Education in the West Indies", *Social and Economic Studies*, Vol. 7 (March, 1958), 76-108.

BROOM, LEONARD, "Urban Research in the British Caribbean: A Prospectus", *Social and Economic Studies*, Vol. 1 (February, 1953), 113-119.

———. "The Social Differentiation of Jamaica", *American Sociological Review*, Vol. 19 (April, 1954), 115-125.

BROZEN, YALE, "Determinants of the Direction of Technological Change", *The American Economic Review*, Vol. XLIII (May, 1953), 301.

BURNS, A., "Towards a Caribbean Federation", *Foreign Affairs*, Vol. 34 (October, 1955), 128-40.

CATER, JOHN, "The Forest Industries of Trinidad and Tobago", *The Caribbean Forester*, Vol. 9 (January, 1948), 1-14.

CHAMPION, HAROLD, "Industrial Era for Jamaica", *New Commonwealth*, Vol. 29 (February 7, 1955), 130-133.

CHARLES, L. J., "Malaria in Leeward and Windward Islands, British West Indies", *American Journal of Tropical Medicine and Hygiene*, Vol. 1 (November, 1942), 941-961.

CHEVALIES, LOUIS, "Population Movements in the Caribbean Dependencies", *Population*, Vol. VI (April-June, 1949), 356-361.

CLARK, EDITH, "Land Tenure and the Family in Four Communities in Jamaica", *Social and Economic Studies*, Vol. 1 (August, 1953), 81-118.

181

CLARKE, A. M., "Is Infanticide Practiced in China?", *Catholic World*, Vol. 60 (March, 1895), 769-81.

COHEN, YAHUDI A., "Structure and Function: Family Organization and Socialization in a Jamaican Community", *American Anthropologist*, Vol. 58 (August, 1956), 664-686.

——. "The Social Organization of a Selected Community in Jamaica", *Social and Economic Studies*, Vol. 2 (March, 1954), 104-133.

COON, F. SEAL, "Research in the Jamaican Sugar Industry", *The Caribbean*, Vol. 12 (October, 1958), 54-57.

COWGILL, DONALD O., "The Theory of Population Growth Cycles", *The American Journal of Sociology*, Vol. LV (September, 1949), 163-170.

CRIST, RAYMOND E., "Static and Emerging Cultural Landscapes in the Islands of St. Kitts and Nevis, B.W.I.", *Economic Geography*, Vol. 25 (April, 1949), 134-145.

CUMPER, G. E., "Population Movements in Jamaica, 1830-1950", *Social and Economic Studies*, Vol. 5 (September, 1956), 261-280.

——. "Labor Productivity and Capita-Labour Rates in Jamaican Manufacturing Industry: Their Relation to the Problem of Selective Industrialization", *Social and Economic Studies*, Vol. 1 (No. 1), 61.

——. "Employment in Barbados", *Social and Economic Studies*, (June, 1959), 105-146.

——. "A Modern Jamaican Sugar Estate", *Social and Economic Studies*, Vol. 3 (September, 1954), 119-160.

——. "Labour Demand and Supply in the Jamaican Sugar Industry, 1830-1950", *Social and Economic Studies*, Vol. 2 (No. 4), 37.

——. "Two Studies in Jamaican Productivity", *Social and Economic Studies*, Vol. 1 (No. 2), 3.

CUMPSTON, I. M., "A Survey of Indian Immigration to British Tropical Colonies", *Population Studies*, Vol. 10 (November, 1956), 158-165.

DAMBAUGH, LUELLA N., "Jamaica: An Island in Transition", *Journal of Geography*, Vol. 52 (February, 1953), 45-47.

DANIEL, GEORGE T., "The Role of Trade Union Leaders", *The Caribbean*, Vol. 10 (June, 1957), 272-275.

DAVIS, KINGSLEY, "Population and Spread of Industrial Society", *Proceedings of the American Philosophical Society*, Vol. 96, No. 1, 16.

——. "Population and Change in Backward Areas", *Columbia Journal of International Affairs*, Vol. IV (Spring, 1950), 46.

——, AND CASS, ANNA, "Urbanization in Latin America", *Milbank Memorial Fund Quarterly*, Vol. 24 (April, 1946), 186-207. Also June, 1946, 292-314

DEMAS, WILLIAM G., "The Economics of West Indies Customs Union", *Social and Economic Studies*, Vol. 9 (March, 1960), 13-28.

DICEY, E., "Infanticide Amongst Poor of England", *Nation*, Vol. 1, 270.

DORAN, EDWIN, JR., "Cultural Connection in the Leeward Islands", *The Caribbean*, Vol. 11 (July, 1958), 274-277.

——. "Inbreeding in an Isolated Island Community", *Journal of Heredity*, Vol. 43 (November-December, 1952), 104-133.

DORN, HAROLD F., "The Effect of Public Health Developments upon Population Growth", *Ann. New York Acad. Sc.*, Vol. 54 (1952), 742-749.

EARLE, A. F., "Incentives to Private Investment as an Aspect of Development Programmes", *Social and Economic Studies*, Vol. 1, No. 3, 141.

EDGE, P. GRANVILLE, "Infant Mortality in B.W.I.", *Transactions of the Royal Society of Tropical Medicine and Hygiene*, Vol. XXXVIII, No. 2, 117-132.

EDWARDS, DAVID T. "An Economic Study of Agriculture in the Yallahs Valley of Jamaica", *Social and Economic Studies*, Vol. 3 (December, 1954), 316-341.

ENKE, STEPHEN, "The Gains to India from Population Control: Some Money Measures and Incentive Schemes," *The Review of Economics and Statistics*, Vol. XLII (May, 1960), 175-181.

ERICKSEN, E. GORDON, "An American Consultant Faces a Foreign Social Environment", *The Journal of Educational Sociology*, Vol. 29 (December, 1955), 184-190.

———. "Bad Houses, Bad People?", *The Caribbean*, Vol. 9 (August, 1955), 9-11.

FERMOR, PATRICK LEIGH, "The Caribs of Dominica", *Journal of Geography*, Vol. 23 (October, 1950), 256-264.

FLEMING, PETER, "The Lesser Antilles of the West Indies", *Holiday*, Vol. 5 (March, 1949), 99-124.

FOSTER, ALICA, "Barbados: A Geographical Study of the Densely Populated Island in Tropical America", *Journal of Geography*, Vol. 22, No. 5, 205-216.

FRAMPTON, A. DEK., "Land Tenure in Relation to B.W.I.", *Caribbean Economic Review*, Vol. 4 (December, 1952), 113-139.

GARBER, C. M., "Eskimo Infanticide", *Science Monthly*, Vol. 64 (February, 1947), 98-102.

GOODE, WILLIAM J., "Illegitimacy in the Caribbean Social Structure", *American Sociological Review*, Vol. 25 (February, 1960), 27-30.

GOODHART, C. B., "Natural Regulation of Numbers in Human Populations", *Eugenics Review*, Vol. 47 (1955), 173-178.

GOTTLIEB, MANUEL, "The Theory of Optimum Population for a Closed Economy", *The Journal of Political Economy*, (December, 1945), 289-316.

GREENIDE, C. W. W., "The Present Outlook in the B.W.I.", *International Affairs*, Vol. 25 (April, 1949), 175-181.

———. "The British Caribbean Federation", *World Affairs*, Vol. 4 (July, 1950), 321-334.

HALL, DOUGLAS G., "The Apprenticeship Period in Jamaica, 1834-1838", *Caribbean Quarterly*, Vol. 3 (December, 1953), 142-166.

HAREWOOD, J., "A System of Labour Force Statistics", *Social and Economic Studies*, Vol. 5 (March, 1956), 1-18.

HARRISON, L. C., "Dominica: A Wet Tropical Human Habitat", *Economic Geography*, Vol. XI (1935), 62-76.

HEESTERMAN, J. E., "Industrial Use of Natural Gas", *The Caribbean*, (January-February, 1957), 161-164.

HENRIQUES, FERNANDO, "Color Values in Jamaican Society", *British Journal of Sociology*, Vol. 2 (No. 2, 1951), 115-122.

———. "West Indian Family Organization", *American Journal of Sociology*, Vol. 55 (July, 1949), 30-37.

HUGGINS, H. D., "Employment, Economic Development and Incentive Financing in Jamaica", *Social and Economic Studies*, Vol. 1 (No. 1), 3.

————. "Seasons, Variations and Employment in Jamaica", *Social and Economic Studies,* Vol. 1 (No. 2), 85.

Hunt, Chester L., "Cultural Barriers to Point Four", *The Antioch Review,* Vol. 14 (Summer, 1954), 162.

Ibberson, D., "A Note on the Relationship of Illegitimacy and Birth Rates", *Social and Economic Studies,* Vol. 5 (March, 1956), 93-99.

Islam, Nurul, "Foreign Aid and Economic Development", *Social and Economic Studies,* Vol. 8, No. 3, 265.

Jolly, A. L., "Some Economic Aspects of the Depression in Trinidad's Cacao Industry", *Tropical Agriculture,* Vol. 16 (December, 1939), 272-274.

————. "Small Scale Farming in the West Indies", *World Crops,* Vol. 8 (May, 1945), 173-176.

————. "Peasant Agriculture: An Economic Survey on the La Pastora Land Settlement", *Tropical Agriculture,* Vol. 23 (July, 1946), 117-122.

Kondapi, C., "Indians Overseas: A Survey of Development in 1946", *India Quarterly,* Vol. 3 (March, 1947), 54-65.

————. "Indians Overseas", *India Quarterly,* Vol. 4 (March, 1948), 60-77.

————. "Indians Overseas, The Position in Trinidad", *India Quarterly,* Vol. 4 (July-September, 1948), 265-273.

Le Page, R. B., "The Language Problem of the British Caribbean", *Caribbean Quarterly,* Vol. 4 (January, 1955), 40-49.

Lewis, W. Arthur, "Employment Policy in an Undeveloped Area", *Social and Economic Studies,* Vol. 7 (September, 1958), 42-67.

————. "The Industrialization of B.W.I.", *Caribbean Economic Review,* Vol. 2 (May, 1950), 1-61.

Lindholdm, R. W., "Accelerated Development with a Minimum of Foreign Aid and Economic Controls", *Social and Economic Studies,* Vol. 9 (March, 1960), 57-67.

Lowenthal, David, "Population of Barbados", *Social and Economic Studies,* Vol. 6 (December, 1957), 445.

MacColl, E. Kimbark, "Poverty and Politics in the Caribbean", *International Journal,* Vol. 7 (Winter, 1951-52), 12-22.

Mason, K. E., "Differences in Testis Injury and Repair after Vitamin A-Deficiency, Vitamin E-Deficiency and Inanition", *American Journal of Anatomy,* Vol. 52, 1933, 15.

Maunder, W. F., "The New Jamaican Emigration", *Social and Economic Studies,* Vol. 4 (March, 1955), 38-63.

Midas, Andre, "Constitutional Evolution", *The Caribbean,* Vol. 10 (May, 1957), 236-240.

Milstead, H. P., "Cacao Industry at Grenada", *Economic Geography,* Vol. 16 (1940), 195-203.

Morais, Allan, "Tide of Industry", *The Caribbean,* Vol. 9 (August, 1955), 5-8.

Nash, E. F., "The Problem of Overseas Markets", *Social and Economic Studies,* Vol. 7 (September, 1958), 120-135.

Ogburn, W. F., "The Historical Method in the Analysis of Social Phenomena", *Publications of the American Sociological Society,* Vol. XVI (1921), 70-81.

BIBLIOGRAPHY

O'LAUGHLIN, CARLEEN, "The Economy of Antigua", *Social and Economic Studies,* Vol. 8 (September, 1959), 229-264.

———. "The Economy of Montserrat", *Social and Economic Studies,* Vol. 8 (June, 1959), 147-178.

———. "The Economy of St. Kitts - Nevis - Anguilla", *Social and Economic Studies,* Vol. 8, No. 4, 377.

PARRY, JOHN H., "Plantation and Provision Ground: A Historical Sketch of the Introduction of Food Crops into Jamaica", *Revista de Historia de America,* (Junio, 1955), 1-20.

———. "Salt, Fish and Ackee", *Caribbean Quarterly,* Vol. 2 (No. 4), 29-35.

PECK, H. AUSTIN, "Economic Planning in Jamaica", *Social and Economic Studies,* Vol. 7 (December, 1958), 141-169.

PITMAN, FRANK, "Slavery on the British West Indian Plantation", *Journal of Negro History,* Vol. XI (October, 1926), 606-608.

PLATT, RAYE R., "Economic and Social Problems in the B.W.I.: A Review", *Geographic Review,* Vol. 30 (October, 1930), 672-675.

PROCTOR, JESSE H., JR., "The Development of the Idea of Federation of the British Caribbean Territories", *Revista de Historia de America.* Number 39 (June, 1955), 61-105.

RADIN, M., "Exposure of Infants in Roman Law and Practice", *Classical Journal,* Vol. XX (March, 1925), 337-343.

RICHMOND, ANTHONY H., "Immigration as a Social Process—The Case of the Coloured Colonials in U.K.", *Social and Economic Studies,* Vol. 5 (June, 1956), 185-201.

ROBERTS, G. W., "Some Demographic Considerations of West Indian Federation", *Social and Economic Studies,* Vol. 6 (June, 1957), 262-285.

———. "A Life Table for a West Indian Slave Population", *Population Studies,* Vol. V (1952), 238-243.

———. "Population Trends in the British Caribbean Colonies, 1948-61", *Caribbean Economic Review,* Vol. III (October, 1951), 179-200.

———. "Some Aspects of Mating and Fertility in the West Indies", *Population Studies,* Vol. 8 (March, 1952), 199-227.

———. "Immigration of Africans into the British Caribbean", *Population Studies,* Vol. 7 (March, 1954), 235-262.

———. "Motherhood Tables of 1946 Census", *Social and Economic Studies,* Vol. 2 (1953), 173-186.

———. "Emigration from the Island of Barbados", *Social and Economic Studies,* Vol. IV (September, 1955), 245-288.

———. "A Note on Mortality in Jamaica", *Population Studies,* Vol. IV (June, 1950), 64-85.

———, AND MILLS, D. O., "Study of External Migration Affecting Jamaica, 1953-55", *Social and Economic Studies,* Suppl. to Vol. 7, No. 2, 1-126.

ROBINSON, WARREN C. AND ROBINSON, ELIZABETH H., "Rural-Urban Fertility Differentials in Mexico", *American Sociological Review,* Vol. 25 (February, 1960), 77-81.

RODMAN, HYMAN, "On Understanding Lower-class Behavior", *Social and Economic Studies,* Vol. 8 (December, 1959), 441-450.

ROTTENBERG, SIMON, "Income and Leisure in an Underdeveloped Economy", *The Journal of Political Economy*, Vol. LX (April, 1952), 96.

SAUNDERS, HAROLD W., "Human Migration and the Social Equilibrium", *Journal of Business*, (March, 1942), 221.

SEERS, DUDLEY, "Federation of the British West Indies: The Economic and Financial Aspects", *Social and Economic Studies*, Vol. 6, No. 2, 197.

SHEPARD, C. Y., "Economic Survey of the Cacao Industry of Trinidad, B.W.I.", *Economic Geography*, Vol. 3 (1927), 239-258.

———. "The Sugar Industry of the British West Indies and British Guiana, with Special Reference to Trinidad", *Economic Geography*, Vol. 5 (1929), 149-175.

SIFFLEET, NORA M., "National Income and National Accounts", *Social and Economic Studies*, Vol. 1 (July, 1953), 5-135.

SIRES, RONALD V., "Sir Henry Barkley and the Labour Problem in Jamaica", *Journal of Negro History*, Vol. 25 (April, 1940), 216-235.

———. "Negro Labour in Jamaica in the Years Following Emancipation", *Journal of Negro History*, Vol. 25 (October, 1940), 484-497.

SMITH, C. A., "The Effect of Wartime Starvation in Holland upon Pregnancy and Its Product", *Am. J. of Obstetrics and Gynecology*, Vol. 53 (1947), 599.

———. "Effects of Maternal Undernutrition upon the Newborn Infant in Holland", *Journal of Pediatrics*, Vol. 30 (1947), 229.

SMITH, MICHAEL G., "Some Aspects of Social Structure in the British Caribbean about 1820", *Social and Economic Studies*, Vol. 6 (August, 1953), 55-80.

———. "Community Organization in Rural Jamaica", *Social and Economic Studies*, Vol. 5 (No. 3, 1946), 295.

SPENGLER, JOSEPH J., "Population Movements, Employment and Income", *The Southern Economic Journal*, Vol. 5 (October, 1938), 129-157.

———. "The Population Obstacle to Economic Betterment", *American Economic Review*, Vol. XLI (May, 1951), 343-354.

STOCKDALE, FRANK, "The British West Indies", *United Empire*, Vol. 36 (July-August, 1945), 135-140.

STRAW, K. H., "Household Budgets and Nutritional Analysis of Food Consumption in Barbados", *Social and Economic Studies*, Vol. 2 (June, 1954), 5.

———. "Some Preliminary Results of a Survey of Income and Consumption Patterns in a Sample of Households in Barbados", *Social and Economic Studies*, Vol. 1 (No. 4), 5-40.

STYCOS, J. MAYONE AND BACK, KURT, "Contraception and Catholicism in Jamaica", *Eugenics Quarterly*, Vol. 5 (December, 1958), 216-220.

———, AND BLAKE, JUDITH, "Jamaican Family Life Project: Some Objectives and Methods", *Social and Economic Studies*, Vol. 3 (December, 1954), 342-349.

TAX, SOL, "Selective Culture Change", *American Economic Review*, Vol. XLI (May, 1951), 315-342.

THORNE, ALFRED P., "Size, Structure and Growth of the Economy of Jamaica. A National Economic Accounts Study", *Social and Economic Studies*, Vol. 4, No. 4, (1955), 112.

VANCE, RUPERT B., "Is Theory for Demographers?", *Social Forces*, October, 1952, 11.

Fertility in Puerto Rico." University of Puerto Rico: Social Science Research Center, 1954 (mimeo.).

JOLLY, A. L., "Peasant Farming." Trinidad: Caribbean Commission, 1954 (mimeo.).

LANDY, DAVID, "Childbearing Patterns in a Puerto Rican Lower Class Community." University of Puerto Rico, 1952.

"Population Movements in the Caribbean Dependencies." Jamaica: College of the West Indies (Anglo-American Caribbean Commission), Undated (mimeo.).

ROBERTS, G. W. AND MILLS, D. O., "Study of External Migration Affecting Jamaica, 1953-55." Barbados: Development and Welfare Organization, Undated (mimeo.).

TIETZE, CHRISTOPHER, "Report of the Government of Barbados on Research Related to Family Planning Service." Barbados: Government Offices, 1957 (mimeo.).

TOKUHATA, GEORGE K., "Behavioral Factors Affecting Fertility Expectations: Introduction to Behavioral Demography," Unpublished doctoral dissertation, State University of Iowa, 1956.

————. "Configuration and Dynamics of Fertility Expectations." Paper presented at the annual meeting of the American Sociological Society, Seattle, Washington, August, 1958.

BIBLIOGRAPHY

WALKER, 'ARENCE, *A Report on Jamaican Migration to Great Britain.* Kingston:
19. 'overnment Printer, 1953.
W₁ ⸱ ⸱ ᵗⁱ *Inventory of the Barbados Rocks and Their Possible Utilization.*
⸱ ⸱ ⸱ ᵗᴮarbados Dep't of Science and Agriculture, Bulletin No. 1, 1944.
WIL *nd* ⸱. ⸱ *he Labour Force* (No. 1, 1955). Trinidad: Central Statisti-
ral Office, 1956.
WIRTn *in the West Indies* (Occasional papers, reprint series no. 22, parts 1-2)
/ Francisco: California State Library, Sutro Branch, 1940.
WRIGHT, ¹ᵒⁱˢ P., *Commercial Geography of the Eastern British Caribbean.*
V₀. ᵗ ᵗⁱᵍton, ᵗd., Technical Report No. 1, June, 1961.
⸱ ⸱ ⸱ ᵗⁱⁱᵒ⁵ RAY, *Hurricanes: Their Nature and History, Particularly of*
⸱ ⸱ ⸱ ⸱ *Indies and Southern Coasts of U.S.* Princeton: Princeton
⸱ ⸱ ⸱ ⸱ ᵗᵉᵉˢ, 1938.
A ⸱ᵒʷᵇⁱⁱ ⸱ᵒᵇⁱᵗᵃᵗⁱ ᵗⁱ *and Economic Development in the Caribbean Area* (Results of the eighth meeting of the Caribbean Commission), Vol. 21, No.
Ad ⸱ ⁷25. Washington D.C.: Dep't of State, July 25, 1949.
⸱ ᵗᵗ *Budget Plan,* San Marcos, Calif., Space Ltd., undated.
Adm⸱ ⁿ., *Report on the Conditions of Indians in Jamaica, Br. Guiana, and*
⸱ ⸱ ⸱ ᵗᵈ ⸱Simla: Government of India Press, 1939.
ᵗ⸱ ⸱ ⸱ᵗ ᵗᵗ *rt on the Work of Blair Health Center, 1944-1951.* St. Vincent:
⸱ ⸱ ⸱ ⸱ ᵗ854.
ᵗ ⸱ᵗ *ᵗ⸱* ⸱ ⸱ ⸱ ᵗ⸱ᵗ⸱ᵗⁱ46. Jamaica: Government Printer, 1948.
West Indian ᵗᵉ ᵗ ᵗ ᵗ *Commission, 1938-39, Recommendations.* London: HMSO,
Command ⸱ ⸱ ᵗᵗ 1940.
WILLIAMS, E., *Documents on British West Indian History, 1807-1833.* London:
HMSO. 1952.
Yearbook of Caribbⁱⁿ Research. Trinidad, Caribbean Commission, 1949.
Vital Statistics of ᵗ⸱e British Caribbean Territories, Appendix IV. Jamaica:
Government 'rinter, 1950.

UNPUBLISHED MATERIAL

BROWN, ANN. D., "British Possessions in the Caribbean Area." Washington D.C.:
Library of Congress, Division of Bibliographies, 192 pp. (mimeo.).
COMBS, J. W., "Human Fertility in Puerto Rico." Unpublished doctoral disserta-
tion, Columbia University, 1954.
ERICKSEN, E. GORDON, "Infanticide in a Disorganized Society: A Study in 'Fringe
Demography'," University of Kansas, 1959, (mimeo.).
FREEMAN, A. KOEHLER, "Blue Mountain Coffee District, Jamaica." Unpublished
Master's thesis, University of Chicago, 1940.
HADDEN, JEFFREY K. AND ERICKSEN, E. GORDON, "Contraception and Catholicism
in the Caribbean." University of Kansas, 1960 (mimeo.).
———. "An Attitudinal Survey of Fertility Expectations in the West Indies."
Unpublished Master's thesis, The University of Kansas, 1960.
HARDY, F., "The Soil of Barbados," Trinidad: Imperial College of Tropical
Agriculture, 1952 (mimeo.).
HILL, REUBEN, BACK, KURT, AND STYCOS, J. MAYONE, "Family Structure and

Index

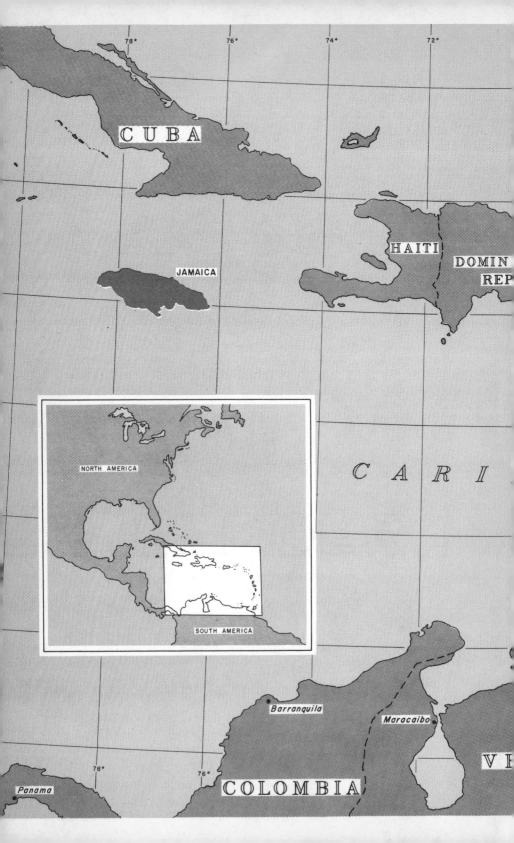

The West Indies Federation

68° 66° 64° 62° 60°

C

PUERTO RICO

ANGUILLA

St. KITTS
NEVIS   ANTIGUA
MONTSERRAT

LEEWARD ISLANDS

B E A N   S E A

DOMINICA

St. LUCIA

WINDWARD ISLANDS

St. VINCENT

BARE

GRENADA

TOBAGO

TRINIDAD

ZUELA

Caracas

0   100   200
MILES

60°